The
Condominium
Community

Contributors:
Joseph T. Aveni, CPM®
Steven P. Bloomberg
R. Bruce Campbell, CPM®
Aaron M. Chaney, CPM®
John N. Gallagher, CPM®
R. Don Larrance, CPM®
Robert McLallen
Jack L. Moyer, CPM®
William D. Sally, CPM®
Thomas A. Scapillato, CPM®
Joseph L. Yousem, CPM®

The Condominium Community

**A Guide for
Owners, Boards,
and Managers**

Institute of Real Estate Management
of the NATIONAL ASSOCIATION OF REALTORS®

430 North Michigan Avenue • Chicago, Illinois 60611

Standard Book Number: 0-912104-22-8
Printed in the United States of America

Second Printing

Coordinating Author and Designer, Nancye J. Kirk
Jacket Designer and Photographer, Bud Moon

Contents

v

3   Transferring Control   35

4   The Board of Directors   49

5 Conducting Effective Meetings 61

6 The Committee Structure 75

9 Managing the Human Element   129

Preface

RESIDENTIAL CONDOMINIUMS probably will never fully replace traditional single-family homes. However, they have become important alternatives to home ownership in many parts of the country. Condominium ownership involves a person's exclusively owning an individual dwelling unit and sharing ownership of areas used commonly by all residents, such as hallways, swimming pools, and parking lots. Unfortunately, this new and complex form of real-property ownership often is not fully understood by people who buy condominium homes or by those who become involved in the governance of their condominium community.

Usually a condominium unit owner's problems begin when he makes his purchase without being informed about the meaning of condominium ownership, basic condominium law, condominium management, maintenance problems and costs, rights and restrictions and obligations, and the condominium association that governs the community. The new owner also may not be prepared for living with others in an often densely populated community, usually consisting of many units in a single building, which relies on social interdependence and practices self-government.

However, despite the unfamiliarity with the concept of owning—as opposed to renting—a place to live in a multifamily housing development, the move toward condominium building and living with all its economic and social implications seems irrevocable. This new type of home ownership appears to be here to stay, and condominiums likely will play increasingly important roles in the nation's housing market. It has been projected that the same factors that influenced early condominium growth will influence its growth in the future. Real estate and construction costs are not likely to decline and possibly will continue their upward trends, and condominiums should continue to bring home ownership within the financial reach of people who otherwise might be excluded from owning. In addition, the same kinds of people who have been attracted to condominium ownership in the past should be attracted to condominium ownership in the future because of the financial benefits of income tax deductions and equity accrual coupled with the relatively maintenance-free living it promises. It is essential to the overall success of the condominium industry that people who have bought and will buy condominium units and become responsible for making decisions affecting their condominium community understand what they are doing and why.

Although the condominium concept of home ownership initially was greeted in the United States with skepticism, acceptance and a construction boom soon followed. According to some professionals in the real estate industry, however, this occurred much too quickly. They theorize that not enough research and thought had gone into condominium planning, and many problems arose, leading to confusion, misapprehension, and more skepticism. The main difficulties were poor construction, lack of suitable insurance coverage or an income tax system for this residential arrangement, shoddy selling techniques, and inexperience on the part of both professionals and unit owners with condominium management and association administration. The condominium image became blemished.

But time has been a good teacher. Many problems have been recognized, and steps have been and are being taken to eliminate them. A second wave of state condominium legislation is providing improved guidelines for developing and governing condominiums, and consumer standards are being set to eliminate sales abuses, leading to greater satisfaction with condominium living. Based on the experiences of the first decade of condominium ownership, the future can bring together the best of the individual home and the best of multifamily living. New condominium unit owners can benefit from earlier owners' experiences to widen their knowledge and enable them to set the proper balance for working with professionals.

Experience has shown that the association form of government is the most practical and desirable method for maintaining a condominium's open spaces and recreational facilities and enforcing the legal covenants. A set of governing documents gives the association its authority and provides its legal framework. Serious difficulties and problems are not as likely to occur in associations where a sound legal foundation is created through these documents. However, while this legal basis is important, the success of an association's ability to govern a community hinges on the people who live there. With effective leaders who understand their obligations and how to fulfill them, the association should operate smoothly through its board of directors, the official policy-making body of the association, and a network of complementary committees.

The Institute of Real Estate Management (IREM), aware of the problems connected with managing a condominium and running an association, recognized the need for a comprehensive textbook to be used as a reference for persons involved with condominiums. Therefore, *The Condominium Community: A Guide for Owners, Boards, and Managers* was developed to assist all condominium unit owners and especially those involved in the governance of their condominium associations. It should help the new board of directors that is accepting the transfer of control from the developer and provide suggestions for the ongoing board that wants to improve its operation so the condominium can become a more stable community. It should benefit small associations of only a few units that manage themselves and assist large associations that use total professional management. It also should be useful to property managers who are involved with condominium communities.

The Condominium Community is not an operational manual. It does not intend to describe the "only" way or the "right" way to finance and operate a condominium association and maintain the physical plant. For one thing, the size of a condominium plays an important part in determining the way it can function most effectively. Also, because condominium legislation is made by states, not centrally by the federal government, associations in different states may have different legal obligations. Given the size and statutory variations, however, there are common managerial and operational premises upon which most condominium associations may make decisions, and there are certain problems with which most condominiums will be confronted.

The Condominium Community outlines these premises and suggests ways of solving the problems that will be common to most condominiums. It defines condominium ownership and explains the powers and responsibilities of the association and the board of directors. It deals with accepting control of the association from the developer, creating an effective administrative system, conducting effective meetings, deciding on a condominium management plan, maintaining the common areas, establishing lines of communication, setting up sound fiscal procedures, insuring the condominium, and understanding the tax status of the association and the unit owners.

Of course, condominium ownership is not the only form of multifamily ownership, nor is the condominium association the only organization designed to govern a community of home owners. Communities in many parts of the country have formed other kinds of homeowners' associations as the means for building better and stronger neighborhoods. A homeowners' association is an organization of persons who own homes in a subdivision or other housing development whose major function is to maintain and provide community facilities and services. The homeowners' association typically owns the common property for which it is responsible. This is different than the situation in a condominium, where the unit owners own these areas in common, and the association, which usually owns nothing, administers them. Although homeowners' associations and other similar community associations are not governed by the strict real estate laws that govern condominiums and often are made up of owners of conventional houses, the general operations and requirements of the covenants may be similar. In both kinds of associations, all owners automatically belong. Both rely on assessments of owners as the principal source of funding their operations. Both have similar problems in the areas of government, management, and human relations. Consequently, many of the operational and administrative guidelines provided here could be applied to other kinds of associations of home owners.

Similarly, there are kinds of condominiums other than the strictly residential one, on which *The Condominium Community* is focused. For example, there are time-sharing condominiums, in which an owner receives a deed that entitles him to the use of a condominium unit for a certain length of time each year. There are resort condominiums that are not used as primary places of residence but usually as vacation getaways. There are commercial condominiums that are used for all kinds of businesses. Again, although each form of condominium will have specific legal requirements and unique problems, some of the concepts that apply to residential condominium operation may be applied to operation of condominiums created for other uses.

The Condominium Community was developed as a means of exchanging experiences by making available to condominium unit owners, association leaders, and property managers the lessons that have been learned about living in and working with condominium communities. This was accomplished by compiling research materials, ideas, theories, documents, forms, personal accounts, and suggestions provided by a number of professionals who have experience assisting condominium associations.

Professional property management agents who long have been involved with condominiums of all sizes and whose contributions were invaluable to the development of *The Condominium Community* were:

R. Bruce Campbell, CERTIFIED PROPERTY MANAGER® (CPM®), president of Wallace H. Campbell & Co., a management and investment property consulting firm that assists over 30 community associations in the Baltimore, Maryland, area. The firm has been involved with condominium associations since the first one was formed in Baltimore in 1967. In response to the growth of the condominium industry, Wallace H. Campbell & Co. expanded its involvement in the condominium field and is active in various local and national organizations whose goal is to improve condominium living through legislative and management changes. In addition to being an active member of IREM and the 1977 second vice president of IREM's Maryland Chapter, Campbell is a sustaining member of the Community Associations Institute (CAI). He also has served as local president of the Home Builders Association (HBA) of Maryland Apartment Council and second vice president of the Baltimore Chapter of the Building Owners and Managers Association (BOMA).

John N. Gallagher, CPM®, senior property manager specializing in condominium and community management with Shannon & Luchs Company, of Rockville, Maryland. Gallagher conducts the firm's community management operations in Montgomery County, Maryland, and has direct responsibility to boards of directors and developers for the property and financial management of 10 condominium communities there. He has been involved in most facets of the condominium industry, including conversion of multifamily rental property to condominium ownership, development of land into new condominium homes, builder developer relations, provision of counseling and assistance of condominium sales techniques, and all phases of association management and maintenance. In addition, Gallagher is on the special condominium committees of the Washington, D.C., Board of Realtors and the NATIONAL ASSOCIATION OF REALTORS® and on the faculties of IREM and Howard University's Real Estate and Housing Management Program. Gallagher also serves on the Board of Directors of the Property Management Association of Greater Washington, D.C.

Jack L. Moyer, CPM®, president of J.L. Moyer Company, an ACCREDITED MANAGEMENT ORGANIZATION® (AMO®) in Sepulveda, California, that has been involved with thousands of condominium and cooperative developments varying in size from 12 to 6,000 units. His firm has managed many individual associations for more than 10 years. Moyer has been in the community management field since graduation from the University of California in 1939, having served as a community manager with the United States Department of Agriculture and Director of Management for the Housing Authority of Los Angeles. He has written many articles on condominium management for the California Real Estate Association, the HBA national organization, and IREM's *Journal of Property Management*. Moyer also has taught property management courses offered by the University of California extension division and been a frequent speaker at real estate and property management seminars. In addition to these activities, Moyer was 1977 president of the Western Los Angeles-San Fernando Valley-Ventura County Chapter of the CAI.

Thomas A. Scapillato, CPM®, an assistant vice president of First Chicago Realty Services Corporation, a subsidiary of First National Bank of Chicago. Scapillato has been involved with the management, development, and sale of condominiums ranging in size from 36 units to 600 units and including projects in Florida, California, and Illinois. Scapillato is a graduate engineer of Illinois Institute of Technology and now serves on the IREM faculty and on the real estate faculties of several community colleges in the Chicago area. In addition, Scapillato is a sustaining member of CAI.

Others who contributed to *The Condominium Community* were:

Joseph T. Aveni, CPM®, president of Hilltop Management Company in Cleveland, Ohio, a firm active in the management and development of condominiums, apartment buildings, office buildings, and shopping centers. In addition to being the 1977 president of IREM, Aveni has served the Institute in a variety of other capacities, including regional vice president, chairman of the Experience Exchange Committee, and chairman of both the Membership Services and Communications Division Councils. A past president of the IREM Cleveland Chapter, Aveni received that chapter's 1973 Manager of the Year Award. He also is a recipient of the Cleveland Apartment Homeowner's Association's Man of the Year award and served as president of that association in 1971, 1972, and 1973.

Steven P. Bloomberg, a law partner with Moss and Bloomberg, Ltd., which practices law in DuPage, Will, and Cook counties in Illinois. As a specialist in municipal law, corporate law for profit and not-for-profit corporations, and condominium and homeowners' association law, Bloomberg represents more than 30 condominium and homeowners' associations and eight municipal districts and associations in the Chicago area. After graduating from DePaul University Law School and prior to forming Moss and Bloomberg, Ltd., Bloomberg worked in the Illinois Attorney General's office, first as Assistant Attorney General and head of the Litigation Division of the Consumer Fraud and Protection Division and later as Special Assistant Attorney General assigned to major cases by the Attorney General.

Aaron M. Chaney, CPM®, president of Aaron M. Chaney, Inc., AMO, a Honolulu firm which manages condominium and cooperative apartments, office buildings, a shopping center, and special-purpose properties throughout Hawaii. Chaney was the 1973 president of IREM and also has served as president of both IREM's Hawaii Chapter and the Honolulu Board of Realtors, which named him Hawaii Realtor of the Year in 1959. He has lectured on property management throughout the United States, as well as having been a lecturer for various educational courses offered by IREM. In addition to this service, Chaney has been vice president of National Association of Real Estate License Law Officials and chairman of the Hawaii Real Estate Commission.

R. Don Larrance, CPM®, vice president of Perry & Co., a full-service real estate firm in Denver, Colorado, engaged in the management of condominium associations and conversion of rental properties to condominium ownership, as well as the management of all types of income properties. Long active in IREM, Larrance was elected a 1977 regional vice president, has chaired the Chapter Activities Committee, and has served two terms as president of IREM's Northern Colorado Chapter. Larrance is on the faculties of IREM, the University of Colorado, and Metropolitan State College in Denver.

Robert McLallen, president of Condominium Insurance Specialists of America of Hoffman Estates, Illinois, an independent agency formed to serve associations and owners in the highly specialized area of condominiums and cooperatives.

William D. Sally, CPM®, vice president of Baird & Warner, Inc., and general manager of the Chicago-based company's property management division. A licensed real estate and insurance broker, Sally also is trustee of Baird & Warner Realty and Mortgage Investors, a Real Estate Investment Trust. In 1977 Sally, who serves on the Board of Trustees of CAI, was elected president of that Institute, which was founded to assist the nation's community and condominium associations. In addition to his CAI activity, Sally is past chairman of the Property Management Council of the Chicago Real Estate Board, a charter member of IREM's Academy of Authors, and a charter member of the Management Advisory Council of the National Housing Partnership.

Joseph L. Yousem, CPM®, a founder of Joseph L. Yousem Company in Los Angeles, California. He has headed the firm, which manages more than 4,000 condominium units in Los Angeles and Orange County, for over 20 years. Yousem's professional career was highlighted by his election as 1976 president of IREM. He also has served as president of IREM's Los Angeles Chapter, which named him Manager of the Year in 1971, chairman of the California Association of Realtors (CAR) Property Management Committee, and director of the NATIONAL ASSOCIATION OF REALTORS®. In addition, he has been a member of the Junior College Advisory Committee and was one of the founding directors of the California Housing Council. Recognized as a leading authority on real property management, Yousem has conducted special seminars on syndication, apartment house management, and condominium conversion and has lectured throughout the United States for IREM and throughout California for CAR.

Chapter 1

What Is a Condominium?

TRADITIONALLY, THE United States has been the land of plenty, including plenty of land. Part of the American dream has been to own a home and some of that land. For a long time, most people were able to realize that dream, but the dream is fading quickly for many. The harsh reality is that land is becoming increasingly scarce in the more heavily populated areas of the country. Today, few families can afford the luxury of a large rambling house set amid several grassy acres. For that matter, even a modest split-level on a quarter-acre lot is beyond the reach of many. As a result, alternative forms of housing that use the land more economically have begun to increase in popularity.

The dwindling land supply and consequent rising cost of land, together with skyrocketing interest rates and construction costs, unquestionably have affected the housing market. However, there are other factors that also have had significant impact. Most importantly, personal attitudes about home ownership are changing, and these are affecting the country's housing industry.

Attitudes about ownership responsibilities are changing. Many people want to own their own homes but do not want to be tied to houses that require a lot of time and money to maintain. They are looking for ways to enjoy the benefits of ownership without being burdened by the maintenance responsibilities that usually accompany them.

Attitudes about families are changing. The couple who might have had three or four children several decades ago now may have only one child or even decide to remain childless. As a result, more households are being formed, but the size of the average household is smaller. Thus, while more housing units are needed, they need not be as large as they once were.

Attitudes towards careers are changing. It is no longer unusual for both husband and wife to work, increasing the average couple's total income. This increase in income usually is accompanied by an increase in the desire for home ownership and the status that goes with it.

Attitudes of older persons are changing. Many retired men and women who can afford to are choosing to live in warmer climates. They also want recreational facilities near at hand to help them enjoy their later years. Empty nesters, that is, parents whose children have grown up and left home, no longer need large houses. They often want smaller, more conveniently located residences that require less work.

Attitudes of unmarried men and women are changing. Women who are single, divorced, or widowed want the security of owning a home but do not want the problems of maintaining one. Single men increasingly want to invest in homes but do not want accompanying responsibilities or suburban living. They tend to prefer more informal surroundings and conveniently located recreational facilities.

All of these—small families, working couples, older and single persons—have needs and desires that promise to be met by multi-family, housing developments commonly known as *condominiums*.

What Is a Condominium?

"Condominium" has become an accepted and frequently used term, but there remains some confusion about what it actually means. A person may say he owns or lives in a condominium, but he is not using the word in the way that the law defines it. The law defines "condominium" not as a building or an apartment but as a form of ownership of a dwelling unit located in a multiple-family development, as well as of the land and all the other assets of the development. When a condominium is conveyed—that is, when title to a dwelling unit is transferred—the buyer receives two things: exclusive ownership of the individual unit and common ownership of certain areas and facilities.

The Condominium Unit and the Common Areas

A *condominium unit* is that part of the condominium development that is privately owned and independently and exclusively used by the condominium buyer. In other words, it is the unit in which he lives and for which he receives a deed. Ownership of a condominium unit (or, as it is referred to in some states, condominium apartment) is, from the point of view of the law, no different from ownership of a single-family dwelling in that the unit can be sold, taxed, mortgaged, insured, and leased. Nonetheless, there are some obvious differences between condominium unit ownership and single-family home ownership. The single-family home owner usually owns and has virtually unrestricted use of a house and the land on which it is built. In contrast, a condominium unit often is legally defined as a space of air or a three-dimensional area located within the walls, floor, and ceiling of a condominium structure.

In consequence, the owner of a condominium unit rarely has exclusive title to the walls, roof, and floors that enclose his cube of air. These are *common areas* or common elements—that is, they are owned in common with all the other owners of the development. Common areas include the land on which the building is built; any other buildings or facilities that are not part of the individually owned units, such as swimming pools, tennis courts, parks, and playgrounds; and hallways, basements, elevators, lobbies, stairways, boilers, pipes, conduits, parking areas, air vents, exterior walls, and any other structural or mechanical elements.

Condominium Ownership

All unit owners share an *undivided interest* in the common areas of a development. That fact is what distinguishes condominium ownership from ownership of a single-family dwelling. The term "undivided interest" means exactly what it says—ownership cannot be divided. For example, if there are 50 units in a project that covers 100,000 square feet of land, all of the unit owners own the land, but the land cannot be divided among them; that is, no one owner can claim that he owns a specific 2,000-square-foot area of that land. Common areas are owned jointly by all of the unit owners, and they all have joint responsibility for them.

Ownership of a condominium unit and the undivided portion of the common areas generally is legally defined as a *fee simple absolute interest*. Fee simple absolute interest gives the title holder ownership of the property without restriction, as well as the right to use it and dispose of it as he chooses. Some condominium buyers may acquire a *leasehold interest*, which means they are leasing the estate for a definite but usually very long period of time. This gives them the right to possess, use, and enjoy their property for a certain period of time, during which they may transfer the title of the unit to others, mortgage it, or do anything else with it that the owner who has a fee simple absolute interest can. However, when the lease expires, the leasehold interest terminates, and the use and possession of the property is returned to the owner of the estate.

A person who holds title to a condominium unit and the undivided interest in the common areas usually is referred to as a *unit owner*, or sometimes as an apartment owner or a co-owner. The term "unit owner" may refer to one person or to a combination of persons, such as a married couple, a corporation, or a partnership. (For simplicity, this book will refer to the unit owner as though he or she were one individual. The reader should keep in mind, however, that this is not necessarily so in all cases.)

Kinds of Condominiums

The word "condominium" usually conjures up visions of high-rise luxury buildings lining ocean beaches. True, the high-rise condominium is very popular, but there are other kinds of condominium structures, some in even greater demand. In fact, condominium ownership easily lends itself to many forms of residential architecture.

A *high-rise condominium* is a vertical arrangement of units placed one on top of the other. Although a high-rise condominium can be as many stories as is physically possible, most high-rises are 20 to 30 stories tall. This condominium structure utilizes land with maximum efficiency and therefore is popular in locations where land is at a premium.

The *mid-rise condominium* ranges in height from six to nine stories. Typical characteristics of the mid-rise are a single front entrance and lobby, common corridors, and similar apartment plans on each floor.

The *garden condominium*, or, as it sometimes is called, the *low-rise condominium*, usually is no more than three stories tall. The garden condominium is an arrangement of units attached horizontally as well as vertically. It usually is built around a courtyard or has a front lawn.

A *townhouse condominium* is an arrangement of units attached side by side. It usually consists of single-family rowhouses that have individual entrances and occasionally offers private patios or yards for each resident.

A condominium containing two units might be called a *duplex condominium*, and there also might be *triplex, quadraplex*, and even *fiveplex condominiums*. The condominium concept can even be applied to a group of detached single-family houses whose owners have undivided interest in common areas. In fact, the structural possibilities of the condominium are endless.

One important trend in condominium development is the conversion of rental properties to condominiums. *Conversions*, as these condominiums are called, may involve high-rises, townhouses, garden buildings, or any other kind of multifamily development that originally consisted of rental units. From a legal standpoint, a conversion occurs when the owner of a rental development transfers its ownership to others through the sale of individual living units.

The primary impetus for converting apartments to condominiums is financial. The owner of a rental property may decide to dispose of it because he is unable to receive a good return on his investment due to such things as rent controls, increased maintenance costs or real estate taxes, high interest rates, loss of depreciation, or other inflationary factors. Converting the rental property to a condominium often is a profitable alternative to selling it to a single investor. Selling the apartments one at a time as condominium units usually brings the seller a higher return than would selling the entire apartment building as a single piece of property.

Conversions serve many good purposes. A condominium conversion usually is accompanied by improvements in the property and increases in the tax base (condominiums usually are assessed at a higher rate than rental buildings) and can help to stabilize a neighborhood. However, conversions also can create problems. Although a condominium theoretically can take any physical form, some existing apartment buildings simply are not designed to accommodate condominium usage, and many lack amenities commonly associated with newly constructed condominiums. Conver-

sions also pose serious concerns among tenants who cannot or do
not want to buy their apartments, especially older persons who may
have difficulty obtaining long-term mortgages.

A condominium, then, may be a new or old structure. It may
be large or small. It may include as few as two units or as many as
hundreds or even thousands. A condominium may be a luxury
building or a low-income development. It may contain one building or include several buildings. It may come complete with a
swimming pool, tennis courts, and even medical services, or it may
offer no recreational or other amenities. Therefore, a condominium cannot be defined as any particular type of building. It only
can be defined as a building or development that has a particular,
and increasingly popular, form of ownership.

How Did It All Begin?

The condominium form of property ownership is neither unique
to the United States nor a creation of the twentieth century. In
fact, its history goes back to the time of the Roman Empire, when
its leaders, faced with a shortage of land, solved their housing
dilemma by passing a law permitting Roman citizens to own individual dwelling units in multifamily structures. Although there is
some question about the details of this Roman law, it is generally
believed to be the predecessor of the condominium concept as we
know it today. Condominiums became popular again for a time
during the Middle Ages when many cities in what is now Western
Europe feared attack by outside enemies. This fear drove people
to live within the confines of defensive walls. As populations grew,
the land within these enclosed cities became increasingly scarce
and valuable, and the idea of dividing a single building into many
separately owned homes reemerged.

The condominium concept lay dormant until the early years
of the twentieth century, when it was revived in Europe, becoming an increasingly popular form of home ownership in Spain,
Italy, Germany, Belgium, France, and Great Britain. But the
United States did not adopt the condominium idea from Europe.
The concept first spread to South America, when, in 1928,
Brazil became the first South American country to pass a law
permitting the sale of *horizontal property*, as condominiums were
known there. Several decades later, Puerto Rico, troubled by a

booming population, a housing shortage, and a scarcity of appropriate land on which to build new homes, looked to its South American neighbors and passed its Horizontal Property Act of 1958. This act defined the ownership of real property under the condominium concept.

The situation in Puerto Rico set the immediate precedent for enactment of condominium legislation in the United States. The first action to stimulate interest in condominiums came in 1961. That year, the National Housing Act was amended to include Section 234, which extended to condominiums government mortgage insurance provided by the Federal Housing Authority (FHA) of the Department of Housing and Urban Development (HUD). While the act did not empower the FHA to actually lend money, it did permit it to insure loans made by private lenders for the construction, rehabilitation, and/or purchase of single-family or multifamily housing for rent or ownership. This protection by FHA insurance made it easier for developers to obtain loans to build condominiums and for buyers to purchase them once they were built.

Real estate laws are under the jurisdiction of the individual states. Thus, following the adoption of Section 234, the FHA in 1962 drew up a condominium statute based on the Puerto Rican Horizontal Property Act and intended as a model for state use in drafting condominium legislation. By 1968 all of the states had enacted legislation that enabled condominiums to be created and constructed.

Initial acceptance of this new and different form of ownership was not immediate. However, by 1970 condominiums were in demand in most parts of the country. Condominium construction activity has been greatest in ten states—Florida, California, Ohio, Texas, Illinois, Michigan, Arizona, New York, Pennsylvania, and Maryland. According to the *HUD Condominium/Cooperative Study* published in 1975, these ten states account for approximately two-thirds of the condominium housing in the country, with Florida and California having the greatest shares.

Making A Choice

The acceptance and increasing popularity of the condominium concept in the United States has been attributed in large measure to the advantages that condominium ownership offers. Although condominium ownership does have drawbacks, its benefits are numerous. In effect, condominium ownership combines the convenience of renting an apartment with the financial advantages of single-family home ownership.

Condominium or Rental Unit?

The condominium unit owner enjoys several benefits that the typical apartment tenant does not. Tax advantages are a major benefit. The unit owner is treated as a home owner under federal income tax statutes and can realize the same tax advantages as the owner of a conventional single-family home. Specifically, if he itemizes his deductions, the unit owner can subtract from his taxable income the amounts paid for property taxes and interest on his unit mortgage.

As a real estate title holder, the unit owner also enjoys the economic benefits of equity accrual and capital appreciation. *Equity* is the owner's interest in his property or the value of the unit less the amount of any mortgage on it, and equity accrual is the buildup in his interest. For example, the person who obtains a $35,000 mortgage to purchase a condominium unit and reduces it by payments over a period of time to $20,000 then has $15,000 ($35,000 − $20,000) worth of equity, which accrues as he continues to pay off his mortgage. This equity may be even greater if the market value of the unit has increased. To continue with the example, assume that the market value of the unit increased by $3,500 during the time the mortgage was reduced by $15,000. The owner's equity therefore would be $18,500 ($15,000 + $3,500). These economic benefits offer the unit owner a hedge against inflation, an advantage the renter does not enjoy.

Occupancy security is another advantage of condominium ownership. The unit owner knows he cannot be evicted from his home by a landlord. He also knows that his monthly mortgage and interest payments will remain stable, despite inflation, while apartment rents may be increased drastically with little warning.

The person who owns a condominium unit can participate through an organization of unit owners in the operation of his community. He has a voice in how the project is run, something a tenant is not likely to have. This does not mean that a person should buy a condominium unit solely because he is tired of rules and regulations imposed by a landlord. A condominium also imposes a set of restrictions. In fact, because the condominium's rules and regulations have their basis in state law, they may be more readily enforceable than those of an apartment building or other rental property. Nor should a person buy a condominium only because he wants more privacy than he would have in an apartment. The average condominium unit usually offers no more privacy than the average apartment. In fact, because unit owners have an organization and share use and ownership of common areas, the amount of interaction between neighbors may, of necessity, be even greater in a condominium than in an apartment building.

The unit owner holds title to his unit. Therefore, he has greater freedom to decorate the interior of his unit than does the tenant who is bound by the terms of a lease. In addition, the owner knows that any improvements he makes in his unit should increase the value of his investment. On the other hand, improvements made by a tenant increase the value of the property owned by someone else—the landlord.

Of course, in some respects and for some people, renting does have advantages over buying a condominium unit. There are two financial drawbacks to condominium ownership. First, the purchase of a condominium unit requires a large commitment of cash. The tenant need not make a down payment, but the person buying a condominium must. Second, the monthly cash payments for a condominium usually will exceed a month's rental fee for a similar residence because the unit owner must directly share the cost of maintaining and repairing common areas and delivering common services, as well as pay off his mortgage and the interest on the mortgage loan.

Condominium ownership probably is not a good choice for the person who wants to retain his mobility. In fact, any kind of ownership is likely to be incompatible with a mobile lifestyle. After all, a mortgage is far more permanent than a lease. The tenant also can call on a janitor or property manager any time something goes wrong inside his residence. Unlike the renter, the condominium unit owner is responsible for the interior maintenance of his unit. He generally has no one to whom he can voice complaints about it. In addition, if the owners' association embarks on a self-help program in an effort to reduce common expenses, the unit owner may have to accept some responsibility for exterior maintenance and repairs as well.

Condominium or Traditional House?

The condominium unit owner and the owner of the conventional single-family home enjoy many of the same advantages. Each has certain income tax advantages, each can obtain a deed of ownership, each benefits from equity accrual, each can secure a separate mortgage, and each can treat the interior of his dwelling as he wants to. But condominium ownership offers some benefits that single-family home ownership does not.

The multifamily ownership concept offers a way of increasing services and amenities by prorating costs. The condominium unit owner may enjoy convenient and comparatively low-cost management and maintenance through collective bargaining of rates and prices by the unit owners' organization. The condominium owner also may enjoy recreational amenities that are not available at a comparable cost to the average home owner. Obviously, a swimming pool intended for use by 80 families is more economical than a swimming pool intended for use by one. Similarly, the condominium probably may provide a better security system than most single-family home owners can afford to provide for themselves.

Condominiums generally are conveniently located. While there are many suburban condominium developments, numerous condominiums are located closer to downtown areas than are single-family homes. Living in these urban condominiums is considered by many to be a major advantage, as they provide better locations at less cost than would a similarly located house. This is especially important to persons who work in metropolitan areas and want to be near their places of business. Of course, to some, a convenient location means being on a beach and in a warm climate. Condominiums usually can offer this kind of lifestyle less expensively than can conventional houses.

The cost factor also is a major boon to the condominium market. The price of the average condominium unit usually is less than the price of a typical single-family dwelling, bringing condominium ownership within the range of a greater number of people. The condominium's utility costs probably will be lower too.

But, in weighing the characteristics of condominium ownership, the prospective buyer should look at both sides of the picture. There are disadvantages to multifamily ownership and living that should not be ignored. One of the major drawbacks is a result of the very nature of high-density living. A person moving from a single-family home may encounter severe difficulties in adjusting to living in the condominium's typically closer quarters. The high level of social interaction required by condominium life does not suit everyone. In addition, the typical condominium unit usually offers less space than the typical single-family home of similar value. This fact applies not only to the space within the unit but also to private space within the common areas. To put it more simply, the condominium resident can expect to have greater difficulty finding a place to be alone.

When buying a house, most people negotiate the price and terms of the sale with the seller. This is rarely, if ever, done when a person buys a unit in a newly formed condominium. Because condominium documents often are prepared prior to construction or conversion of the development and the sale of the units, the unit purchaser usually must accept the prescribed price and conditions of sale and rarely is able to negotiate them. However, price and terms of sale are subject to negotiation when a condominium is resold by a previous owner.

Joint ownership also implies certain social obligations and restrictions that are not required of owners of single-family homes. The condominium unit owner must learn to conduct himself in accordance with a set of regulations that are not typically imposed on owners of conventional houses. In addition, architectural limitations frequently are imposed to preserve the value of the other condominium owners' investments. These may restrict the unit owner's ability to make structural or decorative additions and modifications or exterior changes, no matter how small. Although single-family home owners also may be subject to restrictions imposed by zoning regulations, these generally are not as stringent as a condominium's architectural controls.

Condominium or Cooperative?

Although condominium living requires a great deal of cooperation, a condominium is not synonymous with a *cooperative*, another form of multifamily housing. A cooperative is a corporation that owns real estate—the building or buildings, the land on which they are built, and any other real property. Unlike the condominium owner, the person who purchases housing in a cooperative does not actually own either his own unit or a share of common real estate. Instead, he owns a share in the corporation that owns all the real estate, and he has the right to live in one of its units. Like the term "condominium," the term "cooperative" refers to a form of ownership rather than to the physical plan of a building. The cooperative—or co-op, as it often is called—can take any physical form, including that of a high-rise, a garden building, or a row of townhouses.

The cooperative concept has a longer history in the United States than does the condominium concept. It appeared on the scene several decades ago, declined during the Depression, then gained in acceptance during the more prosperous post-war period. However, development of cooperative housing has slowed considerably since 1970, perhaps as a result of the increase in condominium construction.

One of the disadvantages of being a shareholder in a cooperative relates to the way in which cooperatives are financed. Cooperatives usually are financed by a single mortgage on the entire property. No individual shareholder can personally negotiate better mortgage terms or obtain a personal loan. Instead, each shareholder is responsible for a proportionate share of the total mortgage. This usually presents no problem in sound economic times, but in more difficult times, some shareholders may be unable to meet their obligations, leaving defaults in payment to be made up by the other shareholders. In contrast, the condominium unit owner has no liability for the mortgage debts of other unit owners (although any unpaid assessments must be made up by the other unit owners). In addition, the purchase of shares in a cooperative usually requires a larger down payment than does the purchase of a condominium unit.

However, the cooperative form of tenancy is not without benefits. The primary advantage of cooperative housing frequently is its cost—it generally is less expensive than a condominium unit of comparable size. In addition, many cooperatives are financed at lower rates of interest and their mortgages are payable over longer periods of time. Because a single mortgage is obtained to finance the purchase of the cooperative, the interest rate remains constant when a shareholder sells his stock in the corporation to a new shareholder. In contrast, a condominium unit must be refinanced whenever it is sold, and, as a result, the new owner is likely to pay a higher rate of interest on the mortgage.

Chapter 2

The Association and
Its Governing Documents

MOST CONDOMINIUMS are designed to make economical use of land. As a result, people who live in condominiums live in close quarters. Some condominiums tend to attract one type of owner. In fact, some have *occupancy restrictions* that define who may and may not buy units, such as condominium developments that accept only persons beyond a certain age or those that prohibit children. But such rigid owner restrictions are rare. Because condominium ownership appeals to people in a wide range of circumstances, condominium communities may be made up of residents of various ages and interests. In a condominium with no occupancy restrictions, older couples may live next door to young single people, animal haters may have neighbors who own a menagerie of pets, and childless couples may find themselves across the hall from families of four.

Despite the diversity of their lifestyles, interests, ages, and backgrounds, all of these condominium unit owners have at least one thing in common—membership in a private, involuntary, usually nonprofit organization. This organization is the *condominium association*, which is responsible for operation of the condominium community. Each unit owner becomes a member of the association when he signs the papers that complete the purchase of his unit. The association of unit owners is the condominium community's government and unites in a joint venture those who otherwise might have no common bond.

The Condominium Association

The condominium association is known by various names in various states. In some, it is called a council of co-owners or owners, in others an association of apartment owners, in others by some other similar names. Whatever it is called, the purpose of every organization of condominium unit owners is the same—to encourage cooperation and to deal with all facets of the working condominium community. This formal organization acts as a small government to settle differences of opinion among residents, collect and allocate funds to operate the community and maintain common areas, and make all those decisions that are vital to the unit owners.

Each and every owner belongs to the association and therefore is responsible for the economic and social success of the condominium community. Unfortunately, the role of the association often is not explained to the buyer by the sales representative even though many potential problems could be avoided if it were.

The condominium association usually does not hold title to any property. However, it does serve as the vehicle for making decisions that affect property owned by all its members. Its responsibilities typically include (1) providing common services to and repair and maintenance of the common areas, (2) protecting the unit owners' investments, (3) establishing and collecting assessments to pay common expenses and establish reserves, (4) enforcing the rules and regulations of the association, and (5) helping members live together and share common facilities. These responsibilities and the ways in which they are to be fulfilled are set forth in a series of governing documents specifically designed for condominium ownership.

The Governing Documents

Most people know that the developer plans and finances the condominium project. Few may realize, however, that the condominium actually is created on paper. In the beginning, the developer holds the title to a plot of land that is recorded as an estate covered by only one deed, or a *single deed estate*. The law then requires the developer to commit this land to the condominium form of ownership. He does this by converting the single deed estate into numerous   single deed estates—the individual condominium units—

classifying the remaining property as common areas. In effect, the developer sets aside the land for the purpose of building a condominium and creating a condominium association to run it. It is the developer, then, and not the people who someday will live there, who establishes the condominium association.

The single deed estate is committed to the condominium plan when certain legal documents are recorded with the appropriate local government office. The number and kinds of documents the developer is required to prepare vary from state to state. Most states, however, require the developer to file three basic documents—the *declaration*, the *bylaws*, and the *individual unit deed*. These documents define who owns what in the condominium and outline the association's administrative procedures. Although not always required by state law, two additional documents—the *articles of incorporation* and the *house rules and regulations*—also govern the condominium. Certain states also require that certain other documents be recorded with the primary governing documents.

The Declaration

The declaration—known in some states as the enabling declaration, the master deed, the plan of condominium ownership, or the declaration of conditions, covenants, and restrictions (CC&Rs)—is the most important legal document related to a condominium. It commits the land to condominium use, creates the condominium association, describes all of the physical elements that make up the condominium development, and defines the method for determining each unit owner's share of common areas. The declaration tells the unit owner what he is going to own and outlines his responsibilities to the association and the association's responsibilities to him. In effect, it is the constitutional law of the condominium association.

Because of the importance of the declaration, the conscientious developer usually prepares it with the aid of the project's architect, an insurance agent, a professional management agent, and an attorney. Since state laws governing condominium development vary, the content of a declaration written in one state may differ from the content of a declaration written in a neighboring state. In addition to complying with applicable state statutes, declarations also must fit the specific needs of each condominium development. As a result, one document may be 100 pages long while another may be only ten pages long.

Even a well-prepared declaration may at times require amendment. Therefore, procedures for amending the declaration should be incorporated into the document itself. Amendment of a declaration usually requires approval of a large percentage of voters—often as many as 80 to 100 percent. In some instances, lenders also may have the right to approve amendments. In view of the fact that amendment of the declaration may be difficult, the developer should limit the document to only those provisions that are absolutely necessary. A well-written declaration should establish a strong association without at the same time imposing undue restrictions on the unit owners. If it does, the members should amend it only after careful consideration. In addition, the association should confer with legal counsel prior to amending the declaration to assure that any proposed changes are not in conflict with state laws governing condominiums.

The condominium *plat*, a diagram of the total condominium area, usually is filed as an addendum to the declaration. It generally includes a survey map of the surface of the land, a metes and bounds description of the parcel of land, and floor plans of all buildings, showing common areas and the individual condominium units. The plat is especially useful in locating the property and indicating adjoining parcels and possible easements and rights-of-way.

The Articles of Incorporation

Most states consider a condominium association to be unincorporated and thus do not require the developer to record its articles of incorporation. In states where they must be filed, the articles set up the condominium association as a corporation (usually a nonprofit one) under the laws of the state. When an association is incorporated, the individual members cannot be personally liable for any actions taken by the association. The articles also provide guidelines for the association's administrative functions.

In addition to filing articles of incorporation for the single condominium association, the developer also may file articles of incorporation to form a *master association*. A master association, also called a common association, is a nonprofit corporation that owns and is responsible for recreational facilities shared by residents of several condominiums. For example, a single condominium may not be large enough to support recreational amenities, while, on the other hand, three condominiums may be. The developer, therefore, may set aside a separate section of land conveniently located to these condominiums to build a swimming pool and tennis courts. He then would file articles of incorporation to establish a master association that would be responsible for the facilities' maintenance, repair, and operation. The articles of incorporation of a master association should state that each of the participating condominiums' unit owners automatically is a member, each has a vote in the decision-making process, and each is responsible for a share of the expenses. The operations of single condominium associations are unaffected by the operation of a master association.

The Bylaws

The declaration and, in cases where they are filed, the articles of incorporation create the condominium association and give it its legal power. The bylaws—sometimes known as the code of regulations—state how this authority may be exercised.

The declaration establishes a broad administrative framework for the association, while the bylaws provide rules for handling routine matters. The two documents may cover similar subjects and, at first glance, appear to duplicate each other; however, the bylaws usually are more detailed, outlining specific procedures for the administration of the association and the day-to-day operation of the condominium community. Again, because state requirements vary, the content of the bylaws may vary from state to state.

The bylaws should be drafted to accommodate future needs and possible problems. Procedures for making changes in the bylaws may be written into either the declaration or the bylaws themselves. Amendment usually requires the approval of a specific percentage of voters, ranging from as few as 51 percent to as many as 75 percent. Although the bylaws generally are easier to amend than the declaration, this document also should be prepared carefully by the developer and his attorney in order to set up an administratively sound association.

The Unit Deed

The individual unit deed is the document that legally transfers the title of a condominium unit and its undivided portion of the common areas from the developer to the purchaser. Similar to the contract signed by the buyer of a traditional single-family house, it outlines the basic provisions of a contract of sale. These include the purchase price, a description of the unit that is being purchased and of any easements, the conditions of the sale, the percentage of the common areas that are being purchased, and any other specifications required by state law or the particular condominium project.

There is, however, one key clause that distinguishes the unit deed from the deed to a conventional house. It states that the purchaser has received copies of the declaration, bylaws, house rules and regulations, and any other pertinent documents. In effect, the unit deed serves as a prospectus of the condominium and includes samples of the documents related to it. When the new unit owner signs the agreement, he acknowledges that he has read the documents and accepts all of their provisions.

In addition to the principal governing documents, the file that is submitted with the unit deed might include an *initial operating budget*, a *management agreement, recreational leases,* and *maintenance* or *service contracts.* These are disclosed in an effort to alert consumers to possible abuse by the developer and enable them to make decisions about the purchases accordingly.

An initial operating budget should indicate clearly the cost of operating the association, maintaining the common areas, and providing common services. The initial budget often is used as a sales tool to indicate to the buyer the cost and complexities of operating common areas. If the developer underestimates the budget either accidentally or intentionally, the buyer may believe maintenance costs to be much lower than they actually are. Therefore, the prudent developer will prepare his budget carefully and honestly with professional assistance to avoid the association's being faced with drastic increases after it assumes control of the common areas. Nor should there be operating deficits that the association members must cover at the time the developer leaves the condominium.

A condominium management agreement is a contract between a professional management firm and, in this case, the developer of the condominium project. It outlines those management functions for which the firm is responsible and indicates the rates of compensation. This disclosure gives prospective buyers the opportunity to identify any "sweetheart" agreements— contracts calling for excessive lengths of service or excessive rates of compensation—that may exist between the two parties. Any service contracts with outside contractors to perform maintenance tasks or deliver common services also should be disclosed.

A recreational lease is a long-term agreement under which the developer retains ownership of a condominium's swimming pool, tennis court, golf course, or other recreational facilities and leases them to the unit owners. These leases usually are binding contracts that cannot be broken. Under the terms of most leases, the unit owners must make periodic rental payments to the developer, who can foreclose on a unit if the payments are not made. In addition, most recreational leases have an escalator clause that provides for automatic payment increases to keep up with the rate of inflation. Recreational leases have been abused, primarily in Florida during the early condominium boom. However, they now have been virtually eliminated throughout the country.

Most unit deeds allow the purchaser a period of time during which he may withdraw from the sale without losing his down payment or deposit. Some states have passed laws relating to this provision to protect the consumer who does not understand or does not receive an explanation of what it means to own a condominium. If the unit deed does not give the purchaser the right to reconsider the purchase without penalty, he should not sign it until he has studied all the accompanying documents carefully and fully understands his obligations. This set of documents may be as much as two inches thick, but the time required to read it is an essential investment for the prudent buyer. An even better idea is to review these documents with a lawyer.

The House Rules and Regulations

The house rules and regulations are the guidelines to day-to-day personal behavior, and each resident of the condominium community is required to comply with their restrictions. They tell the residents how they must conduct themselves in the common areas and also may include measures that affect relations among neighbors. Ideally, house rules and regulations will assure that living in a high-density condominium is a pleasant experience for all without impinging on any one resident's personal freedom.

The house rules and regulations should be based on the provisions of the other governing documents. The developer usually writes rules and submits them to purchasers with the other documents. However, as association members gain experience in living in the condominium community, they may wish to change, add, or delete regulations. One of the other governing documents should outline a procedure for doing so. There has been some legal question regarding whether or not unrecorded rules are enforceable. Therefore, it is a good idea to consult a lawyer whenever rule changes are considered.

What the Governing Documents Do

While laws governing condominium ownership vary from state to state, governing documents everywhere commonly deal with certain general subjects: (1) the definition of the individual units and the common areas, (2) the method of determining percentages of ownership interest in the common areas, (3) the creation of the association and an outline of its administrative procedures, (4) maintenance responsibilities, (5) management requirements, (6) the assessment system and other fiscal policies, (7) insurance requirements and damage or destruction provisions, (8) rules, regulations, and restrictions, and (9) the transfer of control from the developer to the association. A checklist that notes which subjects are treated in which documents can be a valuable reference. *(See Appendix A for sample Governing Document Content Checklist.)*

Define What's What

The declaration is the primary descriptive document. It defines the common areas—the buildings, grounds, and other facilities in which every unit owner has an undivided interest—and identifies the individual units.

The condominium units occasionally are defined merely as all the property that is not owned in common with all the other condominium unit owners. Usually, however, the unit is defined in very specific terms. The following is an example of the detail that can be used in defining a condominium unit:

Unit shall mean an individual air space unit which is contained within the unfinished perimeter walls, floors, ceilings, windows, and doors, together with all interior nonsupporting walls, fixtures, and improvements therein contained, and those installations within such air space unit for electricity, gas, water, and heating, including, but not limited to, pipes, wires, ducts, cables, conduits, public utility lines, equipment, tanks, boilers, and hot water heaters, pumps, motors, fans, and compressors which serve only the individual unit and do not serve any other unit, commencing at the point at which such installations enter the unit; provided that the unit shall not include any of the foundations, roof, columns, girders, beams, or other structural components of the building as shown on the condominium map or any other common areas as hereinafter defined.

Similarly, although common areas occasionally are defined as all property other than the individual units, they usually are defined in much greater detail. Typically, they include the land upon which the condominium project is constructed; the foundations, load-bearing walls, columns, girders, beams, supports, and roofs; exterior surfaces; steps, lobbies, halls, stairways, entrances, fire escapes, exits, and communication ways; yards, private streets, parking areas, garages, and open-space gardens; the clubhouse, pool, and other recreational facilities; central utility services that are used by the common areas or that serve more than one unit; elevators, garbage containers, and incinerators; and any enclosed air spaces in the building that are not included within a unit. The dwelling unit of an on-site manager or janitor also may be classified as a common area.

Any *limited common areas* that may exist also are described in the declaration. Limited common areas are those that are physically part of the common areas but reserved for the exclusive use of a specific unit owner or group of owners. Legal definitions of limited common areas vary among states. In some, areas defined as limited common areas might include a patio or balcony attached to a unit, a storage locker, a parking space, an outside front door, or stairs leading to a single unit. However, at least one state's laws classify these elements as the property of the individual unit owner, even though they are not within the boundaries of the unit.

Some states recognize as limited common areas such elements as corridors or stairways that lead to a group of units and are designed for the exclusive use of the residents of those units. In addition, a laundry room or similar facility in one building of a multibuilding project might be reserved for use by the residents of that building and therefore classified as a limited common area. Whatever the requirements of a given state, the declaration of a condominium should define the limited common areas accordingly.

Units and common areas also should be described in the individual unit deeds. However, the unit deed definitions may be less detailed than the declaration definitions or may even simply refer to the declaration to identify the unit. The unit deed also usually defines a unit by reference to its post office address and the corresponding unit number on the condominium plat.

Determine Ownership Interest

The method for determining a unit owner's percentage of ownership interest in the common areas and facilities is set forth in the declaration. The unit deed specifies exactly how much of the common areas the unit owner owns, based on the guidelines given in the declaration. This provision is one of the most important in the declaration, since it determines each unit owner's share of the *common expenses*, which are the costs of operating, managing, maintaining, repairing, and replacing the common areas and administering the association.

The method for assigning percentages of ownership interest may be determined solely by the developer. However, most states have developed guidelines that he must follow. A unit owner's percentage of ownership interest usually is based either on the area that his unit covers or on its original value. The former method is considered to be the more equitable way of assessing financial responsibilities. Because value is relative, the value method seldom is used anymore to determine ownership interest. However, if based on original value, the percentage of ownership interest will be calculated according to this formula:

$$\frac{\text{Original value of unit}}{\text{Total original value of units}} = \text{Percentage of ownership interest}$$

If the percentage of ownership interest is based on the area of the unit, this formula is used:

$$\frac{\text{Area of the unit}}{\text{Total area of all units}} = \text{Percentage of ownership interest}$$

In some cases, a rule of one unit, one share is applied, and common expenses are divided equally among all unit owners. This concept often is used in developments in which units are nearly equal in both size and value.

To understand how value and area ratios are used to determine percentages of ownership interest, let us consider a hypothetical condominium project of 80 units. This hypothetical project consists of 20 one-bedroom units that cover 800 square feet each and originally sold for $20,000 each; 40 two-bedroom units that cover 1,200 square feet and originally sold for $30,000; and 20 three-bedroom units that cover 1,500 square feet and originally sold for $40,000. Thus, the total original value of the condominium units is $2,400,000, and the units cover a total area of 94,000 square feet.

Using the value-of-unit to value-of-whole ratio, the following percentages of ownership interest would be assigned to the unit owners:

$$\frac{\$20,000}{\$2,400,000} = .833 \text{ percent interest (one-bedroom)}$$

$$\frac{\$30,000}{\$2,400,000} = 1.250 \text{ percent interest (two-bedroom)}$$

$$\frac{\$40,000}{\$2,400,000} = 1.670 \text{ percent interest (three-bedroom)}$$

Using the area-of-unit to area-of-whole ratio, these percentages of ownership would be assigned to the unit owners:

$$\frac{800 \text{ square feet}}{94,000 \text{ square feet}} = .851 \text{ percent interest (one-bedroom)}$$

$$\frac{1,200 \text{ square feet}}{94,000 \text{ square feet}} = 1.277 \text{ percent interest (two-bedroom)}$$

$$\frac{1,500 \text{ square feet}}{94,000 \text{ square feet}} = 1.600 \text{ percent interest (three-bedroom)}$$

Both the declaration and the unit deed should clearly indicate that the percentage of interest in the common areas is undivided and that the owner cannot sever his share of the common areas. The unit and its accompanying percentage of ownership also are inseparable and must be conveyed together whenever the unit is resold.

Although the percentages of ownership interest usually remain constant once they are determined, a declaration may contain a provision that would allow the percentages to be changed. Changes in ownership interest usually occur in conjunction with *expandable condominium projects.* An expandable condominium project is one that is designed to permit the developer to add additional multifamily living structures to the original structure or structures. For example, a developer may wish to give himself a chance to assess demand for condominium units before committing himself to building the maximum number of units a project can consist of. To permit himself this option, the developer may include a clause in the declaration that would permit changes in the percentages of ownership interest in the event of expansion of the project.

Establish Administrative Procedures

No community can run efficiently and successfully without some form of orderly government. The condominium community is no exception. A condominium association is created to fill the need for government. The bylaws of the association usually establish most administrative procedures, although it is not uncommon for the declaration to contain some administrative provisions. Because most states require the bylaws to be submitted with the declaration, the declaration usually will discuss association issues in general terms only, referring the unit owner to the bylaws for specific rules of operation. Articles of incorporation also may provide certain administrative guidelines.

The declaration usually does two things to establish administrative procedures. It usually recognizes the *board of directors* —sometimes referred to as a board of trustees or by some other similar name—as the official governing body of the association and indicates how many votes each unit owner is entitled to. For example, each owner may be entitled to a number of votes equal to his percentage of ownership interest. Alternately, a one-unit, one-vote rule may be applied.

The various governing documents may outline additional administrative procedures, such as the method of election of the board of directors, the number of board members and their qualifications, their terms of office, and the powers and duties of the board. They should specify which officers are to be elected (usually, a president, vice president, secretary, and treasurer), their duties, and the method of election. The documents also should establish the association rules for calling meetings, requirements for notifying members of meetings, voting procedures, and a model order of business for the annual membership meeting. They also may contain provisions relating to such matters as filling vacancies on the board, removing directors, calling and conducting board meetings, and establishing a committee system.

Because of the differences among state laws, some of these provisions may be found in the bylaws in one state and in the declaration in another state. Therefore, a careful review of all the governing documents is essential to full understanding of how the association should operate. An information sheet that lists administrative requirements would be a useful reference to most associations. *(See Appendix A for sample Condominium Association Record of Administrative Requirements.)*

Outline Maintenance Responsibilities

The governing documents should specify which maintenance responsibilities belong to the individual unit owner and which belong to the association to assure that clear lines are drawn between common and individual expenses. They should state clearly that the unit owner is liable for the costs of all maintenance and repairs inside his unit, including the costs of redecorating, upkeep of interior surfaces of windows and doors, most utilities (in some condominiums, certain utilities are provided by the association), and any other costs that affect his unit. They should further state that the condominium association is obligated to operate and maintain the common areas, perhaps listing the services for which the association is directly responsible. These services might include, among others, the provision of water, sewer services, trash collection, and all utility services to the common areas, as well as the provision of materials and labor necessary to operation of the common areas.

Delegate Management Authority

Although the board of directors is ultimately responsible for managing the condominium, most condominium documents—usually in either the declaration or the bylaws—specify that the association may hire a professional management agent to assist the board

in fulfilling its duties. Some documents may authorize the board
to delegate any or all of its duties to an agent; others may list the
duties that the board may delegate. Some may include further
provisions for cancelling an agent's contract, requiring unit owner
approval of an agent's contract, or limiting the length of an
agent's contract. In rare cases, the documents may make no men-
tion of professional management.

Establish Fiscal Procedures

Running a condominium association can be a very expensive un-
dertaking. Fortunately, the legal documents provide a means for
adequately funding the operation by outlining procedures for assessing unit owners for common expenses. The documents require the association to adopt a yearly budget based upon the
estimated cost of maintaining and repairing the common areas
and operating the association. Each unit owner is assessed his
share of this cost based upon his percentage of ownership interest. The documents should state how the assessments should be
collected and may offer guidelines for penalizing delinquent unit
owners and setting limits on assessment levels. The documents
also may specify how often assessments are to be collected. (Typically, unit owners are billed each month, although some documents call for quarterly payments.)

A unit owner's assessment is determined by this formula:

$$\text{Percentage of ownership interest} \times \text{Yearly estimated common expenses} = \text{Unit owner's annual assessment}$$

If, for example, a unit owner's percentage of ownership interest is
1.09 percent and the total annual estimated common expense is
$55,000, then the following calculation is made to determine his
share of common expenses:

1.09 percent interest × $55,000 = $599.50 per year

If this unit owner is billed monthly, he then would receive an
assessment bill for $49.95 ($599.50 ÷ 12) each month.

An important fiscal responsibility of the association is to
establish *reserve funds*. Most documents require it to set up
two reserve funds: a *capital reserve fund* for the repair and replacement of common areas and facilities and an *operating contingency
reserve fund* to cover emergencies and unusual expenditures that

are not anticipated when the annual budget is drafted. Because these reserves may not be sufficient to cover all emergencies, the documents usually also include provisions for making special assessments.

The governing documents often contain guidelines for internal fiscal controls. For example, they may require that financial records be audited each year, that all checks or drafts be signed by a person or persons specifically designated by the board of directors, or that records be open to any unit owner who wants to see them.

Outline Insurance Requirements

Individual unit owners are liable for their privately owned units. However, responsibility for protecting common areas from liability falls to the association through its board of directors. Determining how to adequately insure all the elements that make up a condominium raises certain questions. Although the documents cannot provide all the answers, they should offer guidelines to help the association protect itself against liability.

Declarations usually outline a set of basic insurance requirements, varying widely in the degree to which they are detailed. Some offer broad generalizations, others precise specifications. Nonetheless, most address a few of the same fundamental issues. In general, most documents require an association to obtain adequate physical damage insurance coverage against fire and certain other calamities, to carry liability insurance, to appoint an insurance trustee, and to treat insurance premiums as a common expense. Some also may offer guidelines for obtaining appropriate amounts of physical damage and liability coverage.

The declaration should outline steps for repairing or replacing common areas in the event of fire or other casualty. It also may prescribe how to obtain bids for the repair or reconstruction of damaged common areas, how to levy special assessments against unit owners if insurance proceeds are insufficient, and how to handle reconstruction funds. The unit owners may not wish to rebuild a project that is destroyed or badly damaged; the declaration should establish ground rules for dealing with such a situation. Declarations commonly hold that if a large portion of the project is destroyed, the condominium association does not have to rebuild it, providing that a certain percentage of unit owners agree that it need not. This clause also may specify how insurance proceeds and any other funds held by the association are to be distributed if the association were terminated.

Establish Rules, Regulations, and Restrictions

The social success of the condominium community depends in large part on the rules, regulations, and restrictions that govern how residents are expected to conduct themselves. Typically, the declaration subjects all unit owners to general covenants, while the bylaws and house rules and regulations provide specific guides to day-to-day living. Without these restrictions and a means to enforce them, the communal living experience could become chaotic indeed.

The condominium community must have two categories of restrictions: *use restrictions* and *architectural restrictions*. The former attempt to regulate human behavior; the latter outline procedures a unit owner must follow if he wishes to change the outward appearance of his unit. Both sets of restrictions are essential to the proper use of common areas and the preservation of the design and character of the condominium development. In addition to specifying rules, regulations, and restrictions, the documents also may specify how violations should be treated.

Use restrictions may appear in the declaration, bylaws, and/or house rules and regulations. It is not uncommon for the declaration to state only that the "common areas should be used for the purpose for which they were intended, as long as that use does not hinder or encroach upon the lawful rights of the other owners," leaving details to the other documents. Use restrictions will be listed somewhere in the documents and usually are prohibitive in tone. For example, use restrictions may prohibit loud noises, certain kinds of pets, obstruction of the common areas, trash accumulation in the common areas, or construction of outdoor structures on the common areas. Occupancy restrictions also may be listed, for example, prohibiting children under a certain age or restricting the number of persons who may live in one unit. Such restrictions are essential to the protection of the community's character and rightly belong in one of the principal documents.

House rules and regulations that relate to day-to-day living, on the other hand, may be subject to more frequent change.

Therefore, the board of directors typically is authorized to modify, delete, or adopt new rules and regulations. Subjects covered by house rules and regulations usually include such matters as parking, the conduct of children and pets, noise levels, guest provisions, and use of common areas for personal property. House rules and regulations may include or be supplemented by rules and regulations governing any recreational facilities. For example, a set of swimming pool rules might require women to wear bathing caps when in the pool, restrict breakable articles from the pool area, or require children to be accompanied by an adult. Other sets of rules might regulate use of a clubhouse, a tennis court, or even a laundry room.

Architectural restrictions or controls are designed to protect the condominium's character and, hopefully, to enhance its value. The standards they set for design, material, color, use, and replacement are not intended to stifle individual freedom or creativity but to preserve the project's original design. To adequately fulfill the purpose of protecting the condominium's value, architectural restrictions should be extremely detailed. Here, for example, is a detailed set of restrictions drawn from one set of bylaws:

It shall be prohibited to install, erect, attach, apply, paste, hinge, screw, nail, build, alter, remove, or construct any lighting, shades, screens, awnings, patio covers, decorations, fences, aerials, antennas, radio or television broadcasting or receiving devices, slabs, sidewalks, curbs, gutters, patios, porches, driveways, fences, walls, or to make any change or otherwise alter, including alteration in color, in any manner whatsoever to the exterior of any condominium unit or upon any of the common elements within the project until the complete plans and specifications, showing the location, color shade, height, material, type of construction, and/or other proposal for change shall have been submitted to and approved in writing as to the harmony of external design, color, and location in relation to surrounding structures and topography by the board of directors of the corporation or by an architectural control committee designated by it.

Almost without exception, condominium documents require the board of directors to form an architectural control committee. This committee generally is responsible for reviewing and recommending to the board of directors approval or rejection of applications for exterior architectural changes or making the decisions itself.

Define How Control is Transferred

The legal documents serve one additional important function —they state explicitly how control of the association is transferred from the developer to the association of unit owners. Control is transferred officially when the unit owners elect a board of directors from among their own ranks. This transfer of control usually occurs at an organizational or first *annual membership meeting*, the date of which is prescribed in the documents either as a specific date, as the end of a specific period of time, or as the time when a certain percentage of sales has been closed.

Chapter 3

Transferring Control

MANY PEOPLE BUY condominium units with the expectation of settling into the carefree life but quickly discover that the protection of their investments may depend on their willingness to become involved with the management of the condominium project. A unit owner has no choice about joining his condominium association; he becomes a member automatically as soon as he buys his unit. At first, he may be totally unaware of the existence of the condominium association or expect to play no role in it. Later, he may realize that he must participate in it more than he had ever anticipated. Most first-time condominium unit owners know little about how to operate an association or manage property. These owners must prepare themselves to assume their new responsibilities. They must learn the fundamentals of how to financially and physically maintain the condominium project and enforce the community's rules and regulations.

Condominium associations go through three stages of development. The first is the *interim period*, the time during which unit owners have begun to live in the condominium but the developer still retains control of the association. Real responsibilities for an association—and sometimes real difficulties—begin in the second stage, which occurs immediately after the developer transfers control of the association to the unit owners. This is the *transition period*, when the residents become personally accountable for all the problems previously handled by the developer. The third stage, the *period of ongoing governance* when the unit owners have accepted their responsibilities, begins and continues throughout the rest of the life of the association.

The shift of responsibility from the developer to the owners should begin even before the legal transfer of control and not be completed until the owner-controlled association is firmly established. Some condominium projects sell out almost immediately, permitting virtually no interim period. In such cases, the unit owners assume control without having had an initial period of reliance on the developer. In other cases, the interim period can take at least a year and may extend as long as two or three or even longer. Whatever its duration, this phase is crucial, as the association begins to make decisions and set precedents that will influence its operation for many years to come.

The transfer of control of the association to the unit owners presents them with a new and complex enterprise. Some conscientious developers assist new unit owners in assuming their new responsibilities. Unfortunately, some do not, and, as a result, many owners are not adequately prepared. Ideally, the developer should inform, train, and assist new owners in how to run their organization, explaining the governing documents that provide guidelines to condominium management and familiarizing them with the process of making decisions and doing the necessary work. As the popularity of condominium living increases, more and more developers are realizing the importance of adequately preparing owners for the new demands that will be placed on them. However, some developers ignore this responsibility. In those cases, alert unit owners must assume responsibility for their own education.

The Interim Period

Whether the transfer of control is smooth or rocky may depend in large part on the way in which the developer treats the association during the interim period. To understand the developer's crucial role, the unit owner should first know how the developer establishes and controls the association.

The governing documents authorize the board of directors to govern the association. The first board of directors is formed at some time during the early stages of the condominium's creation. This board is appointed by the developer and usually is comprised of persons employed by or representing him, such as financial partners in the project. The board governs the association, and the developer controls the board. In effect, the developer therefore controls the association. Although the developer has his own financial interests to consider, he also has a fiduciary responsibility to the unit owners. This situation results in conflict, requiring the developer, whose interest in the condominium project is short-term, to make decisions that will affect the association for many years to come. This conflict usually results in the developer exercising his power in one of three ways.

One developer may run the association as a dictatorship, either failing to organize it or dominating it so completely that the residents play only unimportant roles in it. Once all the units in the project are sold, this developer may leave the residents to fend for themselves. This developer probably will do a good job of protecting the initial value of the condominium development, thereby increasing the rate of sales. However, by making all of the association's decisions, he fails to prepare the unit owners to handle their responsibilities after his involvement in the project is ended.

Another developer may transfer control of the association too soon—that is, before leaders have been adequately trained. These unit owners probably will be forced to manage by trial and error, perhaps making decisions without considering their long-term effects. This often is a problem in condominium projects that sell out quickly.

A third—and model—developer controls the association through the early stages of occupancy, at the same time training potential leaders. Unit owners should experience a smooth transition to responsibility if they are fortunate enough to purchase their condominium homes from a developer who educates his owners, provides a guiding hand to the association, and prepares for the time when he is to relinquish control.

Orientation Needs

Unfortunately, studies indicate that few developers provide association members with the counseling they need. In some cases, the developer may be unable to perform this invaluable service. In fact, the developer himself may not fully understand how a condominium association functions. He can overcome this handicap by employing a professional management agent to assume the role that the developer may be unequipped to play. As a rule, associations whose developers initially hire professional managers experience much smoother periods of transition.

New unit owners should be brought into the operation of the association as early as possible. Residents new to the condominium community usually are eager to get involved with it, and this is an especially good time to tell them about the association, the role it will play in their lives, and the role they should play in it. The consumer orientation program should begin in the sales office. The developer or his sales representative should explain to the purchaser exactly what the association is and how it operates. Unfortunately, the condominium lifestyle too often is romanticized in an effort to sell a unit.

If the developer and/or his management agent provide adequate counseling and orientation to the condominium lifestyle and the association form of governance, unit owners need only take advantage of these training programs. But what if the advice given by the developer is limited or nonexistent? What if he fails to hire a management agent to compensate for these deficiencies? In such cases, the new owners may have to assume the initiative themselves. If the developer shows no interest in the association, someone must do something to awaken the unit owners to its importance. Concerned residents may plan a breakfast or luncheon meeting, giving themselves the opportunity to get together, become acquainted with their neighbors, and discuss the governing documents and the association concept. With good fortune, they may find some second- or third-time condominium owners among them who can provide invaluable insights into how a condominium association works.

Interim Assessment Practices

While the developer controls the association, he is responsible for all operations and management of the condominium. To exercise this responsibility, he needs money, which usually is collected through assessment procedures. However, the method of handling assessments during the interim period can create some problems.

Once the condominium association has been established, the developer is, in theory, one of the unit owners and, by law, is subject to monthly assessments on each unit he still owns (in other words, on all unsold units). In practice, it does not always work that way. Many developers do not pay monthly assessments on each unsold unit. Instead, some pay only the difference between total operating expenses and the assessments paid by the other unit owners. Others pay all operating expenses during an interim period while the other unit owners pay no assessments at all. In still other cases, the unit owners each may pay flat rates to cover expenses until an owner-controlled board of directors is elected; the developer makes up the difference between the amounts they pay and total expenses. Other developers may adopt still other practices.

Although most of these alternative approaches are practical, any interim assessment method may cause some disagreement. Problems usually arise when assessments have been underestimated or developers have subsidized common expenses without the knowledge of the owners. The reason assessments may have been underestimated is obvious—low assessment rates can be used to promote sales. However, this can result in special assessments being imposed to ensure the association's financial stability. Assessments sometimes are low in part because the developer does not establish operating and replacement reserve funds. If such is the case, an association may find itself with inadequate reserves when the period of developer control ends. This situation can result in a major problem when, because sales have been slow, the developer has been in control for a long period of time. By the time control is transferred to the association, major repairs may be needed but no funds will have been set aside to make them.

The Transition Board of Directors

In the interim period, while the developer controls the association, he can do a great service to the unit owners by appointing one or more of them to a transition board of directors. Some states require such a board by law. The Florida Condominium Law, for example, requires one unit owner to be named to the board of directors when 15 percent of a project's units have been sold and closed. At the present time, however, only a few states do. Since many developers offer no more orientation than is required by state law, the association members may wish to form an ad hoc administration committee to determine whether a transition board is desirable. If the committee identifies a need for a transition board, it may ask the developer to relinquish some seats on the board to unit owner representatives.

New unit owners of condominiums whose units are sold within a short period of time may have a very different problem—they may find themselves in control of the association before they are ready to assume it. Usually, however, sales continue over a relatively long period of time while unit owners have no voice in the operation of the project. The ad hoc administration committee can be a useful tool for pressing the developer to share his influence with the unit owners through an interim board of directors.

Ad Hoc Interim Committees

The ad hoc administration committee is only one of several ad hoc interim committees that the unit owners may wish to form during the time that the developer controls the association board. Various committees may be established to advise the developer and his board. Although the formation of ad hoc interim committees is not required by law, these transition committees can involve unit owners in the activities of the association from early in its existence. Once control is transferred, the ad hoc interim committees usually cease to exist or are replaced by standing committees.

As soon as residents begin moving into a condominium, someone—the developer, the management agent, or other residents—should begin to attempt to identify individuals who show leadership potential. Once the condominium is sufficiently filled (say, when 15 to 20 percent of the units are occupied), a meeting of residents should be called at which to outline the legal basis and purpose of the association and emphasize the importance of participation by all members. Ad hoc interim committees also may be formed at this orientation session. If neither the developer nor his management agent convene an orientation meeting, a member of the association may have to assume the initiative and do so.

The Ad Hoc Acceptance Committee. The most important committee that can be established during this early stage in the condominium's life is the *ad hoc acceptance committee*. The purpose of this committee is to work with the developer to resolve any construction or landscaping defects in the common areas. Any unit owners with experience in landscaping, engineering, building construction, plumbing, or electrical contracting would make ideal members of this group.

Unlike the transfer of control of the association, which occurs on a specific date, transfer of ownership of the common areas and facilities shifts gradually from the developer to the unit owners as, with the closing of each sale, each unit owner acquires his share of the common areas. Although ownership shifts gradually, the common areas must be delivered in total free of flaws and with any special facilities promised by the developer. Since it is impossible for each owner to accept all the common areas, there is need to designate a representative group of owners who can legally accept the common areas on behalf of all the owners. This need may be filled by the ad hoc acceptance committee.

Formal acceptance of the common areas requires an inspection of the project. The committee may wish to invite the developer along on a walk through the common areas and to invest in the consultative services of an independent structural engineer or architect. The quality of the construction should be judged, the completed project compared to the original plans and specifications, and compliance with building codes should be verified. After inspecting the condominium project, the acceptance committee should list any defects found in the common areas and present this list to the developer. Any areas of disagreement should be negotiated at this time. Then, the developer should prepare a schedule for completion of any incomplete or unacceptable items and submit it to the committee.

The ad hoc acceptance committee need not necessarily be disbanded when control is transferred to the association. Rather, it should remain intact until all of the developer's promises have been fulfilled, even though this may occur one or more years after control is transferred. The committee should have no reservations at the time it recommends acceptance of the common areas to the board of directors, and the board should give the developer no releases until it is satisfied with the condition of the project.

Other Ad Hoc Interim Committees. The establishment of other ad hoc committees can ease the transition period. Those whose functions are social in nature should be established during the early stages of the project's occupancy to encourage residents' interest in the association and their participation in it. For example, an *ad hoc welcoming committee* could help residents adjust to their new homes and introduce them to the association. An *ad hoc social and recreation committee* could plan programs that encourage owner interaction and ensure good use of the recreational facilities. An *ad hoc communications committee* could provide unit owners with information on new residents, association functions, and the progress of the development's construction.

After these social committees become active, the unit owners should begin their involvement with the actual management and operation of the condominium. Other ad hoc committees should be formed at this time to work with the developer and/or his property management agent and to familiarize those who serve on them with the operation of the association. Such ad hoc administrative and operational committees might be involved with architectural controls, the association's finances, insurance, maintenance, and rules.

An *ad hoc architectural control committee* could establish standards for modifying exteriors of individual units, as well as a process for seeking proposed approval of modifications. An *ad hoc finance committee* could advise the developer on capital and operating budgets. Its members could review the developer's bookkeeping policies, his budgets, and all available information on the association's tax status. An *ad hoc insurance committee* could study all association insurance policies, the insurance requirements prescribed in the governing documents, and the association's liabilities. An *ad hoc maintenance committee* could review all maintenance contracts signed by the developer. And an *ad hoc rules committee* could review existing rules and regulations and recommend changes suggested by the experience of living in the development.

No one set of ad hoc committees will fit the needs of every condominium project. The size and structure of each project must dictate which committees are needed. In addition, the success of the ad hoc committee structure will depend in large measure on the attitudes of the committee members. Meetings of the ad hoc committees should have specific goals; they should not be allowed to become complaint sessions.

Although the ad hoc committees serve only as advisory bodies, they can smooth the way for the transfer of control by permitting unit owners to become involved in the operation of their community prior to the formal election of the owner-controlled board of directors.

The Transfer of Control

Ideally, the developer gradually hands over responsibility for operating the condominium association to its members. However, the legal transfer of control occurs at a specific time, the time at which the association members elect a board of directors composed of unit owners. This owner-controlled board is elected at the first formal membership meeting (often called the organizational meeting), the date of which is prescribed by the governing documents. Once this election has been held and the votes counted, the real life of the condominium association begins.

The date of the membership meeting generally depends upon when a certain percentage of the project's units have been sold and closed. Alternatively, the governing documents may call for the meeting to be held after a certain period of time following the sale of the first unit or on a specified date. Most state laws require the first annual meeting to be held when 75 percent of the units have been sold and closed. Some require that it be held after only 51 percent of the units have been sold, while others require transfer of control after the sale of 80 to 90 percent of the units. In addition, the governing documents may state that control must be transferred no later than a certain number of months or years after the first closing. This time period can range from six months to three years. Many documents include a whichever-comes-first clause stating, for example, that "control of the condominium association must be transferred to the individual unit owners no later than three years after the closing of the first unit or when 75 percent of the units are sold and closed, whichever is the first to occur."

The Transition Period

The time immediately following the legal transfer of control may be the most difficult in the life of the association. It also may be the most important. The period during which an association adjusts to self-government usually lasts for at least a year following the transfer of control. During this time, unit owners must begin to make important decisions that can have a major impact on the future value of their property and on their satisfaction with condominium living.

If construction of the project is incomplete, the developer may continue to remain involved in its completion after control has been transferred. He has the opportunity to begin or to hopefully continue to train the leaders of the association. A professional management agent employed by the developer also may continue to work with the association. The newly elected board of directors may include knowledgeable and competent businessmen, but rarely will it include anyone who is versed in property management in general or condominium living in particular.

In its first year, the board of directors can expect to have to deal with a number of problems. In the interest of a smooth-running and relatively peaceful operation, the developer and/or his management agent should be available to provide counseling. The developer's obligation to the unit owners should not end with the legal transfer of control. Unfortunately, many developers see the first annual membership meeting as their signal to withdraw completely from a project, requiring the new board to seek out the developer if it needs assistance. Even worse, it may be left with no one to whom to turn for help.

The new board of directors should ask the developer for all association records, especially a detailed accounting of all monies collected and paid out during the time he controlled the association. The new board should obtain a certified audit of the funds of the association, which should immediately alert them to potential financial liabilities. The audit should indicate to the board the costs of managing and maintaining the condominium, assist it in preparing budgets and setting assessments, and provide a basis for reviewing operating contingency and replacement reserves. Developers seldom set aside reserves for future expenditures, and the new board should set about this task at once to eliminate, for the most part, the need for costly and unpopular special assessments. In addition to this audit, the status of delinquent assessments should be determined. Developers may be reluctant to take action against unit owners who are late in payment of their regular fees, and the new board may find itself with large uncollectable assessments.

The new board also should obtain original copies of association insurance policies and enlist the aid of a qualified insurance agent to review the adequacy of the condominium's insurance coverage. The board then should inform all unit owners of what is covered by the association's policy and advise them regularly as to what supplemental insurance they need to be completely protected.

The board also should obtain a record of contract and bidding activities, copies of all governing documents and architectural plans of the development, copies of warranties on all equipment, and files of all correspondence related to the association. The board's most important task then is to review and approve these records and to adopt an operating budget. It may ask the developer and/or his manager to make budget recommendations for the next fiscal year.

A myriad of questions must be answered and important decisions made about contractors, insurance coverage, maintenance, and common services. Most—perhaps all—of these problems may be eliminated if professional management has been provided throughout the life of the project. In fact, a professional manager may provide crucial liaison between the developer and the unit owners.

Proper orientation by the developer can make the transition process much smoother, but the first owner-controlled board of directors always will be faced with problems related to financial management, legal matters, and the inevitable disputes among neighbors. The ultimate responsibility for all decisions rests with the board of directors and, even with the help of an able professional management agent, overseeing the operation of even a small condominium project can be a very time-consuming business. The board members must help the other owners realize that they are not tenants in an apartment building or residents of detached houses but members of an association whose success depends on them.

Chapter 4

The Board of Directors

THE REAL WORK of the condominium association begins after the developer transfers control to the unit owners. While certain matters that affect the condominium must be put before the entire membership, most decisions are made by the board of directors, the official policy-making body of the association. (The board of directors is referred to in some states as a board of managers.)

Although it is unlikely that anyone in the community will have had experience managing a multifamily housing development, there probably will be individual unit owners who possess basic leadership qualities. A member of the board of directors must be a negotiator and a communicator, a leader and a partner, a supervisor and an organizer. Although a strong vocational background can be an asset, leaders should be judged principally on the time they have to invest in association activities and the sincerity of their interest in the future of the association. He or she may be a lawyer, an insurance agent, an architect, an accountant, an electrician, a gardner, or a retiree or other individual who is at home most of the day and, thus, familiar with the community's everyday problems.

Elections

The governing documents usually require the association to elect an uneven number of unit owners—usually from three to nine —to serve on the board of directors. The declaration and the bylaws also prescribe methods of election, terms of office, and methods of removing directors and filling vacancies, and outline the role of the board.

Notifications and Nominations

The primary purpose of the annual membership meeting is to elect the board of directors. All of the seats on the board must be filled at the first annual meeting. In contrast, only a few seats may be open on the board of an ongoing association with a staggered-term policy. Prior to the annual meeting, all unit owners should be notified of the upcoming election according to procedures outlined in the governing documents and invited to run to fill vacancies on the board.

The invitation can take the form of a nomination application or questionnaire, which can be answered and returned by anyone interested in serving on the board. *(See Appendix A for sample Nomination Application.)* The application, a copy of which should be sent to each unit, might ask potential candidates for general personal information, business and educational data, and any other information that may be necessary or helpful. Potential candidates also may be asked to state why they believe they could serve the community well and why they want to be seated on the board of directors. Many associations also require an owner's candidacy to be endorsed by a certain number of other unit owners.

An *ad hoc nominating committee* often is appointed to review these questionnaires objectively. The committee should be comprised of persons representing various interests of the association, including young and old persons, housewives and professionals. After studying the questionnaires and evaluating the respondents' qualifications, the committee should nominate those who appear to be most capable of serving the association. An information sheet about each of the nominees (perhaps a copy of the application) should be sent to each unit owner with the official meeting notice. This provides the residents with adequate time and information to decide for whom to vote.

In addition to those nominated by the ad hoc nominating committee, nominations for candidates also should be accepted from the floor. Customarily, all nominees are introduced and given a few minutes to tell the membership why they believe they should be elected.

Balloting

Balloting or secret voting can be a complicated process, and certain voting procedures should be outlined in the governing documents. Some documents allocate one vote to each unit. Others state that each unit owner may cast a vote equal to his percentage of ownership interest. For example, if a unit owner has a share in the common area equal to 1.27 percent, then he can cast 1.27 votes for the nominee of his choice.

One ballot per unit should be prepared in advance of the meeting. Ballots should list in alphabetical order those persons nominated by the ad hoc nominating committee and provide blank spaces in which to add floor nominations and write-in candidates. Ballots may be distributed at the door of the meeting room. As each member enters, he may be handed a ballot and his name crossed from a membership roster. Elections that permit each unit owner to cast a vote equal to his percentage of ownership interest in the common areas present special problems. Because some unit owners may not remember their percentage of interest, the percentages should be shown on the roster and written on the ballots as they are handed to members. An alternative method is to attach an identification slip showing each voter's name, unit number, and ownership interest to his ballot. The slip can be removed easily to ensure the secrecy of the election. *(See Appendix A for sample Ballot.)*

Some documents call for *cumulative voting*. When cumulative voting is required, each unit owner is allowed a total vote equal to his regular vote multiplied by the number of directors to be elected. If the one-unit, one-vote rule is applied, he has as many votes as there are seats to be filled. For example, if three directors are to be elected, the unit owner will have three votes. If the percentage of interest rule is applied, the owner's percentage of interest is multiplied by the number of vacant seats. For example, if three directors are to be elected, the unit owner with a 1.27 percent ownership interest can cast 3.81 votes (1.27 × 3). Subject to the provisions of the documents, he may be able to distribute his vote. For example, he may be permitted to cast 1.27 votes for each of three nominees or 3.81 votes for one candidate or divide the votes in any other way he wishes to. When votes are not accumulated, each unit owner is allowed one vote or a vote equal to his percentage of interest, depending on the voting requirements in the governing documents. This is *noncumulative voting*.

Elections of condominium associations that operate under a one-unit, one-vote or a noncumulative voting rule are less complex. However, no matter how the election is conducted, voting procedures should be explained to all association members prior to the actual balloting. After the balloting, the votes should be tallied and the results announced immediately. Tabulation of an election conducted according to cumulative voting requirements may be a time-consuming and difficult task, especially in larger associations. One possible solution is to retain the services of a tabulating or accounting firm. A management agent also may assume responsibility for tabulating the vote, as well as be charged with the preparation for the annual meeting. Among other things, he may prepare the notifications, send out the nomination questionnaires, and prepare the ballots.

Very small associations may be able to conduct elections less formally. For associations of fewer than twenty units, for example, all nominations may be made from the floor, and blank sheets of paper on which each unit owner can cast his vote may serve as ballots.

Terms of Office

Terms of office of board members typically range from one to three years. Many documents also specify that directors be elected to staggered terms. For example, a clause in a typical condominium association's bylaws states:

At the end of the first annual meeting of the Council of Unit Owners, the term of office of two members of the Board of Directors shall be fixed at three years, the term of office of two members of the Board of Directors shall be fixed at two years, and the term of office of one member of the Board of Directors shall be fixed at one year. At the expiration of the initial term of office of each respective member of the Board of Directors, his successor shall be elected to serve a term of three years.

Some documents may go further, stating, for example, that the two directors with the highest and second highest number of votes are to serve on the board for three years, that the two directors with the third and fourth highest number of votes are to serve for two years, and that the director with the fifth highest number of votes is to serve for one year. The purpose of staggered elections is to encourage continuity by eliminating the possibility of a complete turnover of the board of directors at each election and facilitate the ongoing operations and activities of the condominium association.

Removing Directors and Filling Vacancies

The governing documents also should provide for the removal of directors from the board and the filling of vacancies. Language that is typical of condominium documents states that "any one of the members of the board of directors may be removed with or without cause by an affirmative vote of a majority of the unit owners." Prior to a vote to remove a director, a public hearing should be held to permit the board member in question to present his side of the issue to all the unit owners. The documents usually further require that an election be held immediately to replace a member removed in this fashion. Vacancies created in other ways usually are filled by appointment by the board.

The Association Officers

The board of directors must meet as soon as it is elected to select its officers, holding what usually is referred to as the *organizational board meeting*. Most governing documents specify when this meeting should be held. Some require that it be held immediately after election results are announced. Others call for it to be held within a certain number of days—usually no more than ten—following the election.

One of the governing documents (the bylaws, usually) lists the titles and duties of the various officers. Titles usually are *president*, *vice president*, *secretary*, and *treasurer*. Occasionally, the roles of secretary and treasurer are combined. The documents typically state that the officers must be elected by the board from the board. However, some condominium documents require only the president to be a member of the board of directors, permitting the other officers to be drawn from among the membership-at-large.

The President

The president is the chairman of the board of directors and chief administrator of the association. His ability, judgment, and enthusiasm often will determine whether or not the association is a success. The president is charged with presiding at all meetings of the membership and the board of directors and usually is given, to quote one set of bylaws, "all of the general powers and duties which are usually vested in the office of president of a corporation." Even in projects that employ a property manager, the president has the chief responsibility for the condominium's operations, and must be willing to assume that responsibility.

As the most visible representative of the condominium association, the president probably will become a sounding board for many of the unit owners. Ideally, he will be an impartial and diplomatic mediator for complaining residents. He must take the time to listen to all grievances, follow the will of the majority, and serve the best interests of the association. Many controversial issues may arise during the president's term of office. He must take a statesmanlike attitude and not abuse the power of his office by attempting to influence the other board members.

The documents probably will authorize the president to appoint committee members. Therefore, it is important that he know the other unit owners and their strengths and weaknesses in order to make intelligent appointments.

The Vice President

The vice president presides at meetings from which the president is absent and takes the chair when the president wishes to participate in a discussion or exercise his right to vote. (The chief executive should not exercise this right often, although there will be issues about which he feels strongly enough to speak.) The vice president also may serve in various other capacities specified in the bylaws or assigned by the board, for example, as coordinator of all standing committees.

The Secretary

The secretary is the official record keeper of the association and, as such, is responsible for keeping accurate minutes of all meetings and filing them in a minutes ledger. All other official records of the association, such as contracts, membership rosters, correspondence, and proxy votes, also are maintained by the secretary. The person who accepts the secretaryship should realize fully the importance and value of accurate records, which may at some time be needed to support legal commitments.

A good system of communications is essential to every association, and much of the responsibility for establishing this system may fall to the secretary. Among other things, he may be responsible for preparing and sending all official information relating to the association, especially notices of meetings. However, if a management agent is employed by the condominium, the agent usually will do much of this work.

The Treasurer

The treasurer oversees all of the association's financial affairs. For example, he may be responsible for keeping a record of all financial transactions, maintaining a list of unit owners whose assessments are delinquent, hiring an accountant to conduct an annual audit, reviewing the monthly operating statement and comparing it with the budget, and collecting, disbursing, and depositing all of the association's money. Although most of this work actually may be done by a management agent, the ultimate responsibility for it is retained by the treasurer.

The Responsibilities of the Board

As the official governing body of the association, the board of directors has many obligations. Although it always should remain open to ideas and suggestions of all members of the community, the board will have the ultimate responsibility for decisions about the operation of the association. Its decisions must be in line with the powers and duties outlined in the governing documents. These may include any or all of the following:

(1) Providing for the care, upkeep, operation, maintenance, and surveillance of the condominium.

(2) Preparing and adopting an annual budget and determining the amount of common expenses required for the proper operation of the condominium and for administrative business.

(3) Making assessments against unit owners, establishing the method of collecting assessments, and determining the frequency of the installment payments of the annual assessment.

(4) Opening bank accounts on behalf of the association and

designating their signatories.

(5) Collecting assessments, depositing them in proper accounts, and using the monies to carry out the administration of the property.

(6) Enforcing payment of the assessments from unit owners and adopting methods for handling delinquent payments.

(7) Designating, hiring, and dismissing the personnel required to maintain, operate, and repair the condominium.

(8) Acquiring and maintaining adequate insurance.

(9) Making additions, repairs, improvements, and alterations to the common areas in the event of damage or destruction by fire or other casualty.

(10) Enacting rules and regulations governing the use of the property and the conduct of the unit owners.

(11) Enforcing architectural controls.

(12) Levying fines against unit owners for violation of rules and regulations.

(13) Keeping books with detailed accounts of the receipts and expenditures related to the property and administration of the condominium.

(14) Establishing reasonable reserve funds for future common expenses, including repair and replacement of common areas and unforeseen contingencies.

(15) Selecting an auditor, an attorney, and any other professionals whose assistance may be required.

(16) Employing management agents and contractors and outlining their duties.

(17) Bonding all officers and employees who have fiscal responsibilities.

Methods of Fulfilling Its Responsibilities

How the board may best carry out its obligations depends, in large part, on the size of the condominium and the number and kinds of common areas. A development with few or no parks, swimming pools, or recreational buildings probably will not require a great deal of membership involvement in its association. The board of directors of such a project may best act as the dominant decision-making authority. Although the board should remain open to ideas of the other members, it should be able to make decisions without discussion with the total membership.

A condominium with parks and recreational facilities at which unit owners meet and talk presents its board with a different situation. These areas encourage communication among residents, and greater interest in the association is likely to result. The success of such a community may hinge on democratic participation in the decision-making process. In addition, where more functions are to be performed and more common areas maintained, the work of the board of directors is more visible and residents usually will be more willing to lend it a helping hand.

Of course, these are generalities, and many other factors may dictate how a board may best run its association. A very small, homogeneous association, for example, tends to encourage social relationships even where there are no common areas. In such situations, an informal structure that permits all members to participate in decision making may be the best form of governance. On the other hand, large associations, even those with numerous recreational amenities, may operate more efficiently under an authoritative board of directors.

Policies and Resolutions

In order for the board of directors to make consistent and methodical decisions, it must establish administrative policies for handling specific needs or problems through resolutions. A *policy resolution* is a formal statement that is adopted by the board of directors to chart its plan of action.

As a first step in adopting policy, the board should provide all residents with an opportunity to voice their opinions about any policy resolutions that it is considering. This is especially important in the case of resolutions that relate to the residents' rights and obligations, such as, for example, resolutions to establish guest parking guidelines or set rules governing the use of common areas. Copies of such resolutions should be made available to all members of the association, either by mail or through the association newsletter, together with a notice of a public hearing at which they will be discussed. Although the board must make all final decisions adopting or defeating resolutions, these hearings (which may coincide with a regular or special meeting of the board of directors) give the members an opportunity to participate in the policy-making process.

A public policy hearing should not be mistaken for a special membership meeting and therefore need not comply with the membership meeting requirements set forth in the governing documents. By properly advertising the hearing as a special meeting of the board, the board can expect only those persons who are genuinely interested in the resolution at issue to attend and state their views, giving the board background for making a reasonable decision.

When a policy resolution is adopted, the original copy should be filed in a book of resolutions and additional copies sent to each unit owner and/or published in the condominium newsletter. Some associations have found it convenient to adopt a standard form for use in stating policy adopted by resolution. *(See Appendix A for sample Policy Resolution.)*

Some associations have encountered difficulty enforcing resolutions that have not been recorded and made a matter of public record. As a result, some states are considering legislation that would allow policy resolutions to be recorded with the condominium governing documents, giving the association greater power to enforce them.

Chapter 5

Conducting
Effective Meetings

MEETINGS CAN BE the lifeblood of a condominium association, or they can strangle it. Properly conducted meetings can provide a forum for reasonably discussing differing viewpoints and adequately dealing with administrative needs. Meetings that are not run in a businesslike manner may discourage unit owners' interest in the association, jeopardizing its overall soundness.

The governing documents establish requirements for calling and conducting meetings. These must not be overlooked. The success of meetings of the membership and board, however, requires more than merely satisfying the prescribed requirements. Their success may depend in large part on how effective the board is in establishing guidelines for conducting meetings and how faithful it is in following these guidelines.

Membership Meetings

The board of directors has the authority to make most of the decisions that affect the condominium, but certain important matters, including election of directors, must be brought before all the members of the association. It is essential that as many residents as possible attend membership meetings. One of the goals of every board of directors, therefore, should be to persuade the residents of the community that they are needed and wanted at membership meetings.

Notification Procedures

To encourage attendance at membership meetings, every unit owner must be given proper notification. The governing documents should outline basic requirements for notifying unit owners of meetings. The secretary usually is responsible for preparing and mailing the official meeting notice, or where professional management is employed, the agent may prepare and mail the notices. The governing documents probably will prescribe how far in advance of the meeting the notice must be sent. *(See Appendix A for sample Notice of Annual Membership Meeting.)*

The board of directors, however, should take steps beyond these basic requirements. Advance publicity should generate interest in an issue that concerns many of the residents and improve meeting attendance. For example, the board may place an announcement of the meeting in the association newsletter, outlining the business to be discussed. The president also may send each member a personal letter stressing the importance of the meeting. Contact by telephone or on a person-to-person basis also is an appropriate method of encouraging attendance. Board members may visit the units personally, or block chairmen may be assigned to call on various residents.

When and Where

The annual membership meeting is the session that the entire membership is expected to attend. The governing documents should be very specific about the date and time of this meeting. Although the date of the first annual meeting is usually determined in relation to the date on which the first or a certain number of units have been sold, most documents prescribe a certain day of a certain month as the date of all subsequent annual meetings. This permits the members to know the date of the meeting well in advance. For example, the bylaws of a condominium in Maryland state that, after the first annual, or organization, meeting, "the annual meeting of the Council shall be held at 8:00 p.m. on the third Thursday in the month of October of each succeeding year, if not a legal holiday, then on the next secular day following." If the documents do not specify the time of the meeting, the association should consider scheduling an evening session when more residents should be free to attend.

In providing guidelines for the location of a membership meeting, most documents state only that meetings "shall be held at such place as may be designated by the board of directors." The board should find a meeting room that is large enough to accommodate all those who may attend. A condominium clubhouse generally is an ideal meeting place. Very small associations may be able to meet in one member's unit or even in the condominium lobby. Other associations may need to look outside their condominium for meeting rooms. They often will find such facilities available without charge at banks, churches, and other institutions that may offer meeting rooms as a public service to the community.

It is advisable that meetings which must be held away from the condominium project be held as close to it as possible. Typically, there is a direct and inverse relationship between the distance from the condominium that a meeting is held and the number of persons who attend it. To state it more simply, as the distance increases, attendance usually decreases. In addition, if the meeting is held some distance from the condominium, the board must be sure that adequate parking facilities are available.

Special membership meetings of the association also can be called either by the board of directors or the unit owners who represent a certain percentage of votes specified in the governing documents. Proper notification also must be given of special meetings, and the nature of the business to be discussed should be stated in the notice of the meeting. Only the business for which the session was called should be discussed and transacted at a special meeting. The board should exercise discretion in calling special meetings and call them only in the case of emergencies or when matters arise that require the vote of the total association membership.

Quorum Requirements and Voting Rules

A *quorum* is the minimum number of votes held by unit owners that must be represented in person or by proxy before business at a membership meeting can be conducted legally. Governing documents usually hold a majority of the total votes to constitute a quorum. The quorum requirement protects the association from dictatorship by a small number of residents whose decisions may not accurately reflect the majority consensus.

Voting procedures also should be outlined in the governing

documents. The declaration prescribes the number of votes assigned to each unit owner in one of two ways. Unit owners may be assigned one vote per unit or a number equal to their percentages of ownership interest in the common areas. To retain their rights to vote at membership meetings, association members usually must be in good standing; for example, there should be no liens against their units for delinquent assessments.

The vote of a majority of unit owners present at a meeting usually is sufficient for action on most issues brought before the membership. However, some, such as amendment of the declaration, may require a greater percentage of the total vote.

Most associations permit *proxy* voting. A proxy authorizes one unit owner to vote for another who is absent from a meeting. A proxy usually must be filed with the association secretary within a certain number of days prior to the meeting at which it is to be used. Some documents may limit the number of proxy votes each unit owner can cast. *(See Appendix A for sample Proxy.)*

The Order of Business

To assure that membership meetings run smoothly, an *order of business* establishing the sequence in which business is to be considered should be carefully planned and followed. The order of business may be prescribed by the governing documents. If it is not, the board should adopt an order for use at the membership meetings. The following is an example of such an order:

Order of Business for Membership Meetings
Call to order by the president
Roll call
Reading and approval of minutes of last meeting
Reading and acceptance of treasurer's reports
Report of board of directors
Reports of standing committees
Reports of special committees
Report of management agent
Election of officers, if applicable
Approval of budget for the next fiscal year, if applicable
Unfinished business
New business
Announcements
Adjournment

A well-organized order of business should facilitate the democratic process without stifling opinion and ideas.

Board Meetings

With the exception of those few matters that require the vote of the entire membership, all responsibilities related to administration of the condominium association are discharged by the board of directors. Thus, a great deal of business must be transacted and a number of important decisions must be made at board meetings.

Notification Procedures

The governing documents require the secretary to notify the association directors of approaching board meetings and often indicate how far in advance each meeting notification should be made. Although it is not required by the documents, it is equally important that upcoming board meetings be announced to the membership at large. All boards should hold open meetings, thereby giving every resident an opportunity to play a role in the board's decision-making process.

When and Where

Requirements for convening regular meetings of the board of directors should be spelled out somewhere in the governing documents. Documents often specify that "regular meetings of the board of directors may be held at such time and place as shall be determined, from time to time, by a majority of the directors." Many boards find monthly meetings sufficient to handle most administrative matters. However, very small associations may need to meet only quarterly, while very large associations may need to meet as often as weekly. Some documents require that a minimum number of regular board meetings be held each fiscal year, usually two or four. The documents also should provide for calling special board meetings to handle urgent business.

To encourage participation, regular board meetings should be held at regular times—for example, at a certain time of a certain day of each month, such as at 8:00 p.m. on the third Thursday of each month. Most board meetings are held in the evening to permit the greatest number of residents to attend.

Board meetings should be held in the condominium club-house, if there is one, or in some other convenient and, if possible, regular location. Whatever the size of the board, the meeting place should be large enough to comfortably accommodate the membership at large, all of whom should be invited to attend.

Quorum Requirements and Voting Rules

A quorum—that is, a majority of directors—must be present before any business may be transacted to protect the association against domination by one or two board members. Motions may be carried by the vote of a majority of the directors present at a meeting.

The Order of Business

Board meetings also should follow a standard order of business. The governing documents probably will not prescribe one; therefore, the board should adapt the order of business followed by the association's membership meetings to its own meetings. The following order has been successfully followed by several condominium association boards:

Order of Business for Board Meetings
Call to order
Reading and approval of minutes
Reading and acceptance of treasurer's report
Reports of standing committees
Reports of special committees
Report of management agent
Unfinished business
New business
Public discussion
Adjournment

Making Meetings More Effective

Adherence to parliamentary procedure is essential to keeping debate focused on the appropriate subject. Therefore, every association should refer to *Robert's Rules of Order* for guidelines to conducting all business meetings. Indeed, most governing documents require that the basic parliamentary procedures outlined in the *Rules of Order* be followed at business meetings. These rules assist in smoothing the flow of a meeting and provide a method for dealing with any questions of procedure that may arise.

Adherence to parliamentary procedure is even more important at membership meetings which, because they are attended by a greater number of persons, require a greater degree of formality to transact business and protect each member's rights.

Making and Acting on Motions

Parliamentary procedure requires every item of business to be brought before the association membership by means of a *motion*. A motion is a formal proposal by a member on which the membership must act.

Making and acting on a motion requires seven steps:

(1) The member who wishes to make a motion *obtains the floor* when the chairman formally recognizes him and gives him the exclusive right to speak.

(2) The member *makes a motion*. The motion or proposal usually is introduced when the member says, "I move that...." A long or complex motion should be submitted in writing to the secretary. After the motion has been made, the member is seated.

(3) The motion is *seconded* by another member. The second to a motion indicates that at least one other member believes the subject to be important enough to be brought before the membership. If there is no second, the chairman should go on to other business. It is not necessary for another member to obtain the floor in order to say, "I second the motion."

(4) The chairman *states the question* on the motion, that is, he restates the motion and opens it to debate by the membership. If the wording of a motion does not clearly state its intention, the chairman should put it in suitable form without changing its meaning. Before the question is stated, the person who made the motion has the right to change its wording or to withdraw it completely. Once the question has been stated, no changes in it can be made, nor can it be withdrawn without the consent of the membership.

(5) The motion is *debated*. If the person who made the motion wishes to speak, he should be the first person called on. Each

person who wishes to speak should be given the opportunity to do so before anyone who already has spoken is called on a second time. Debate should be limited to the motion that is before the membership.

(6) The chairman *puts the question* by repeating the motion and asking the members to vote on it. Most motions are passed by a simple majority of the votes present.

(7) The president *announces the results* of the vote, specifically stating whether the motion has been adopted or rejected by the membership.

Kinds of Motions

Most motions can be classified under four categories—*main motions, subsidiary motions, privileged motions,* and *incidental motions*. A main motion brings business before the association members, who are required to take action on it. The other three categories of motions, commonly called *secondary motions,* either relate to the main motion or involve emergency or procedural questions.

Subsidiary Motions. A subsidiary motion changes or affects the way in which a main motion is handled and must be voted on before the main motion is put to a vote. For example, a subsidiary *motion to postpone indefinitely* may be taken when the assembly prefers not to take action on the original motion. If a motion to postpone indefinitely is adopted, it kills the main motion for the duration of the meeting and forestalls a vote on the question. It is a tactic that may be used when an ill-chosen motion has been made or when a motion can be neither appropriately adopted nor rejected.

A member who wishes to change the wording of a main motion may make a *motion to amend*. This is a motion to modify, within certain limits, a main motion before it is acted on. Passage of a motion to amend only changes the wording of the original motion; it does not mean that the original motion has been adopted.

If a member believes that not enough information has been presented to permit an intelligent decision on a subject, he may make a *motion to commit* or *refer* a pending question to a committee for study and resubmission to the assembly at a later date. A member who wishes to delay a decision on a pending question may make a *motion to postpone definitely* or *to postpone to a certain time*, which would delay action on the pending question until a certain time in the future. The motion to postpone definitely also may specify the date on which the question is to be recalled.

A common problem of many association meetings is debate that goes on indefinitely. To avoid this situation, a member may make a *motion to limit* (or *extend the limits of*) *debate*. Such a motion may state that debate should be limited to a certain amount of time or that it should end at a prescribed time or that each speaker should be allowed only a limited amount of time for debate. Another method of speeding the conduct of a meeting is to *move the previous question*—that is, to bring the members to an immediate vote on the pending question. If the motion is passed, debate on the question and amendment close immediately.

The *motion to lay on the table* is one that often is abused or misused. Such a motion permits the membership to set aside temporarily a pending question when a more urgent matter arises. No specific time is set for taking up the matter again. The motion to table is a necessary tool to enable the membership to deal with emergencies when they arise. However, it should only be used to delay consideration of a question and not to kill it.

Privileged Motions. A privileged motion usually relates to urgent or special matters. Privileged motions interrupt consideration of other matters. One, a *motion to call for the orders of the day*, requires the assembly to conform to the prescribed order of business and may be moved if the chairman does not adhere to the agenda. A member also may make a *motion to raise a question of privilege*. This permits him to interrupt pending business to state an urgent request or make a motion on an immediate problem, as, for example, when there is too much noise in the room to hear the business that is being conducted.

A *motion for a recess* proposes that a short intermission be called. Passage of such a motion does not end the meeting, whose business should be resumed when the recess ends at the point at which it was interrupted. A recess might be called to permit members time to count ballots, gather necessary information, or hold informal consultations.

A meeting can be ended by a *motion to adjourn*, which can be made and passed even while business is pending, provided that the time for the next meeting is established by the members.

Under certain conditions, the assembly may wish to set a date and hour at which to hold another meeting prior to the next regularly scheduled meeting. In such cases, a *motion to fix the time to which to adjourn* can be made.

Incidental Motions. An incidental motion involves questions of procedure that arise out of another motion and must be considered before the motion in question is voted on. Most incidental motions are undebatable and must be acted on immediately before business can proceed. Although numerous kinds of incidental motions may be made, five should adequately serve the needs of most associations.

A member who believes that the chairman is not enforcing parliamentary rules may call attention to that fact by moving the *point of order*, thereby calling on the chair to make a ruling. In cases in which the membership wishes to take up a matter in violation of parliamentary rules, a *motion to suspend the rules* may be made. A member who does not wish a main motion to be discussed may make a *motion to object to the consideration of the question*. Such a motion can only be made before debate on the main motion has begun and before any subsidiary motion has been stated.

If a pending main motion or an amendment to it consists of two or more parts that are capable of standing as individual questions, the assembly can vote to treat each part separately. This course of action is proposed by a *motion for division of a question*.

Some decisions may be made by voice vote or a vote by show of hands, the result of which is announced by the chairman. A member who doubts the accuracy of the chair's announcement of the result of such a vote can demand a *division of the assembly* requiring the members to stand to indicate their votes.

Motions to Renew Motions. *Robert's Rules of Order* also provides for a set of specific main motions that bring a question before the membership a second time. One such motion is a *motion to take from the table*, which reopens a motion tabled in the current or a previous session. A *motion to rescind* cancels a previous action, while a *motion to amend something previously adopted* can be made to change, in part, the text or wording of a motion that already has been passed.

Often a question will be referred to a committee but, for various reasons, the committee will not make a final report on it.

As long as the question is in the committee's hands, the members of the assembly can consider no other motion involving it or a similar question. A *motion to discharge a committee* removes the question from the committee's consideration and puts it before the members. This is one parliamentary method of dealing with a subject when a committee fails to do so.

The members may adopt a motion but, for one reason or another, subsequently wish to reconsider it at the same meeting. To reopen the question, a *motion to reconsider* can be made by a member who voted with the prevailing side. Passage of such a motion brings the question before the members as though it had not been considered previously.

Parliamentary procedure also prescribes that certain motions take precedence over certain other motions, that some motions do not need to be seconded, that some motions may not be amended, debated, or reconsidered, and that some motions require more than a majority vote. *(See Appendix A for Parliamentary Rules Governing Motions.)*

Facilitating Business Meetings

Parliamentary procedure can facilitate the functioning of both board and membership meetings. However, an association may wish to adopt additional guidelines to make its meetings more effective.

The first requirement for effective meetings is advance preparation. An order of business should be prepared prior to the meeting and a copy sent to each person who will take part in it. Thus, the order of business should be sent to each unit owner prior to an annual meeting and to each director prior to a board meeting. Then, the agenda must be carefully adhered to. This is not to suggest that resident participation in meetings is not needed or wanted. Adequate time should be allowed at membership meetings to permit debate on pending motions. Even at board meetings, at which the board has the decision-making authority, time should be allocated to discussion of subjects that are of concern to unit owners.

In addition, all meetings should begin and end on time, and the time at which a meeting is scheduled to end should be announced prior to the meeting. Chairmen will find it much easier to adhere to an agenda when all participants know when the meeting is to end.

Understanding parliamentary procedure can speed a meeting, and the use of appropriate motions can facilitate the decision-making process. All members can contribute to the efficiency of the meeting by limiting their debate on motions, planning motions carefully to avoid unnecessary amendment and discussion, and presenting their motions to the chair in writing. The chairman should see to it that motions are phrased properly and that no one member speaks to a question twice until all other members have had an opportunity to speak. A competent secretary is especially important to the efficient operation of a meeting, and the president and secretary should work together as a team to keep the meeting running smoothly. In addition, the president may consider appointing a *parliamentarian* to advise him during meetings as to the rules of parliamentary procedure.

Chapter 6

The Committee Structure

ONCE THE BOARD of directors and its officers have been elected, the next step is to appoint committees. A committee system can relieve the board of some of its workload and facilitate business sessions by researching issues prior to their debate at meetings. Committees should be assigned specific tasks and encouraged to make brief but complete reports and recommendations to board and membership meetings. No board of directors consisting of as few as three or even as many as nine persons can function adequately without the assistance of others. Almost every condominium community consists of a broad range of members. A committee structure of *standing committees* and *special committees* can enable the board to draw upon the expertise of the association's various members to help it run the community.

The Standing Committees

Standing committees are created to perform ongoing functions for the association. The board of directors should appoint a standing committee for each recurring need of the condominium community. A condominium of average size with some recreational amenities probably will have at least ten basic categories of need that may be served by committees. These needs are for architectural control, oversight of the landscaping and grounds, budget and finance and insurance matters, maintenance, development and review of rules and regulations, production of the newsletter, and coordination of social, welcoming, and recreational activities. Later, as it gains experience, the board may wish to restructure its committees, perhaps combining standing committees or establishing new ones. How many and what kinds of committees a condominium project needs depends upon its circumstances. Small associations probably need only a few committees, while larger groups may need and be able to support numerous highly specialized committees. Generally, standing committee members are appointed to one-year terms.

The president usually is responsible for making committee appointments but should seek the advice of other board members in doing so. The process should begin with a careful survey of all unit owners to determine who may contribute to the association's success. One way to do so is to send a questionnaire to all unit owners to determine who would be interested in volunteering to serve on committees, asking members to specify which committees, if any, they are interested in working on. The questionnaire also might ask how much time the unit owner has to devote to committee work and if he has any applicable experience. *(See Appendix A for sample Committee Interest Questionnaire.)*

The board must decide how large each committee should be. The size of a committee should reflect the relative amount of work associated with its function. For example, three members may be adequate for a social committee, while seven may be needed for the more active architectural control committee. A balance must be reached both in number and types of persons who are appointed to a committee. Because the members must interact with each other, it is imperative that they be able to work together. At the same time, they must be able to debate the issues intelligently and consider all sides before arriving at a consensus.

The Architectural Control Committee

Each association should have an architectural control committee to preserve the architectural integrity of the condominium development. In fact, the governing documents of most condominiums require such a committee to be formed. Its goal should be to maintain the appearance and value of the property. Its primary function should be twofold: to recommend architectural standards and to review all proposed changes that would affect the appearance of the condominium in relation to those standards.

The architectural control committee usually is assigned the task of establishing a system for considering and acting on all proposed architectural changes. Most governing documents offer it guidelines for this system that usually call for a four-step process: formal application, review by the committee, recommendation to the board, and approval or rejection by the board. Alternately, some associations' governing documents call for the committee to approve or reject requests, and as a result the third step is omitted.

To speed this process and ensure fair and consistent decisions, the committee should adopt architectural standards. Architectural standards may deal with such things as fences, patios, exterior paint colors, and porch railings. In fact, anything that can be done by a unit owner to his unit or by the association to the common areas may be subject to architectural standards. In some cases, the developer will guide the committee in adopting standards. In most cases, however, the committee must develop its own specifications consistent with the governing documents and state and local law.

Even in those projects that employ professional management to assist it, membership on the architectural control committee may be the most demanding assignment in the entire community. This is especially true of garden and townhouse communities, all or most of whose units may have outdoor entrances that the owners often may wish to modify. In many associations, the architectural control committee may have to meet even more often than the board of directors. For this reason, appointees should be available to meet regularly as well as to periodically inspect proposed areas of change.

The Landscaping and Grounds Committee

Many condominium communities include numerous outdoor common areas for playgrounds, parks, parking lots, and driveways, and a considerable portion of their budgets often is earmarked for landscaping and grounds care. In such a community, the landscaping and grounds committee (sometimes called the outdoor maintenance committee) serves a vital function.

Although few unit owners wish to be concerned with the maintenance of the grounds, everyone is aware of the outdoor environment. Residents usually are quick to complain about lawns and shrubbery that do not meet their personal standards. Because the exterior of a condominium development creates the first impression of visitors, much time and effort is invested in care of the grounds. This committee probably will be responsible for outlining specifications for landscaping and gardening contracts, detailing them in writing, preparing bid packages, evaluating formal bids, and making appropriate recommendations to the board of directors. Once the board of directors has negotiated a contract for outdoor maintenance, the committee may be assigned to supervise the contractor's performance. If professional management is employed, this responsibility may be assigned to the management agent. In such cases, the committee should work with the agent to see to it that contracts are prepared properly and fulfilled adequately.

The landscape and grounds committee makes expense recommendations to the board at the time the annual budget is prepared. In addition to planning for work that will be required on a regular basis, the committee should periodically inspect the grounds and, based on this inspection, recommend any improvements or repairs that are indicated. Many condominium owners formerly lived in single-family houses with grounds and gardens. Finding experienced persons to serve on this committee and make this inspection, therefore, should not be difficult.

The landscaping and grounds committee often is required to review individual owners' requests for planting shrubs or flowers or making other changes to the grounds and acts, as does the architectural control committee, by setting landscaping standards, reviewing all requests for changes, and making recommendations to the board of directors or approving or rejecting applications itself.

The Budget and Finance Committee

One of the most important advisory bodies of any condominium association, the budget and finance committee works with the treasurer, the management agent, and the board of directors on all financial matters.

The committee, of which the treasurer usually is a member, usually assists in preparing the annual budget for submission to the board of directors. This responsibility requires it to meet with the chairmen of other committees to determine the amounts of money they need to operate the various facets of the total community. The committee also may set maximum limits on expenditures in any category of operation, inform the other committees of these limits, and assist them in maintaining their activities within these parameters.

The budget and finance committee must continually review the operating costs of the community, keeping the board apprised of any areas that require re-evaluation. If actual expenses greatly exceed budgeted expenses, the committee may recommend that a special assessment be levied. This would require that a detailed explanation be made to all unit owners. In the event that insufficient funds are generated by existing assessments, the budget and finance committee may recommend that they be increased. Similarly, if the efficient operation of the community or other factors result in lower costs, the committee may recommend a reduction in assessments.

Another function of the finance committee may be to recommend an auditor to perform the annual financial review of the association's books. This may require the committee to obtain bids from accounting firms and make recommendations to the board of directors. Bylaws usually specify how often an audit must be performed.

Additional responsibilities of the budget and finance committee may include deciding who is to prepare the association's income tax return, reviewing its tax status with its attorneys, and supervising reserve funds. It also may be asked to adopt policies to collect delinquent assessments, guidelines for which may be set forth in the governing documents.

The Insurance Committee

Most governing documents address the insurance needs of the condominium association, and because these requirements tend to be complex, the association should consider appointing an insurance committee. This body should be required to review the association's insurance policies each year, as well as immediately prior to their expiration. It also should obtain bids for new policies from various insurers and may be authorized to handle insurance claims. If a management agent is employed by the project, he may be responsible for assisting the committee in handling especially large claims.

An insurance agent who is a member of the condominium community would make an ideal member of this committee.

The Maintenance Committee

The maintenance committee serves in a capacity similar to that of the landscaping and grounds committee but is responsible for the interior and structural portions of the common areas. It may be required to periodically inspect the interior common areas, review work specifications and estimates for contractural work, and inspect and supervise work in progress, working closely with the management agent where one is employed.

The maintenance committee should meet regularly—perhaps monthly or bimonthly, depending on the size of the development —to walk through the common areas, listing any defects noted. It then should make appropriate recommendations for repairs, improvements, and replacements to the board of directors and the management agent. In addition, a large share of the maintenance committee's time probably may be devoted to preparing bid specifications for contracts and presenting recommendations on contractors to the board. A management agent who is experienced in maintenance contracts can be especially helpful to it in drafting these specifications.

Many condominium communities will have members who have experience in construction or home improvement, such as plumbers or electricians, and these persons should be excellent members of the maintenance committee.

Because day-to-day housekeeping also is essential to the preservation of the condominium's integrity, many boards appoint housekeeping subcommittees to work with the maintenance committee. This subcommittee may play a very important role in the self-managed condominium, making regular inspections of the interior common areas and reporting its findings to the management agent and board of directors. It also may be asked to review work schedules of employees with the management agent and to review employees' salaries and benefits and recommend any changes to the board.

The Rules and Regulations Committee

Periodically, it inevitably becomes necessary for an association to change the rules and regulations that govern use of common areas. Bylaws may need to be updated to comply with changing attitudes and demands of the owners and house rules and regulations may require modification. Therefore, there is need for a committee to review the governing documents, react to the experiences that condominium living presents, and suggest whatever changes may be necessary.

State regulations usually require a two-thirds or three-fourths vote of all owners to approve changes in bylaws. However, most documents are flexible enough to allow the board of directors to adopt house rules and regulations. Provided that the rules and regulations adopted in this way are reasonable, they permit the community to function smoothly.

Recent court decisions have struck down house rules and regulations made by certain boards on the ground that they were too stringent and did not permit free expression of the members or the full use of the common areas. Therefore, the rules and regulations committee (sometimes called the bylaws committee) and the board must be reasonable when making decisions that will affect the entire community and consider issues objectively in light of the interests of all community members rather than from subjective or self-serving viewpoints.

The Social Committee

One of the best ways to bring unit owners together to discuss the community and its operations is through periodic social functions. The social committee may consider planning cocktail parties, cookouts, or swimming parties to generate a friendly atmosphere and encourage a sense of community. Easter egg hunts and Christmas caroling are other appropriate social activities of a condominium community.

Although the social committee may receive a minimal amount of money for its expenses, it usually can support its activities by charging a small admission fee to events it sponsors. This committee need not meet regularly but may concentrate its efforts in the weeks immediately preceding each social event.

The Newsletter Committee

The association newsletter is an important link in the network of communications among the entire association and should be prepared and published on a regular basis by a newsletter committee.

Newsletter content should be supplied by the board of directors, committee chairmen, and the management agent. The newsletter should report any decisions made by the board or the committees that affect the membership and keep residents advised of any social functions that are scheduled. The newsletter may be fully funded by the association, or it may support itself in full or in part by selling advertising to local businesses.

The newsletter should bind together the association membership. It should not be a vehicle for debating issues or otherwise creating divisiveness in the community. Obviously, any member of the association with experience as a journalist would be ideally suited to serve on this committee.

The Welcoming Committee

Moving can be a traumatic experience, but a welcoming committee can make the transition from one home to another much more pleasant. This committee may function very much like the social committee in planning activities to bring owners together, but it also should serve as a vehicle for informing new residents about the association form of governance. A member of the welcoming committee should visit all new residents, possibly providing them with information about shops in the area, a map of neighborhood schools and churches, and a list of other unit owners. This committee also may submit the names and addresses of new owners for publication in the association newsletter.

The Recreation Committee

In warmer climates the recreation committee generally functions throughout the year, while in the northern half of the country it may provide services only during the summer months. Small condominiums may have no need for this committee at all, while in some condominium communities, its only function may be to supervise the operation of a swimming pool or tennis courts. In large associations with many amenities, the recreation committee also may run a community clubhouse, plan trips, and organize sports activities and educational classes. The functions of the recreation committee sometimes are performed by three separate committees: a facilities committee, a pool committee, and a recreational activities committee.

Like the other committees, the recreation committee probably will need money to carry out its activities, and the committee members may be responsible for projecting its expenses when the annual budget is prepared. Plans for the upcoming summer season should be made during the late fall and early winter. Such planning may require it to obtain bids for lifeguards, pool chemical service, and resurfacing of tennis courts. Once the summer season begins, the committee should monitor the operation of all recreational facilities and make any recommendations for changes in the rules that govern their use to the rules and regulations committee. Other functions of the recreation committee may be to establish a guest fee structure, be responsible for vending machines, plan such annual events as swim meets, tennis tournaments, and bicycle field trips, and schedule use of a clubhouse.

Special Committees

The board of directors may have special needs that arise for which special committees will be needed. *Special* or *ad hoc committees* are appointed to carry out specific nonrecurring tasks and are disbanded as soon as these tasks are completed. Usually, a special committee goes out of existence when it makes its final report to the board of directors or at a membership meeting. Special committees should never be established to perform functions that fall within the responsibilities of existing standing committees. This disrupts the normal administrative flow and could be demoralizing to the members of the standing committees.

Although special committees often are smaller than standing committees, when such a committee is appointed for investigation of an issue, it should represent, to as great a degree as possible, the various points of view of the association.

Guiding Association Committees

Committees can be useful to the efficient functioning of a condominium community if they are given proper guidance by the board of directors. Appointing committees is only half of the board's job. Guidelines for individual committees should be drafted to direct them in fulfilling their purposes and explaining their exact roles in the overall administration of the association. The tasks of all committees should be carefully delineated and copies of task checklists given to all committee members to avoid misunderstanding about the roles they are expected to play. Because the roles of many committees overlap, the importance of cooperation also should be stressed. In addition, the board of directors should establish administrative guidelines for all chairmen of committees and for all committee members.

Guidelines for Committee Chairmen

A committee chairman serves a very important role. He acts as liaison between the board of directors and the committee membership and must be able to work well with both groups. The effectiveness of a committee chairman is determined in large part by his ability to properly advise and work with the board and its president. He can do this only if he is able to guide his committee toward clearly defined goals. The following guidelines for committee chairmen are offered to assist chairmen in carrying out their responsibilities effectively and to enable them to play appropriate roles in the overall administrative effort.

(1) Begin the meeting on time and announce the time at which it will be adjourned. If the members are aware that the meeting will end at a specific time, the business session probably will move more quickly.

(2) Have an order of business and follow it precisely.

(3) Assign a secretary to keep minutes of each meeting and see that all committee members receive a copy of them.

(4) Do not allow general discussions and extraneous conversations to disrupt the business at hand.

(5) When each speaker finishes his discussion of an issue, sum up what he has said.

(6) Without stifling reasonable debate and constructive disagreement, halt rambling discussion that appears to be leading to no conclusion by appointing a subcommittee to research the issue.

(7) Do not allow hasty actions to be taken because there is not enough time for adequate consideration. Unless the issue is of urgent importance, suggest that discussion be continued at the next meeting.

(8) At the end of the meeting, ask the committee members if they are satisfied that each subject has been given adequate attention.

(9) Use appropriate parliamentary procedures to facilitate the flow of the meeting. (Small committees, however, can use less formal, modified procedures.)

(10) Be prepared to present complete yet brief formal committee reports to the board of directors or the membership. Each report should be submitted in writing and present the findings of any research and, where applicable, specify recommendations based on that research.

Guidelines for Committee Members

While the committee chairman is instrumental to the process of making decisions on issues within the realm of his committee's responsibilities, each committee member must realize his own obligation to contribute to the group's overall effectiveness. The rules that follow should enable the committee members to work together toward meeting the goals of the committee.

(1) Prepare adequately for each meeting. Complete any required research or reading and study the order of business prior to the meeting. If reports have been assigned, prepare them in writing and distribute them to all committee members prior to the meeting.

(2) Ask for the floor when you wish to contribute to the discussion. Speak clearly and loudly enough to be heard by everyone present.

(3) Keep your remarks brief and do not stray from the subject being debated. If a speech must be long, conclude with a summary of your remarks.

(4) Do not bring up issues that are not on the order of business. Refrain from extraneous conversation.

Unit owners may be unfamiliar with committee operation. Therefore, the board of directors of each condominium association should adopt its own guidelines for committee chairmen and members. Lacking such guidelines, the committees' meetings could dissolve into gripe sessions, the purpose of the meetings may be forgotten, and the objectives of the meeting never achieved.

Chapter 7

Management Alternatives

WHETHER OR NOT LIVING in a condominium community is a profitable and pleasurable experience for the unit owners may depend largely on the association's management plan. A well-managed condominium development will permit those who have purchased units to enjoy all the benefits of condominium ownership. When a condominium is managed poorly, condominium living and ownership can become a nightmare.

The term "management," as it applies to a condominium and its association of unit owners, relates broadly to all of the community's activities and encompasses far more considerations than those involving the buildings and grounds. Condominium management is a mixture of many disciplines, including, but not limited to, law, accounting, business, insurance, communications, maintenance, and psychology. It is a unique function that requires special training and skills.

Each condominium unit owner should understand what a *management plan* is and how it works. The association is a self-governing organization that elects a board of directors to make the decisions that affect the operation of the community. One of the most important decisions it must make concerns the management plan. There are three recognized alternatives to condominium management: *self-management, resident management*, and *professional management*. Whichever plan is chosen, the board retains the responsibility for adopting operating procedures and administrative policies. However, the management plan is the means by which it implements these policies and procedures.

91

The best management plan is the one that is designed to fit the specific needs of the condominium community it is designed to serve. The management plan of a 12-unit condominium probably would not work for a 60-unit condominium and certainly would not be practical for a 250-unit condominium. The 12-unit condominium may operate effectively by using volunteers to perform management tasks. The 60-unit condominium may arrange to have a management agent carry out its administrative, financial, and maintenance activities, and the 250-unit condominium may employ a resident manager and staff to work for it exclusively. The size and other circumstances of each condominium must dictate which management plan is most appropriate.

Self-Management

Self-management is the do-it-yourself way of running a condominium association. When a board elects to be self-managed, it is deciding not only to make the policy decisions but to carry them out as well, becoming the supervisor and coordinator of all activities that take place within the community.

Self-management does not necessarily require self-maintenance, as many condominium unit owners mistakenly believe it does. The association that chooses to act as its own manager will not necessarily expect the unit owners to cut the grass or haul away the garbage. But the unit owners, and especially the association directors, will be expected to fulfill a number of administrative, operational, and fiscal obligations.

In order to accomplish the work of the association, the self-managed association may contract for certain services, hire full- or part-time employees, or use volunteers from within the community. The most viable self-management plan combines all three approaches.

Employing Staff

Although a full-time staff probably would be too expensive for small associations, one or two part-time employees may be hired to perform certain tasks in a self-managed condominium community. These might include lawn mowing, typing of minutes of meetings, regular lobby cleaning, or keeping financial records.

When employees are hired to carry out some of the association's duties, they are directly accountable to the board of directors and/or the appropriate committee chairman. Employing staff permits the board to delegate responsibility while still retaining a great deal of control over the operation of the condominium. However, it does make the board's job a very demanding one because it requires the directors to become involved with such personnel matters as hiring and firing, determining Workers' Compensation, withholding requirements, and Social Security, and supervising the work of the employees.

Dealing with Contractors

Even if it has support staff, an association undoubtedly will have to retain contractors to provide certain services. These might include long-term maintenance contracts for such things as landscaping, janitorial, or trash removal services, or special contracts for such jobs as exterior painting or plumbing. Long-term contracts usually cover services performed on a regular basis at a fixed fee.

Although use of a contractor relieves the board of many personnel problems, it requires the directors to take on a new responsibility—contract negotiation. Preparing contract specifications that adequately detail the job can be quite a challenge to the inexperienced board. To avoid possible problems, the board should have all contracts reviewed by legal counsel before they are signed. In addition to contract negotiations, the board also will have to assume supervisory duties to assure that each contractor is living up to the agreement.

Utilizing Volunteers

A self-managed association probably will discover that it has members who would be willing to perform—and even enjoy performing—certain maintenance and repair and management jobs. Someone may volunteer to mow the lawn, for example, or be responsible for overseeing a custodian's weekly cleaning of the lobby. If there are enough active volunteers in a condominium community, the board may let them perform the chores they are interested in. Thus, especially in comdominiums where many retired persons live and are at home much of the time, a self-help program of management can be very successful.

The volunteer self-help approach works very well as long as the volunteers do not tire of their jobs or begin to neglect their responsibilities. However, owners who may have been very maintenance-conscious home owners may not feel the same degree of commitment to a condominium community. Once the novelty of working for the association wears off, volunteers may ignore their assignments, and it is difficult, if not impossible, to force them to do their work. Of course, this does not always happen, and many condominium associations have adopted extremely successful self-help self-management plans.

Choosing Self-Management

The essential ingredient of successful self-management is unit owners who have plenty of time, a certain amount of experience, and a professional attitude toward their work for the association. For example, the treasurer must understand accounting systems and bookkeeping methods and be willing to devote a significant amount of time to maintaining proper financial records and collecting assessments. The chairman of the grounds committee should have some gardening experience and be willing to supervise either a contract landscaping service or a gardener. If the association is fortunate enough to have members who have these three attributes—talent, time, and concern—self-management may be the best route for the association to travel.

Size of the development is another important factor. Although it should not be the ultimate factor in deciding if an association can manage itself, a sound case can be made for limiting self-management to condominiums of fewer than 20 units with few common areas and recreational amenities.

The major advantage of self-management (and a major consideration, especially for very small associations) is its cost. Self-management, especially when it includes an active self-help program, is inexpensive. However, if the motivation for adopting self-management is primarily economic, the board must take care not to be penny wise and pound foolish. It makes little sense to save each unit owner a few dollars a month on the cost of professional management if the value of their property ultimately is decreased by thousands of dollars as a result of poor management.

An equally important consideration is the question of from whom contractors, employees, and volunteers are to receive direction. A self-managed association should not permit every unit owner to be "boss." The board must not permit each resident to give instructions to employees or make decisions that should be made by the board. Instead, it should appoint one person to supervise all ongoing work.

The board also should consider the possible legal liability implications of self-management. Members of the board of directors are legally liable for their decisions. They are responsible to their fellow unit owners as well as to the general public. Even though many governing documents contain a hold harmless clause that tries to protect the board members from legal responsibility for their actions, this may not be adequate to protect them from being sued for mismanagement. The board must decide if its members have enough experience to properly run an association without mismanaging it. In addition, premiums paid for directors' and officers' liability coverage and the cost of fidelity bonds may be higher for associations that do not employ professional management, and this could indirectly raise the cost of self-management.

Individuals embarking on new adventures are sure to be excited about what lies ahead of them. If condominium residents consider the self-management of their community to be an adventure, their level of enthusiasm is likely to be high and self-management may be workable. However, the initial interest of the unit owners may wane, especially when demands on volunteer time are great. Before a board of directors chooses self-management, it should consider how it would operate if the volunteer members began to ignore their duties, a situation that could spell disaster for the condominium association.

It should be clear, however, that self-management need not end in failure. There are success stories of associations for which it has worked well and for a long time. If everyone takes his ownership responsibilities seriously, is professional in his approach toward executing them, and has a cooperative attitude, self-management may be a viable alternative to running the condominium community and a most rewarding experience.

Resident Management

A *resident association manager*, in this context, is one who is hired by and works exclusively for the association rather than as an on-site employee of a property management company. If a condominium is large enough to support the salary of such an individual, hiring a full-time resident association manager may be its best management alternative.

A board may employ a resident manager to oversee all of the operations of the community under its direction. In such a situation, the board plans the course of administrative action and the manager carries out the policies it establishes. The extent of a resident manager's role may vary, depending on the size of the condominium. Based upon the degree of authority a resident manager is given and how closely his work must be overseen by the board, a resident management plan may be more closely akin to either self-management or professional management.

A manager usually will need to hire a crew to facilitate the smooth functioning of the community and may employ maintenance, bookkeeping, and secretarial personnel on a full- or part-time basis. Big jobs and the delivery of certain services will have to be contracted for. A resident manager typically relieves the board of the day-to-day administration and operation of the community. This should enable the board to concentrate on long-range planning. Although the manager works directly with and reports to the board, which is responsible for the overall management plan, committees usually have extremely important and visible functions in associations that adopt a resident manager plan.

A resident manager usually is paid on a cost-per-unit basis, but this cost varies depending on the scope of his assignment. As partial remuneration, the association may provide him with a place to live in the condominium.

A resident association management plan permits the association to retain a great deal of control over the operation of the community while relieving its members of time-consuming daily tasks. In addition, a resident manager can provide some degree of continuity to the association despite changes in the board that occur as new directors are elected each year. However, there remains the possibility that the resident manager will leave the association. A breakdown in management continuity then is likely to occur, especially if the board has become dependent on the manager. Knowledge and experience of the association are likely to be lost when the manager leaves, and problems may arise in training a new resident manager. The resident manager also may occasionally be away from the condominium temporarily because of vacations or illness, and similar problems may surface at these times.

To prepare for occasional absences and possible turnovers in resident managers, the board of directors should institute a system of regular checks to maintain a balance of responsibility between manager and board. This system may involve periodic reviews of the manager's work and maintenance by the association secretary of copies of all financial reports, correspondence, contracts, and other documents that are kept by the manager.

Selecting a Resident Manager

The most difficult job of the board that elects the resident association management plan may be finding an experienced person who is qualified to manage the condominium. The process must be a very careful one if this management alternative is to properly serve the needs of the association.

The board's first step should be to list all of the responsibilities it wishes to turn over to a resident manager. These might include maintaining correspondence, handling all maintenance functions, and working with the unit owners to resolve disputes. Development of such a list should force the board members to agree on the responsibilities of a manager and enable the board to accurately estimate the amount of compensation appropriate to the job.

After preparing a job description based on this list, the board should seek candidates through the best sources available. These may include newspaper classified advertising sections, employment agencies, or local real estate or property management boards. The selection process should include a careful study of each candidate's resume, a check of references, and an interview. The board should consider not only the candidates' practical skills and management experience but also their personality traits, such as their ability to work with boards and committees and to get along with people.

Professional Condominium Management

A plan of professional condominium management relieves the board of directors of much of the burden of personal attention to the details of running the community. When a board of directors is considering which management plan to adopt, it should remain aware that the members of the board will be changing regularly. Through the electoral process outlined in the governing documents, new directors will be chosen periodically by the association members. Even if the terms of the directors are staggered, the character of the board will change from one year to the next because of this continual turnover.

A professional condominium management plan can offer much-needed continuity to the operation of the association. A management agent can serve as the stabilizing force in a community that otherwise would be in a constant state of flux. The agent can bring new board members up to date on the activities of the association and serve as liaison between one board and the next. Even a resident manager cannot offer the kind of long-term continuity that a management agent can. The loss of management firm personnel through vacation, illness, or termination should not affect the management of the association to the degree that the loss of a resident manager may.

Most condominiums of 100 or more units usually are able to support a management fee that covers nearly all management functions and is acceptable to the unit owners. Arranging for professional service for smaller condominiums, however, may present a challenge. Condominiums of 50 or fewer units may need a specially tailored management plan. Nor can they expect to realize savings in the management fee commensurate with their size because there are certain irreducible costs associated with assuming operation of a project.

However, a professional management plan does not have to be all-inclusive. Services provided by management agents can range from consultation to smaller condominiums to the performance of all management functions for larger condominiums. Professional management and association self-help are not necessarily mutually exclusive. The two can go hand-in-hand. Although the board that employs a management agent always retains ultimate responsibility for the operations of the association, professional management may give it more time in which to plan future projects.

Outlining the Role of Professional Management

The board that decides that its association needs professional management must next decide how much assistance to require of the management agent. A 12-unit condominium may need only consultative services, a 25-unit condominium may need only accounting and billing services, and a 70-unit condominium may need an agent to handle all tasks except negotiation of maintenance contracts or decide to turn all management functions over to the agent.

The board should begin to make this determination by listing all of the management functions with which the association is charged. The governing documents should provide guidelines for preparing this list. The specifications of some documents may limit the duties that the management agent can be employed to perform on behalf of the board. However, the major management responsibilities usually fall within one of three categories: fiscal, physical, and administrative. The board members, perhaps working with the various committees, should list all management functions under these three categories and then check off those it wishes to assign to a professional management agent.

It is not necessary for the board to tell the management agent *how* it wants everything done, only that it tell him *what* it wants done. However, an inexperienced board frequently will not really know what services it wants professional management to perform. Therefore, most management firms will agree to hold a preliminary conference with the board of directors to assist it in outlining its needs.

Fiscal Responsibilities. A management agent's fiscal responsibilities may include recommending an operating budget to the board of directors. Although the board retains ultimate responsibility for adopting an association budget, an agent's experience in estimating expenses can be extremely valuable. The agent should have experience in collecting data, analyzing details, and considering various alternatives, experience that most boards of directors could not be expected to have. Of course, both the board and the agent should remember that the agent acts only in an advisory capacity and should not be allowed to dictate how the unit owners are to live or make decisions about how large their assessments will be.

Many associations turn the job of collecting assessments and other income over to a management agent, requiring the agent to bill, receive, record, and deposit all sources of revenue. The agent also may be required to follow up on delinquent payments. The extent of the agent's authority to act in collecting late assessments must be set by the board as a matter of policy. He may be limited to sending out second notices of overdue assessments or authorized to go so far as to institute the filing of liens against delinquent unit owners' mortgages. The agent who is not authorized to pursue collection efforts, or the one who is but fails to collect delinquent accounts, should turn them over to the association's attorney.

In carrying out his responsibilities, a management agent obviously will have to spend some association money. Therefore, the board must decide how disbursements are to be treated. A management agent usually is authorized to make most expenditures provided for in the budget without obtaining formal approval from the board of directors. A limit—often of $500 or $1,000—may be placed on the amount the agent is authorized to spend for any single nonrecurring budgeted expense. Disbursal of any amount exceeding the limit set by the board would require written authorization.

Emergency situations are sure to occur, however, and the board also should consider this possibility when preparing its professional management plan. A management agent should have the authority to make emergency expenditures when the safety of the residents of the community or the value of their property is threatened.

The board also must decide how it wants the management agent to handle the association's money. His fiscal responsibilities, therefore, might include establishing accounting procedures and setting up bank accounts. Typically, the board will want the agent to deposit any money collected from the unit owners in accounts that are separate from the agent's accounts. A checking account is used primarily for the day-to-day operations of an association. Escrow or savings accounts also may be required by the association for replacement or operating reserves and for excess working capital.

In view of the difficulty of preparing financial statements, this fiscal responsibility often is turned over to a management agent. The needs of most boards can be adequately met by the preparation of monthly statements of income and expense. A regular financial report also should show the cash condition of the association, the delinquency status of unit owners, and the balance of reserve accounts. The agent also may be required to prepare annual financial reports as well as certain reports required by the federal government and state agencies. *(See Chapter 10 for a complete discussion of the financial reporting needs of an association.)*

Physical Responsibilities. The management agent also may be delegated responsibility for maintaining and repairing the condominium plant. The board must set maintenance standards; then, it may authorize the agent to assure that the standards are met. Of course, the association must provide adequate funding so that the agent may carry out this responsibility. Therefore, an initial responsibility of the management agent is to develop an annual operating plan, including the scheduling of weekly, monthly, and all other regular maintenance and repair, as well as making provision for irregular and emergency maintenance and repairs. This annual plan of operation also should include a schedule for inspecting work assignments.

To implement this operating plan, the management agent must hire a maintenance staff. Therefore, part of his responsibility is to handle the personnel needs of the condominium, including writing job descriptions and hiring, supervising, and, if necessary, firing staff. The agent also will pay salaries, negotiate collective bargaining agreements, and determine tax withholding and other related employee expenses. Some management firms will insist that maintenance staff be employees of the firm for reasons of control, training, promotional opportunities, and company morale. In other cases, the association may be considered the employer, or the association and the management firm may be considered co-employers. In all cases, the management agent typically is the personnel administrator, but the costs related to employees who work at the condominium are considered association operating costs and are reimbursed to the management firm by the association.

The management agent also may be made responsible for preparing maintenance service contracts and supervising the work of contractors. An agent's background in dealing with contractors should be a major asset to the association, since he should have a good understanding of standard practices.

A major management responsibility is to conduct inspections. The agent should conduct both routine inspections, which should be made on a regular basis to monitor the operating plan of the condominium and help in planning specific programs, and special inspections, which should be made when violations of architectural controls are reported, in case of fire, severe weather, or other emergencies, and when special requests are made by board members or individual unit owners.

Administrative Responsibilities. A management agent is likely to be given some administrative responsibilities. One that every management agent is assigned is that of attending and, often, preparing for meetings. Although he should not be required or expected to attend all meetings, the agent should attend at least the annual membership meeting and certain board meetings. He also may be asked to prepare written reports for meetings that do not require his physical presence.

Many agents are assigned duties in preparation of meetings. For example, the agent may be expected to prepare and send meeting notices, plan the agenda, prepare ballots and proxies and other standard meeting forms, research subjects to be discussed at board or membership meetings, and handle all meeting correspondence, including the minutes.

Administrative record keeping also may be a major part of a management agent's work for the association. The board of directors should list all the records required by the association and decide which the agent should be responsible for. In addition to financial records, these may include transfers of title, resident files, pet and automobile registrations, committee and officer reports, manufacturers' data, all legal documentation, including the governing documents, insurance policies, and government reports, and any other pieces of documentation that relate to the condominium association.

A third administrative responsibility that a management agent may assume is for communications. For example, he may be made responsible for preparation of the condominium association newsletter and mailing of special notices, copies of rules and regulations, or policy resolutions. Correspondence by an agent to unit owners should be prompt, courteous, and direct.

Exclusions. Although a management agent can perform many functions on behalf of the board of directors, there are certain responsibilities that the board should not expect the agent to assume. Specifically, a management agent usually is not professionally trained to offer legal advice, tax help, advice on auditing fiscal records, or advice on architectural or engineering matters.

Nor should a management agent be seen as an arbitrator between unit owners and the developer or as being in any way responsible for the interiors of units or for the association's compliance with the law.

Selecting a Management Firm

Like many of the decisions that the board of directors is required to make, choosing a management firm requires a certain amount of human intuition. But selecting a management firm must involve more than haphazard guesswork. The decision must be based on a complete knowledge of the firm's and the agent's qualifications.

Perhaps the most important requirement of a management firm is that it have some experience in condominium association management. Because condominium development is a relatively new phenomenon, it may not be easy to find such a firm in some parts of the country. While there are some similarities between rental apartment management and condominium management, there are important differences. One has to do with economic motivation. An apartment building is an investment property. The agent who manages rental property is responsible for realizing the highest dollar yield while keeping the property in the best possible condition. The condominium association, on the other hand, is very much aware of costs, but it is not concerned with making a profit.

A second important difference is the presence of resident owners, who can exercise some degree of control over the management agent. The rental property management agent is employed by and reports to a single owner. The condominium manager, on the other hand, deals with an association of owners through its board of directors. The resident owners are likely to demand higher levels of service than tenant residents, who have no ownership interest.

In view of these basic differences, the board of directors should seek a management firm that understands the concept of condominium ownership. Firm members should be familiar with the basic legal documents of condominium associations, be aware of applicable state laws, and understand the differences between owner obligations for the units and for the common areas. Thus, the management agent who has vast experience overseeing the operation of rental properties may not necessarily be the best person to manage the condominium association.

After the board of directors has decided which responsibilities it wishes a management agent to assume, it should prepare a complete and consistent package of information for each firm from which it is seeking bids. The package should contain a complete list of the services it requires, the governing documents, an information sheet showing the number and kinds of units in the project, a list of any outstanding contracts, financial summaries, and any other relevant information about the condominium association. After receiving these bid packages, some management firms may require additional information before they can determine a fee for their services to the association. Some may even have standard questionnaires that they ask the board of directors to complete.

The bid packages should be submitted to the four or five management firms who appear to be of good reputation and have the expertise and integrity required to run the association. In selecting a firm or agent to whom to send bid packages, the board should determine the answers to these questions: Is the prospective agent a CERTIFIED PROPERTY MANAGER® (CPM®) and a member of the Institute of Real Estate Management? Is he a licensed real estate broker or a Graduate of Realtor Institute (GRI)? Is he a member of the Community Associations Institute (CAI) or the Urban Land Institute (ULI)? Is the firm with which the agent is affiliated an ACCREDITED MANAGEMENT ORGANIZATION® (AMO®)? These designations and memberships should give the board an indication of the proven abilities of the management agents and firms it is considering.

After bids have been submitted, the board should interview each of the prospective agents. Standard questions should be asked of each agent, but enough time should be scheduled to permit spontaneous discussion, which may give more insight into a management agent's capabilities than do answers to predetermined questions.

The board needs to ask a lot of questions about the management firm it is considering. For example, what bookkeeping method does it use, and how will it effect the association? How many employees will work at the condominium, and how will they be supervised? Where is the agent's office located? Does he have adequate fidelity bonds? Does the management firm have a round-the-clock telephone number, and, if not, how is it to be contacted in case of an emergency?

Each prospective agent also should be asked to provide references, and the board of directors should check them carefully by calling other condominium associations that the agent has managed. The board members may wish to visit these other projects but should remember that appearances alone do not reflect how well the condominium is managed. In particular, appearances do not reflect the adequacy or appropriateness of the condominium's financial management.

Although cost considerations always will play a key role in its decision, the board of directors should base its selection of a management firm on performance rather than on price. In fact, only after the selection process has narrowed the choice to two or three firms should the price factor be considered seriously. Automatically selecting the least expensive bid without first gauging that firm's potential ability to perform may prove to be a very costly decision in the long run.

The Condominium Management Agreement

After the board of directors has selected the management firm best qualified for the job, a management agreement or contract must be drawn up to formalize the arrangement. This contract identifies the two parties and states what the firm is to do for the association and how much the association is to pay for the firm's services.

A management agreement calling for fair compensation to the manager and a good program of management for the association can be the foundation of a pleasant and lasting relationship, while an inadequate, poorly drafted agreement can cause limitless complications and bitterness. An agreement must take into consideration the benefit and protection of both the agent and the association. By explicitly stating the responsibilities and authority of the agent, it should eliminate or at least diminish the possibility of future misunderstandings.

Although the management firm usually draws up the management agreement, the board of directors should know what an agreement should include. Many firms use standard preprinted contracts. If a standard contract form does not fit the specifications of a particular condominium association, however, the form can and should be modified. Just because a form is preprinted does not mean that it always is appropriate and can never be changed. The agreement should be tailored to fit the needs of the condominium association. It should carefully define those responsibilities that are being assigned to the management agent and omit those that the board wishes to handle itself and should provide guidelines to permit the manager and the board to run the association to the advantage of all the unit owners.

A management agreement need not be a complex document. Rather, it should be easy to understand in order to avoid misunderstandings after it is signed. For this reason, both parties should have the contract reviewed by legal counsel. Although the language of one condominium management agreement may differ greatly from the language of another, there are certain similarities in all contracts. An understanding of the typical provisions of typical management agreements should be of value to the board.

Contracting Parties. Most management agreements begin with a preamble, which identifies the two parties to the contract. Although it may appear to contain only so much unnecessary and complicated legal jargon, this opening paragraph is essential to establishing the legality of the contract. Basically, it verifies that state law gives the board of directors (or, in some cases, the developer) the authority to hire a management agent to act for the association of unit owners.

The preamble not only identifies the employer and the management agent but also states that both the association and the agent wish to enter into the contract, the implication being that both parties will benefit from its terms. Basically, it indicates that the management agent expects to receive adequate compensation for his work and that the association expects to enjoy the advantages of living in a well-managed community.

Property Covered. One of the major differences between rental apartment management and condominium management is that the rental management agent is responsible for the interiors of units. This is not true of condominium management. Therefore, the agreement should describe the property—the common areas—whose management is covered by the contract. The management agent typically has no authority or responsibility for maintenance or repair of the interior of the individual dwelling units. Although irate unit owners are sure to call with complaints anyway, this clause gives the agent a legal basis for refusal to respond to complaints that deal with problems within the units.

Although recognizing that the agent is not responsible for the individual condominium units, some contracts may authorize him to make repairs and provide maintenance to the units, with the understanding that the cost of this work will be payable by the individual unit owner and should not be considered an association expense.

Lines of Authority. One of the characteristics that differentiates condominium management from apartment management is the presence of resident owners. Because each unit owner may consider himself "the boss," the management agreement should clarify to whom the agent is responsible. The contract should designate one individual, often the president of the association, and possibly one alternate to deal with the management agent. The agent should not be expected to spend a great deal of time on unit owners' problems that are not his direct responsibility. Rather, his function should be to act as an agent of and assistant to the board of directors.

Term of Contract. The management agreement must specify how long it is to be effective. Typically, contracts cover one to four years, although two- or three-year contracts are considered by many to be most beneficial to both parties. This timeframe permits the management firm a sufficient period in which to set up its systems and begin operation at full potential, yet is not too long to permit it to develop domination over the association.

An important provision of the management contract is an escape provision that, under certain circumstances, allows either party to cancel the agreement prior to its expiration date. This should relieve the association of concern that it may have no way in which to deal with a management agent who does not perform in accordance with his promises. Most escape provisions require that a certain number of days' notice be given prior to early cancellation. A 30-, 60-, or 90-day clause is typical. The agreement also may provide for cancelling the agreement without this prior notice (usually subject to financial penalty), for automatic renewal, and for ending a contract upon its expiration date.

Responsibilities of the Management Firm. The most important parts of a management agreement are the clauses that list the responsibilities óf the management firm. These responsibilities should be spelled out in detail and be based directly on the specific needs of the association. If the board of directors has made a careful list of the responsibilities it wishes to delegate to the management firm, it should have few problems negotiating this part of the agreement. The board must work with the management agent to include all of those fiscal, physical, and administrative responsibilities that it has decided to delegate. This part of the negotiation process is very important to the successful relationship of the two parties to the contract.

Compensation to the Management Firm. In addition to listing all of the things the management firm is to do for the association, the agreement also must list what the association is to do for the management firm. Specifically, it must list the terms of compensation.

The cost of professional management is based on the amount and kinds of services that are rendered, the number of dwelling units, the number of employees who must be hired and supervised, and other similar factors. A flat monthly fee may be set for small associations that need only consultative or limited services. This should cover the costs of placing the condominium on the management firm's books and initial administrative paperwork. The minimum fee would be slightly higher for larger associations, but it would not necessarily be based on the number of units in a project.

The cost of a complete or near complete professional management plan is determined based on the number of units. Occasionally, however, a fixed charge per period is set. The cost of any on-site labor and office expenses directly related to the association are added to this fixed charge, paid by the management firm, and billed to the association. The board then allocates to each owner his prorated share of this amount based on his share of ownership.

Although most management firms use standard methods to determine their costs, the board of directors should be aware that there are ways to increase—and decrease—the cost of professional management. For example, many agreements will limit the agent's or his representative's required attendance at board meetings to one meeting per month or impose an additional charge for meetings that occur after regular business hours. This additional fee allows the management firm to pay its employees for extra time on the job. However, not every meeting will involve management functions, and the board should use the agent's meeting time wisely. Many meetings are held to discuss topics that have no bearing on the management agent and need not be discussed in his or his representative's presence. In an effort to keep fees reasonable and affordable for smaller associations, some agents may suggest that they not attend these meetings but, instead, consult with the board regarding decisions made at those meetings. As another means of keeping fees down, the board should have the agent prepare only those financial statements that are essential to its control of the association. If it requires the management agent to prepare numerous complicated reports, management costs could be increased.

It is not uncommon for a management agreement to state that any services not expressly listed in the management agreement will be considered expenses of the association. Such additional expenses might be incurred by having a secretary of the management firm prepare the newsletter or in the form of costs of photocopying and postage, and these costs would be charged to the association. If specific areas of responsibility and duties are added to the original management agreement, these duties and their method of compensation to the agent should be listed in amendments to avoid dispute.

Agent Indemnification. Most management agents will insist on *indemnification* or *hold harmless* clauses, which protect the agent by shifting the risk of damages to the association. Lacking these, the management agent is fully liable for the operations of the association and can be held accountable for any acts of negligence, regardless of who is responsible for them. By these clauses, the board acknowledges its full responsibility for the association's operations.

The hold harmless clause may include an agreement by the board to pay legal and court costs incurred if the management agent or firm is sued in relation to the association, to provide adequate public liability insurance and Workers' Compensation, and to pay all legal fees for any alleged violation of laws covering employment, fair housing, and similar statutes.

Chapter 8

Maintaining the
Condominium

THE CONDOMINIUM REPRESENTS a long-term investment for all the unit owners. Thus, maintenance and repair must figure largely in the association's long-term plan. In an apartment building, adequate maintenance is essential to producing a constant flow of rental income. In a condominium, adequate maintenance is essential to preserving and perhaps even increasing the value of the property that is owned by the association members. Therefore, much of the attention of the board of directors—and much of the unit owner assessment revenue—must be allocated to maintenance, that is, to the upkeep, repair, and cleaning of the common areas.

Yet the matter of maintenance is perhaps the most subjective one with which the association must deal. Each unit owner will have his own maintenance priorities. The owner who enjoys being outdoors and often uses the exterior common areas may be adamant about having the lawn meticulously manicured and the grass clipped regularly throughout the summer. Another may be indifferent to the care of the lawns but become upset if the building is not repainted at the first sign of chipped paint.

In order for the board to meet its obligations and appease all the unit owners, it must plan a total maintenance program of inspection, repair, and cleaning. Although outside service contractors or a management agent or resident manager may be responsible for actually maintaining the common areas, the board and the appropriate committees must have a general knowledge of what they have been hired to do. Knowing how things operate and which maintenance procedures are effective should help them deal intelligently with contractors or the management agent and assist the board members in supervising their work.

Physical Maintenance

The initial impression of a condominium is based on the way it is maintained physically, both inside and out. The landscaped grounds and paved areas form a backdrop for the building itself and should serve as an outward reflection of the interior of the building. If the grounds are well cared for and free of litter and debris, they indicate that the inside probably is clean and well maintained and the project a pleasant place in which to live.

A developer usually plans a condominium project to include attractive interior and landscaping features. The unit owners will want to keep it that way. This requires maintenance of the physical elements of the condominium, that is, the grounds, paved areas, roof, recreational amenities, and the interior common areas.

Grounds Maintenance

Many condominium landscaping plans include grass, shrubs, trees, and, occasionally, flowering plants. Although the board of directors may contract with a professional landscape specialist to maintain the grounds, the landscaping and grounds committee must know something about the contractor's work if it is to deal with him effectively. Maintenance of the grounds of a condominium usually requires eight tasks: mowing and trimming grass, pruning and trimming trees and shrubs, controlling weeds and pests, mulching, fertilizing, watering, policing the outdoors, and removing snow and ice.

Mowing. In planning a p ogram for lawn mowing, two questions must be answered: How often should it be cut, and how short should it be cut? Althougl most lawns need to be cut about once a week or when grass is about three inches tall, the answer depends on climatic conditions and the rate of growth. Grass should be cut short enough to present a neat appearance but not so short that its root system is damaged. Cutting grass to a height of one and one-half inches should achieve this balance. If grass clippings are long or wet, they should be raked and carried away before they turn brown and unsightly. If clippings are short and do not lie in clumps, they may be left on the lawn as a mulch. The edges of the lawn that abut driveways, sidewalks, and planted areas should be trimmed to complete the mowing job.

Pruning and Trimming. All trees and shrubs will need occasional pruning and trimming to shape them and remove excess growth. Trees should be pruned as closely as possible to their natural shapes, except where they must be pruned to avoid electrical wires or other obstructions. Although rules for trimming shrubbery vary according to the kinds of shrub and their location, there is one general guideline: early blossoming shrubs usually should be pruned just after they bloom, and late blossoming shrubs usually should be pruned in late winter or early spring. No shrubs should be trimmed in late summer, since the new growth will not be mature enough to endure severe winter weather.

Weed and Pest Control. Dealing with weeds is easier and more economical if it is done before weeds have a chance to grow. Tiny sprouts that begin to emerge in the spring and early summer can be gotten rid of much more efficiently than can mature weeds, especially those that have begun to flower.

Trees and shrubs are vulnerable to attack by aphids, borers, mites, and numerous other kinds of pests and insects. Plants should be sprayed each spring to prevent attacks of these vegetation pests. Herbicides and pesticides for killing weeds, bugs, and insects are toxic and, if not handled properly, can damage other plants, pets, and beneficial insects. Therefore, the board may wish to consider obtaining professional services to handle weed and pest control.

Fertilizing. It is doubtful that any soil will remain rich enough to support a good cover of grass, healthy trees, and shrubs for an indefinite length of time. A soil sample should be taken every three to five years to determine what nutrients may be lacking, and the soil should be revitalized with an appropriate fertilizer. There are many brands of fertilizers from which to choose. Instructions should come with it and indicate how much should be applied, based on the soil analysis. Usually, fertilizer application requirements are based on number of pounds per 1,000 square feet for every month of the growing season.

Mulching. A mulch is a protective covering, usually organic, that is placed around trees and shrubs to protect them against the growth of weeds and to help the soil retain moisture. Straw, dried leaves, peat moss, and lawn clippings make good mulches.

Watering. The secret of a good watering program is to soak the lawn thoroughly but as infrequently as possible, giving it only enough water to keep the grass alive. In other words, a soaking to a depth of about six inches once a week is preferable to numerous light sprinklings. Of course, timing and amounts of water must be determined by weather conditions and the soil.

Policing. The appearance of a healthy lawn and well-maintained trees and shrubs can be ruined by trash, litter, and other debris. Daily checks should be made of all outdoor areas to ensure prompt removal of wastepaper, animal droppings, piles of dirt and leaves, and any other material cluttering the landscaping.

Snow and Ice Removal. Snow and ice removal is a major maintenance consideration in many parts of the country. If the condominium has large open areas, such as parking lots, the board should consider hiring a snow removal service. Snow and ice can be cleared from smaller areas with snow-melting chemicals, salt, or sand or by shoveling. Although rock salt is the least expensive of these methods, it can damage pavements, plants, and, if tracked inside, carpeting. Nor does salt work when temperatures are extremely low. Snow-melting chemicals cost more than salt but do less damage and work at all temperatures. Sand can get the job done, but it often is tracked indoors, resulting in additional cleaning needs. Shoveling snow, of course, if far less harmful than the use of either chemicals, salt, or sand. However, even when snow is shoveled away, sand or salt should be put on icy areas to provide traction for pedestrians.

Maintenance of Paved Areas

Walks, driveways, and parking lots can either complement or detract from the landscaping plan. Paved areas should be clean and free of faults and not be filled with potholes or littered with debris.

Repairing. All paved areas require maintenance from time to time. Changes in temperature and in the level of moisture in the air, as well as normal traffic, will cause cracks, holes, and damage to the pavement. The most efficient approach to pavement maintenance is to detect minor defects early and repair them immediately. Cracks that may be barely visible in their early stages can develop quickly into serious defects that are costly to repair.

Pavement repairs should be made when the air is dry and warm. An inspection of all paved areas should be made each spring, and any potholes or cracks should be repaired at that time. The most common method of repair is cold patching. This involves cleaning the damaged area, applying the product used for the job, and packing and rolling it to form a smooth surface. The use of paving contractors should be considered when large jobs must be done.

Resurfacing. Paved areas cannot be patched again and again indefinitely. Asphalt surfaces should be resealed every several years to increase their total life. An emulsion coating of coal tar placed over the surface should prevent cracking and drying. In addition, resurfaced paved areas present a much more attractive appearance.

Policing. Keeping paved areas clean is another important part of a total maintenance program. Loose paper and rubbish can be blown over the parking lots, oil can drip onto paved surfaces from cars, and careless residents can leave trash on the parking lots. Therefore, daily policing is a necessity. Sidewalks and driveways should be swept and hosed with water, grease spots and oil stains should be removed, and all paved areas should be left in a clean and presentable condition. Occasionally, cleaning of the privately owned streets, driveways, and parking lots of a project is included in a landscaping contract; however, this practice is not common.

Roof Maintenance

It is vital that roofs receive regular care. Sun, wind, water, changing temperatures, and settlement of the building can cause major problems. Unfortunately, many associations overlook the roof until the rainy day that water begins pouring into the building. The best way to adequately and economically care for a roof is to inspect it regularly at least once or twice a year. One inspection should be made in the autumn, prior to approaching winter weather, and another should be made in the spring before the hot summer sun starts doing its damage. Special inspections should be considered after especially violent rain or windstorms. If routine inspections are ignored, small holes may become large holes and the condominium may suffer extensive—and expensive—water damage.

Anybody can find the big holes that result in leaks. But only a qualified individual can be counted on to find the small holes that may grow into big ones. Problems usually develop at those points where the surface of the roof joins something else, such as a stack or chimney. A competent roof inspector should know which areas to be especially attentive to. If a roof receives proper inspection and maintenance, it should last as long as the building. One method of ensuring that it does is to regularly coat the surface. A roof preservative can extend the life of an old roof and prolong the life of a new one. Of course, if the roof is badly deteriorated, a new roof may be needed.

Roof maintenance is not a job for the inexperienced. Repairs should be made only by skilled persons who know what they are doing and know the kind of repair materials that are needed for each kind of roof. Not only is roofing dangerous work, but an unskilled person can cause additional damage.

Interior Custodial Maintenance

All of the common areas inside the condominium—the lobby, laundry rooms, hallways and corridors, stairways, and elevators—must be kept sparkling clean at all times. Walls should be free of fingerprints and smudges, floors should be clean and free of dirt, wood and metal surfaces should be polished, loose debris should be picked up, and any defects, such as inoperable lighting, should be noted promptly. This is not always easy to accomplish, but the board can help achieve the goal by seeing to it that basic housekeeping chores are scheduled and that the schedule is maintained. A regular program of policing and cleaning must be planned. The frequency of all interior cleaning will depend largely on weather conditions, the type of building and its location, the characteristics of the residents, and the amount of traffic through various areas.

The Lobby. Most condominiums have some kind of lobby or foyer that is used by residents and guests. Since the lobby is the first area that people see when they enter the building, it is essential that the lobby present a pleasing appearance. Cleaning should be performed daily, and special care should be given during rainy and snowy weather to remove dirty tracks.

Elevators. Elevators make a strong visual impact on the residents of high-rise condominiums. Cleaning the carpeting in the elevator, polishing the metal, and removing dirt and fingerprints must be included in the daily housekeeping program of an elevator building to ensure its overall attractiveness.

Laundry Rooms. Keeping the laundry room clean is the most important maintenance function connected with this facility. Floors should be cleaned often, and the washing and drying machines should be wiped down regularly. If the association owns the washers and dryers, the maintenance schedule should include removing lint from the filters, cleaning the laundry tubs, and any other maintenance tasks connected with operation of the machines. Often, however, the machines are operated by an outside contractor who is responsible for their upkeep.

Stairways. A large portion of the condominiums in this country are low-rise and garden condominiums. These buildings rarely have elevators but often have stairways, which must be cared for. How frequently stairways should be cleaned depends in part on the amount of traffic they receive. A flight of stairs between the first and second floors, for example, would require more frequent cleaning than a flight of stairs between the third and top floors, which presumably would serve only those who live on the fourth floor. The maintenance schedule should reflect these variances.

When stairways are cleaned and waxed, the residents of the condominium should be warned that such work is being done to avoid the danger of accidents caused by wet landings or stairs.

Corridors and Hallways. Like all other interior housecleaning, the best time to clean hallways and corridors is during the time they are least used by residents. This usually is right after most people have gone to work in the morning.

Windows. Unit owners usually are responsible for cleaning the interior glass of their windows, but the association usually is responsible for cleaning glass in the common areas and, often, the exterior glass of the units. All glass should be clean and free of fingerprints, and windows should be cleaned on a regular schedule. The frequency of cleaning will be based in large part on environmental conditions of the area, the amount of use the glass receives, and the ease with which the work can be done. The windows in especially tall buildings should be serviced by outside contractors.

Window washing should include more than just washing and drying of windows. It also should include washing window sills and frames, dusting the outside of frames and sills, and checking safety catches and frames. Provision also should be made for cleaning storm windows and screens.

Floor Coverings. Carpets and rugs should receive regular care. Those that are in areas of frequent use should be vacuumed each day and cleaned once a year. Professional service should be used to clean rugs and carpeting in the common areas. Not only can professionals get rugs cleaner, but rugs are likely to last longer if they receive the care of an experienced person.

Other kinds of floor coverings also must receive routine care. A well-planned daily maintenance schedule should take into consideration the type of flooring, the amount and kind of flooring, and the degree of cleanliness that is desired. Each kind of floor covering demands a certain kind of attention. Asphalt tile, for example, can be permanently damaged by varnish, and wood floors should never be scrubbed with harsh cleansers or allowed to remain wet. The special needs of the flooring should be determined before any maintenance work begins.

Recreational Amenity Maintenance

The recreational areas of a condominium project probably will be used often by many people. Maintaining these amenities, therefore, requires special consideration. Of course, the areas around swimming pools, tennis courts, and other outdoor amenities should be policed for litter. In addition, each facility will present unique maintenance problems that must not be overlooked by the board of directors.

Swimming Pools. Swimming pools need expert care to prepare them for use at the beginning of the season and to close them down properly at the end of the season. If they do not receive it, costly repairs may be required during the season, during which the pool may have to be closed. Swimming pools need periodic chemical water treatment, performed in accordance with manufacturers' suggestions and local health requirements. Treatment may be done by a lifeguard, or a professional pool service can be retained for this purpose. In addition, a constant water temperature should be maintained.

Tennis Courts. In addition to regular sweeping and cleaning, tennis courts need periodic resurfacing. Depending on the material they are surfaced with, resurfacing usually is required every three to six years.

Mechanical Maintenance

The maintenance program of a condominium must include care of mechanical equipment. It is important that the board of directors and the maintenance committee know the location and repair requirements of all mechanical equipment. Instruction manuals usually are prepared by equipment manufacturers; these should offer some guidelines to repairing and maintaining most equipment.

Guarantees on mechanical equipment may be printed somewhere on the equipment, included in an instruction pamphlet, or printed on a certificate. The guarantee will state what services are covered if the equipment needs repair or replacement. Guarantees printed on pamphlets or certificates should be kept in the association's files. Needless to say, the association should not pay for any maintenance that is covered by a guarantee.

A condominium may have a variety of mechanical equipment, including air conditioning-ventilation systems, boilers, electric motors, elevators and possibly other items. The board and the maintenance committee should become familiar with the basic operations and maintenance requirements of each piece of equipment. Although the board should contract for professional maintenance service, it should know something about the mechanical equipment so that it can deal with the contractors more effectively.

Air Conditioning-Ventilation System Maintenance

In most condominiums, the air conditioning and heating equipment for the individual units will be individually owned. However, the central system that supplies heat or cooling to the units will be the responsibility of the association. It is essential that a routine inspection and maintenance program for the entire year be planned. If it is followed, this equipment should give the unit owners many years of good service.

The air conditioning-ventilation system requires two complete changeovers each year. One occurs in the spring, when the system is changed from heating to cooling; the other is in the autumn, when it is changed from cooling to heating. Although most maintenance work can be done at these times, the equipment needs regular attention throughout the year. For example, air filters should be changed, ducts should be cleaned, and condensors should be drained regularly. A reliable air conditioning service contractor should make regular inspections of the heating-cooling units and outline the maintenance plan for the year.

Boiler Maintenance

A boiler is a pressure tank in which water is heated and from which it is circulated either in the form of steam or water, depending on the needs of the condominium. The maintenance committee should have a basic knowledge of the inspection procedures and the care required by this piece of equipment. If even a minor part of a boiler fails, a rupture or boiler explosion can result. For this reason, the equipment should be inspected and the operation of the pressure valves checked daily. Many insurance companies, as well as municipal or county governments, require such inspections. A knowledgeable person should be contracted to inspect the boilers and clean the equipment. The frequency of cleaning will depend in part on the hardness of the water that is used.

Even with a careful program of inspection and cleaning, there undoubtedly will be times when repairs to the boiler must be made. The system must be shut down whenever repairs are made. This will inconvenience all residents of the condominium. Therefore, to speed the repair process, a supply of principal parts should be kept on hand. In addition, if they can be so planned, any repairs to the boiler should be made during periods of minimal use.

Electric Motor Maintenance

Electric motors are used in condominiums to drive fans, air conditioners, and swimming pool pumps, and for many other purposes, and all of these motors need to be inspected, cleaned, and lubricated regularly. Regular examinations of all motors can keep minor problems from becoming major breakdowns. Inspections should be performed by persons who know electric motors and are able to locate malfunctions in their early stages.

Electric motors can get dirty. In fact, dust is the culprit behind many motor problems. Therefore, in addition to being inspected, all motors should be cleaned regularly with a clean cloth.

The third maintenance requirement of electric motors is lubrication. A bearing will last far longer if the surfaces are smooth and properly lubricated. Although it is possible to apply too much oil, a light layer will separate bearings and prevent metal from rubbing against metal. The manufacturer's instructions regarding the amount and type of oil to use should be followed closely.

Elevator Maintenance

Elevator maintenance requires highly technical expertise and demands the services of a trained specialist. Elevator maintenance usually is performed under a service contract. However, by understanding some important points related to its inspection and routine maintenance, the association can be sure that the elevator is receiving the kind of care it requires.

Before any inspection begins, the main electric power switch to the elevator should be opened. The inspection then should include a thorough examination of the elevator car for structural defects, such as loose bolts or other fastenings. The car switch also should be tested. Regular care of an elevator also includes lubrication. How often lubrication is required depends on operating conditions. However, the elevator manufacturer or the city elevator inspector should be able to provide some guidance in drawing up a regular maintenance schedule.

The Maintenance Program

Understanding all of the maintenance functions that must be performed is only half the maintenance job. The other half is to draw up a program for performing these functions. This program should include not only daily housekeeping and routine maintenance chores but also the regular inspections that are essential to the continuing operation of the community. If an association employs a professional management agent or a resident manager, this scheduling task will fall to him. If the association is self-managed, the board of directors and the maintenance committee may be responsible for preparing a schedule and overseeing completion of the scheduled tasks. An architect, civil engineer, the developer of the project, or a management agent acting as a maintenance consultant should be able to provide assistance in setting up maintenance programs for the self-managed association. If maintenance jobs are contracted for, the board or committee may have to work with the vendor to schedule his work.

Several kinds of maintenance should be considered when a schedule is developed, including *deferred maintenance, preventive maintenance, custodial maintenance*, and *emergency maintenance*.

Deferred Maintenance

Deferring maintenance does not imply that repairs are to be put off forever. Deferred maintenance refers to the type of work that can be scheduled at a future date without permitting a minor problem to become a major disaster. Repair of a hole in a roof, for example, should not be deferred because the hole will get bigger and the problem will get worse. On the other hand, painting the woodwork in the lobby usually may be deferred for a time without harm.

Deferred maintenance should be anticipated by repair and replacement reserve funds for those maintenance tasks that do not require immediate attention. The deferred maintenance schedule is based on the capital improvements reserve schedule, and money should be set aside for deferred maintenance functions through regular assessments. *(See Chapter 10 for a discussion of establishing repair and replacement reserves.)*

Preventive Maintenance

Preventive maintenance is of primary importance. By providing regular care and making regular inspections of mechanical equipment and structural elements, potential problems can be detected early or prevented altogether. Preventive maintenance should be scheduled on a regular basis. A good program of preventive maintenance can keep the condominium's equipment in working order and all of its physical elements functional. Typically, associations with strong preventive maintenance programs have lower operating costs than those that make repairs only when major work is needed.

Setting up a preventive maintenance program involves three steps. The first is to examine the common areas and inventory all mechanical equipment required to provide service to the unit owners and all structural elements. In fact, anything that can break down or disrupt the lifestyles of the unit owners should be listed. This list might include the boiler, electrical motors, air conditioning-ventilation system, and roof. The second step is to note all routine work that is required for each item, including inspection, cleaning, and, in the case of mechanical equipment, lubrication. The third step is to estimate how often each maintenance function should be performed. Manufacturers' handbooks should provide some guidelines to help determine the frequency of schedules. *(See Appendix A for sample Preventive Maintenance Schedule.)*

These preventive maintenance lists should be reviewed at least once a year to ensure that they are still adequately serving the needs of the association. If new equipment is purchased, its maintenance needs must be reflected in the lists.

Custodial Maintenance

Custodial maintenance refers to all policing and housekeeping functions as they relate to the common areas. Preparing a maintenance schedule for routine custodial duties is less difficult but no less important than drafting a preventive maintenance schedule. Although neglect of a preventive maintenance plan can be financially disastrous to an association, the unit owners probably will be more aware of the level of custodial services than they will be of the kind of preventive maintenance that is being performed.

Preparation of a custodial maintenance schedule requires the same procedures as preparation of the preventive maintenance schedule. The first step is to make an inspection. In this case, all physical areas that will need regular attention should be listed, including the lobby, hallways, elevator cars, laundry rooms, grounds, and any other public areas. The second step is to note the housekeeping chores that are connected with each area, and the third is to determine how often each chore should be performed. For example, hallways may need vacuuming daily, while elevator cars may need vacuuming only weekly.

A custodial maintenance schedule acts as a reminder of the work that must be done and provides a guideline to determine if there is adequate staff to perform routine housekeeping tasks. Typically, custodial schedules are put in the form of daily checklists. These list all routine custodial duties and provide spaces for indicating what has been done on what day. *(See Appendix A for sample Custodial Maintenance Schedule.)*

Emergency Maintenance

Even with far-sighted deferred, preventive, and custodial maintenance programs, unexpected repairs are certain to be needed. For that reason, emergency maintenance should be planned for, as much as is possible. One way to prepare for emergencies is to have near at hand a list of important telephone numbers, such as the numbers of utility companies, an electrician, a plumber, all contractors, and police and fire departments. *(See Appendix A for sample Emergency Telephone Number Checklist.)* In addition, the association should maintain a small inventory of parts and equipment with which to make emergency repairs.

Maintenance Service Contracts

Preventive and custodial maintenance schedules are meaningless if no one has been assigned to complete the tasks shown on them. If the association is self-managed and has adopted a self-help maintenance program, many maintenance functions may be assigned to volunteer members or a staff may be hired by the board. If professional condominium management is employed, the management firm probably will set up the maintenance schedules and provide personnel to perform the various tasks. If a resident manager is hired to run the project, he may be responsible for doing much of the work himself or for hiring a staff to work with him.

But no matter what kind of management arrangement the association operates under, there are certain services that must be contracted for with outside vendors. As a general rule, outside service is needed when complex machinery is involved or whenever special equipment or skills are needed. For example, air conditioning and elevator maintenance require very technical skills, and the complicated and expensive machinery they involve demands professional service. Washing windows in a high-rise condominium requires special equipment and should not be attempted by the inexperienced. In addition to those functions that require outside service, others may be performed more efficiently and more effectively by contractors. For example, an association may find it appropriate to contract for janitorial services or grounds care. *(See Appendix A for sample Service Contract Record.)*

If the association recognizes a need for service contractors, it must be prepared to become involved in contract negotiations. First, a bid proposal must be prepared in writing stating the exact services required. *(See Appendix A for sample Grounds Care Program Specifications for Bid.)* Bid proposals then should be submitted to at least three reputable contractors. A deadline should be set for submission of bids, and the board should accept only those bids that are presented in writing.

In evaluating bids, the board should select the contractor who offers the best service at the lowest cost, taking into consideration the contractor's reputation, which can be determined by checking with previous clients, credit bureaus, and banks. The vendor who is selected should demonstrate a desire to cooperate with the condominium association and should prove that he has adequate personnel and the financial ability to perform the functions that the association is contracting for.

To formalize the agreement between the contractor and the association, a contract must be prepared. It should state in as detailed a fashion as possible when and how the services are to be performed. Lacking such specific instructions, the board will have no way in which to evaluate the services that the contractor performs. The service contract also should specify the terms of compensation to the contractor and contain a cancellation clause indicating under what circumstances either party may be released from the agreement. The contract also should contain a statement on the lines of authority. Because the contractor should not be expected to take orders and report to all of the unit owners, someone must be designated to act as liaison with him. The person so designated may be the chairman of the appropriate committee, a member of the board of directors, or some other individual.

All service contracts should be reviewed by the association's attorney before they are signed to assure that the association is protected in the areas of Workers' Compensation, insurance, bonding, and any other potential problem areas. To be sure that contractors hired by the association and their subcontractors have proper coverage, the board should require them to present at the time each contract is awarded certificates of four types of insurance: (1) if a truck or car is to be used on the condominium premises, automobile insurance to protect the association against most vehicle-related injury and property damage claims; (2) comprehensive general liability to cover their employees against bodily injury or property damage while on the condominium premises; (3) fidelity bonds to protect the association if their employees should divert funds illegally or in the case of theft of materials designed for use on the condominium premises; and (4) Workers' Compensation, which provides for the payment of benefits determined according to the law for covered occupational injuries or disease incurred regardless of fault of the employer.

The board also should require contractors to show proof of *completed operations coverage*, a type of liability insurance intended to cover accidents that occur while services that have been contracted for are being performed. For example, this type of insurance could cover claims that could result if a hot water heater were to burst while being installed by a plumber because of faulty installation.

Chapter 9

Managing the Human Element

A CONDOMINIUM COMMUNITY is made up of buildings and parking lots and swimming pools and trees. But above all, it is made up of people. The men, women, and children who live in a condominium form a community bound by a common social and financial interest. They want to enjoy living in the community, and they want the value of their property to be protected. They are the people who create the condominium's social environment. They alone have the ability to make that environment harmonious or discordant.

Buildings and parking lots and trees are easy to manage. There are certain accepted ways to paint a building or patch a hole or trim a tree. People are quite a different matter. Each resident has a unique disposition and interacts in a unique manner with his neighbors. Most of the association's problems probably will involve managing this human element.

Condominium associations manage the human element primarily by establishing a set of mutual promises. When a condominium purchaser signs the deed to his unit, he promises to observe the covenants of the association. The association, in turn, promises to let him enjoy the use of the common areas and facilities. There also are implied, unstated mutual promises. For example, each unit owner agrees to keep noise levels low after certain hours, in return for which he receives the implied promise that other residents will do the same. Cooperation, the key to enjoyment of high-density living, thrives when the value of social interdependence is recognized.

The most important step in alleviating some of the human problems is to establish a strong internal network for informing all residents of what is going on within the community. People cannot be interested in association activities if they do not know about them. They cannot be expected to abide by rules if they have not been informed of them. But, even with the best system of information exchange, there still will be complaints and disputes. The board of directors must establish procedures for handling these grievances and enforcing the rules and regulations.

Communications

Internal communication is the lifeline of the condominium association. The board of directors is directly responsible for setting up this lifeline. Through open channels of communication, the board can create an environment of friendly cooperation. If it is successful in creating this environment, human problems will diminish. To the degree that it is unsuccessful, human problems will increase.

The best way to create a climate of common care and concern is to foster a continuous exchange of ideas and issues. Everyone who is connected with the association—unit owners, the board of directors, the management agent, maintenance and service contractors, and any other persons who serve the community— should be linked by this vital communications system. Because there can be no direct interaction among all these persons, the board of directors or, in some cases, the management agent must act as the gatherer and transmitter of information.

Strong lines of communication should be established immediately, even as early as the prospective buyer's first visit to the salesman's office. Many ill feelings that exist between unit owners and developers could be prevented if the developer told the buyer what his responsibilities as a unit owner will be. A problem common to many condominiums is that buyers do not really understand what a condominium is or what their obligations to it are. Even those who have read the governing documents may not fully comprehend that a condominium association requires their participation or realize that there are rules and regulations by which they must live and social courtesies that they must observe. The association can do little about the communication links established by the developer. But once the owner-controlled board of directors has been elected, it should assign top priority to establishing vehicles of communication. The process of creating an atmosphere of neighborliness and cooperation must begin immediately.

Personal contact is, without a doubt, the best form of communication, and there simply is no substitute for it. In small condominiums with few residents, informal discussions may be the best way to relay ideas. Even in larger condominium developments where common areas form natural gathering places, groups probably will meet informally and talk about issues that are important to the association. But, no matter how effective this word-of-mouth approach may appear to be, a well organized formal program of communication also is needed.

How formal the communications program must be depends in large part on the size of the association. A small association (one that comprises 25 units or less) may need to prepare only those written notifications that are specifically required by the governing documents. Any other information that needs to be relayed to the unit owners probably can be conveyed in an informal, personal way. For example, volunteers may go from door-to-door and pass along any pertinent information or telephone each unit owner. But boards of directors of larger associations must consider adopting more formal communications techniques. In fact, every association is in need of a program for spreading the word to all its members.

The Welcoming Committee

The condominium needs the support of all of its members, and the best time to enlist that support is when someone is new to the community. Moving into a new home can be a very trying experience. A helping hand and a friendly face can make that experience less difficult. When a representative of the association makes sincere gestures of welcome to the newcomer, the association is gaining support and forging a link in the chain of communications.

The association's communications program should not overlook the importance of greeting new members. The board of directors should form a committee to welcome new residents to the community. The whole welcoming committee or, more practically, one or more of its representatives should personally visit each new resident, bringing information on schools, churches, shopping areas, and other facilities, and a list of phone numbers—hospital, fire, police, perhaps even a neighbor's—that may be useful in case of emergency. The committee member also can take advantage of this visit to explain the condominium association to the new resident.

The Newsletter

Although nothing is as effective as personal communication, the association newsletter is probably a close second. It also may be the most practical means of telling the members of the association what is going on in the community. The newsletter can be a very positive force in the community. It can arouse interest and invite participation in association activities and contribute greatly to the creation of a neighborly environment. It should be the vehicle for transmitting official information on board, committee, and membership meetings and public hearings. It may report on committee activities and policy changes and publish annual financial statements. Space even may be allocated to a regular column written by the association's president.

Less official in nature but certainly of interest to many residents of the condominium would be classified advertisements and announcements of neighborhood events and similar items. In this way, the newsletter can serve as a community bulletin board. To further the sense of neighborliness, the newsletter might contain a column of personal news about residents, such as news of births, marriages, and similar information, and the names and unit numbers of new members to the community.

The newsletter does not have to be a stale, boring information sheet. It can contain such things as feature stories on residents with interesting jobs or hobbies, and illustrations can be used to give it vitality. The goal should be to publish the most attractive and informative newsletter possible, within the confines of the budget.

The association budget will dictate what method of printing should be used. A newsletter made up of mimeographed sheets is likely to be least costly, and a local school may have the necessary equipment and be willing to lend it to the association. Alternately, a member of the association or the management agent may have an office copier and make it available to the board of directors. Larger associations may find it feasible to publish a small tabloid newspaper. If the association is large enough, it may even be able to sell advertising space to local merchants, thereby making it totally or partially self-supporting.

The board of directors must study the needs of its association to determine how often the newsletter should be published and how large it should be. While one association may prepare a one-page, mimeographed sheet each week, another association may find its needs better met by a four-page monthly newsletter. The editor, possibly working with the resident manager or management agent, will determine the size of the newsletter but should keep in mind that a newsletter that is too long may discourage readership, thereby defeating its purpose.

The newsletter, in whatever physical form, can help create the environment that is necessary to the success of the association. If it is written well and reflects positively on the community, it may become the cohesive force in the condominium and the one most responsible for fostering the spirit of cooperation among members.

Meetings

Meetings probably provide the best forum for discussing association-related issues. There are three steps that the board should take to assure that meetings realize their greatest potential. The first step is notification, the second, discussion, and the third, follow-up.

The governing documents will require that formal notification be made of membership meetings, but all other meetings of the board, committees, or other groups may be announced through the newsletter or community bulletin board or by mail. Announcements of meetings should spark interest in them and make members eager to attend. If a subject of great concern to many members is to be discussed at a meeting, it should be emphasized. If, for example, there is disagreement over whether or not a swing set for children should be set up, the announcement of a meeting might state: "Do children in this condominium need a swing set? This subject will be discussed at a board meeting at 7:30 p.m. Friday, September 17, in the recreational building." This meeting announcement is sure to draw participation if the swing set issue is really important.

Although a number of items may be on a meeting's order of business, it is important that time be set aside for open discussion.

The order of business can be maintained without stiffling democratic participation. Many associations have found it good practice to set aside 15 minutes of each board meeting for open debate. If members are required to submit their debate topics to the board prior to the meeting, the topics to be discussed can be announced, encouraging those interested in those subjects to attend. The board might consider limiting discussion to one or two subjects per meeting to assure that each issue receives thorough discussion. While encouraging member participation, the board must make it clear that discussion will end at a certain time to keep argument from continuing indefinitely. This can only dissuade members from attending meetings in the future.

Follow-up of all meetings is essential to the communications program. Not everyone who is interested in the association may be able to attend all meetings. Therefore, a report on the meeting should be published in the newsletter or sent by individual letters following each session. Although a complete set of minutes need not be distributed, a synopsis of the business that transpired should be.

Special Communications Problems

Major issues that will require special communications tactics occasionally will come before the board. In anticipation of those occasions, the board should develop careful plans for presenting and discussing highly controversial issues. The board must never attempt to evade an important issue or bypass other members of the association. To do so can only lead to resentment.

One such sensitive issue is the need to increase assessments. Once the board has agreed that a decision on the issue must be made, it should notify the membership that the subject will be discussed at a meeting. The governing documents of many condominiums provide that assessment levels can be changed only with the agreement of a certain percentage of unit owners. Therefore, this subject might best be brought up at the annual meeting, which most residents are likely to attend. To speed discussion and decision making, notice of the meeting should be made far enough in advance to give members adequate time to consider the issue. As a further measure, all appropriate details should be presented to members at the time that notification is given.

Part of the board's strategy should be to inform residents on an ongoing basis about the association's financial status. Members who understand how assessments are set will be less likely to object when the board recommends an increase.

One way in which to improve communication of financial issues is to present information creatively. For example, instead of presenting residents with a set of technical reports that may never be read or understood, the board may consider presenting the breakdown of the monthly assessment in terms of a pie diagram, showing how large a slice of the whole pie is allocated to utilities, how much to insurance, and so on. A careful and meaningful presentation of pertinent facts is essential to effective communication. *(See Appendix A for sample Pie Diagram Assessment Presentation.)*

The same kind of strategy should be adapted to other special issues facing the board. Constant maintenance of open lines of communication will decrease the potential for surprise and hostile reaction when issues are put before the membership.

The Overall Communications Plan

The board of directors should use any and all methods of communication that are appropriate to the condominium community. It should overlook no possible channel of communication, surveying the condominium carefully to identify every possible means for getting news of the association to its members. The conventional bulletin board in the laundry room, the lobby, or other public place should not be overlooked as a way to relay information. An association that employs parking attendants in its garage may have them pass out printed notices, while a smaller association may use volunteers to distribute news bulletins door to door. Nor should board members forget the effectiveness of personal contact when they have the opportunity to discuss association activities with other members on a one-to-one basis.

In setting up the communications program, the board should consider appointing one person to coordinate all forms of communication to assure that the program is properly executed. Lacking central coordination, the program may be undermined, when, for example, everyone believes someone else has done a job or when several persons take on one job. The former situation may result in no information being relayed, the latter in costly duplicated efforts that also would make the board appear unprofessional. The communications coordinator should develop a schedule of activities and decide how they should be carried out, working closely with the newsletter committee. The coordinator also may need to request funds from the board of directors.

Certain communications responsibilities may be assigned to a management agent or resident manager. For example, a manager or agent may be assigned responsibility for notifying members of meetings, distributing copies of the annual budget, or preparing the association newsletter. Some professional management firms use computer billing mailout or addressograph systems that also could be used to mail monthly meeting notices and informational bulletins.

The importance of open channels and a planned communications program cannot be overemphasized. The board of directors cannot afford to lock itself in a room, make all decisions behind closed doors, and fail to inform other residents of its decisions. No matter how lofty their intentions, leaders who do not inform all unit owners of their plans will be unsuccessful. The board's decisions affect everyone who lives in the community, and the board has a responsibility to keep other residents informed of developments. The condominium association serves as a form of government to the condominium. Like any government, if it is to be trusted, its administrative body must be accessible, open to suggestions, and candid about its activities.

Complaints

No matter how good a job the board is doing and how well it is communicating with other residents, there inevitably will be complaints about the maintenance and services provided by the association through the board of directors. Some complaints may involve petty matters, but many will be legitimate. No human relations program is complete unless it provides a means to air all grievances.

Of course the best method of handling complaints is to try to avoid them altogether. The board of directors should attempt to do this by identifying potential problem areas and correcting them before a complaint results. But not all problems can be anticipated or easily resolved. To assure association members of a way to bring problems to the attention of the board, the board should make available to all unit owners grievance forms that provide space in which the unit owner may write his name, unit number, and the nature of the complaint. *(See Appendix A for sample Grievance Form.)*

Complaints related to the association's management of common areas or provision of services should be directed to the appropriate board officer or committee chairman. For example, a complaint about the frequency of garbage pickups should (if the association is responsible for providing this service), go to the chairman of the maintenance committee. If a management agent is employed, the complaint may be directed to him for forwarding to the board. An agent probably will have experience to draw on in resolving problems. However, he should not be used as a scapegoat or offer the board excuses for failure to resolve problems.

After all facts have been gathered, the person assigned to handle the complaint should try to resolve it personally. For example, the committee chairman should try to correct it before he refers the complaint to the committee. If this attempt is unsuccessful, the committee should try to resolve the matter. If it cannot, the committee should make appropriate recommendations to the board of directors, which is ultimately responsible for problem solving. If the same complaint recurs frequently, the appropriate committee and/or the board of directors should study it carefully before making a decision, considering a long-term remedy and perhaps adopting new house rules. *(See Appendix A for sample Condominium Association Complaint Log.)*

No matter how trivial a complaint may seem to the directors, committee chairmen, or management agent, it must never be ignored. Small problems have a way of growing into large ones if they are not handled promptly. As an act of courtesy, the person who files a complaint should receive acknowledgement of receipt of the grievance form and be kept informed of any action taken on it. Actions taken to resolve complaints about the association's operation should be publicized in the newsletter or via some other method of communication. This is especially important if their resolution results in adoption of new rules.

The board of directors may find it helpful to form a community relations committee to act as liaison between complaining residents and the board. Responsibility for establishing grievance procedures may be assigned to this committee. It should be sure that complaint procedures conform to state law and the condominium's governing documents.

Rules, Regulations, and Restrictions

By providing many dwelling units on a relatively small area of land, condominiums fill a vital economic need. But this obvious financial benefit is accompanied by the social disadvantage of requiring many people to live quite close together. As residential density increases, personal complaints can be expected to increase proportionately. Not everyone has a temperament suitable to condominium living. Many persons cannot tolerate living in close quarters. Some may not be willing to abide by the rules and regulations needed to make condominium living comfortable or realize the importance of mutual promises with the association. Unfortunately, there probably will be a few persons living in every condominium community who honestly do not care about the association. They may make loud, unnecessary noises after permitted hours. They may fail to put garbage cans in their appropriate locations. They may park in unauthorized areas. This behavior cannot be allowed to continue. If house rules and regulations are reasonable and do not infringe on individual rights and freedoms, they must be respected.

Use Restrictions

Although the documents filed by the developer will contain numerous restrictions, the board of directors has authority to make house rules and regulations governing the day-to-day operation of the community. Residents who are given a chance to be involved in making the rules should be more cooperative in complying with them once they are passed. Thus, one way to encourage residents to abide by the rules is to encourage their participation in the rule-making process. Rules should be reasonable and not infringe upon personal freedom to too great a degree. Rules also should be enforceable; for example, a rule requiring absolute silence between certain hours probably exceeds the bounds of reason. On the other hand, rules that require dog owners to walk their pets in restricted areas or drivers to park in prescribed locations are reasonable and should be enforced. *(See Appendix A for sample House Rules and Regulations.)*

There is some legal question as to which restrictions are legally binding. In ruling, the courts tend to rely more greatly on restrictions written into the declaration and bylaws than on house rules and regulations, in view of the fact that the former two documents are accepted by all unit owners while house rules and regulations may have been made by the board of directors and do not necessarily reflect a consensus of or acceptance by a majority of unit owners. For this reason, the board may wish to amend the declaration or bylaws when it is considering regulations that would rescind certain rights.

Architectural Controls

Although each condominium owner has a right to the exclusive use of his unit, he does not have the right to make changes to the exterior that would affect the outward appearance of the condominium community. Architectural controls are imposed on each member of the association and, unfortunately, tend to be the root of many problems.

Most governing documents require establishment of an architectural control committee to review all proposed architectural changes and offer guidelines to how the committee should function. In some cases, the board of directors remains ultimately responsible for making final decisions on architectural changes, although the committee has the power to recommend approval or rejection of proposed changes. In other cases, the committee has the power of approval or rejection.

The first step in the approval process should be to require each unit owner who wishes to modify the exterior of his unit to make formal application to the committee. Some associations provide standard architectural control application and review forms for unit owners requesting approval for changes to complete. The form should provide space in which to write a complete description of the change being considered. When appropriate, the unit owner should be asked to include a sample of paint color, construction plans, drawings, or any other materials that would describe the change more fully. *(See Appendix A for sample Architectural Improvement Application and Review Form)* Usually, the governing documents require the committee to give the unit owner a formal response to his request within a specified number of days, usually from 30 to 60. If no response is made within that time, the change usually is approved automatically. However, a change approved by default in this way could result in serious morale and legal problems.

In order to speed reviews and assure consistent decisions, the committee must adopt architectural standards. Architectural standards might relate to such things as fences, patios, gardens, exterior patio colors, porch railings—in other words, to anything that can be done by an owner to a unit and seen from outside the unit. In most cases, the governing documents will provide guidelines for the architectural committee to use in adopting standards. However, the committee may be assigned the task of developing a more complete set of specifications that are compatible with the governing documents.

Once architectural standards have been adopted, the review of proposed changes is systematic. Standards are especially important in that they ensure that every unit owner will be treated equally. A well-written set of standards should tell unit owners which changes probably will be approved by the architectural control review committee and which probably will not be. Again, owner participation should be solicited when standards are developed to encourage their acceptance. *(See Appendix A for sample Guidelines for the Architectural Control Committee.)*

Problems in enforcing architectural controls are likely to arise. The board may be plagued with such infringements as doors painted unapproved colors or patios that extend into common areas. Although requests for all exterior changes should be submitted to the architectural control committee, some unit owners may bypass this requirement, and, to strengthen the authority of the architectural control committee, some associations have issued strong warnings that legal action will be brought against persons who violate design regulations and refuse to take appropriate steps to remedy them. Of course, any enforcement measures must be within the framework of state law and the governing documents.

Announcing Rules and Controls

The job of the board of directors is not finished when it adopts a new rule. It still must publicize it. Rules that have not been announced properly are worth no more than no rules at all, nor can the board expect compliance with them. This is true of both architectural and use restrictions.

Various methods of posting new rules, regulations, and controls have been tried and found successful by various condominium associations. Some associations publish them in the association newsletter; others send a copy of new rules to each unit owner; others merely post new rules on community bulletin boards. Some associations have produced a handbook of rules and regulations; others put the necessary information in a letter. Each method works. The important point is that each association must have a way of publicizing rule changes.

Whenever an association has made many changes in its restrictions, it should consider sending a complete copy of the rules and regulations and architectural controls to each member. The board might even consider adopting a policy requiring this to be done at least once a year. A good time to do so is in the spring, when people probably begin spending more time in the outdoor common areas, to which many rules relate. If the rules and regulations are published in a small, easy-to-use handbook, chances that they will be read and kept are greatly increased.

In addition to the house rules and regulations and the restrictions contained in the governing documents, some associations may adopt sets of rules relating to particular facilities. Such rules should be posted at the facility itself. For example, swimming pool rules should be displayed in a prominent place in the pool area. The bulletin board on which such rules are displayed should be as attractive and eye-catching as possible. In addition, the rules should be written simply to avoid the possibility of any misunderstanding of their intent.

Enforcing Rules and Controls

Few governing documents offer guidelines to administering discipline, requiring the board to establish its own method for handling violations. In doing so, the board should consult with the association's attorney to assure that no unit owner would be deprived of his rights to the use of common areas.

Whenever an apparent violation of a use or architectural restriction has occurred, someone should discuss it informally with the violator. If the association employs a management agent, he may do so, acting as an objective third party in administering the rules. An agent of the board probably can handle problems more impersonally than can the board itself, whose members live among the residents who may be the objects of others' complaints. No one likes to correct or be corrected by his neighbor. Such action only results in discomfort for everyone involved. An agent, however, can mediate impersonally and probably will have previous experience in handling such matters. If the association does not employ an agent, this task might be delegated to the rules and regulations committee or, in its absence, to the board president. In any event, an informal discussion may permit the matter to be disposed of quickly and quietly.

If this informal approach does not produce results, the board should be notified and a hearing should be scheduled. Although the board may hear the dispute, it may be wiser to appoint a special *hearing committee* or *tribunal* made up of objective residents who are neither neighbors nor relatives of the accused violator. The hearing should be open to all members of the association and permit the accused person an opportunity to defend himself. This assures that each accused violator is treated fairly and equally. After the hearing, the committee should convey its recommendations to the board, which then would take any necessary disciplinary action.

Many boards of directors request the rules and regulations committees to establish procedures for enforcing regulations imposed on the association members. This committee also may be used to determine if an infraction is serious enough to require a formal hearing and given the job of keeping a log of all violators of architectural controls and use rules and regulations. Although one violation of a rule may not warrant a public hearing, continued violations may. *(See Appendix A for sample Architectural Control and Use Violation Log.)*

Some documents provide for the imposition of monetary penalties on persons found guilty of breaking the covenants. If the violator refuses to pay the penalty, some state laws authorize the board to sue to collect it. The suit will be successful, however, only if the penalty is reasonable and has been imposed with due process.

Enforcing the rules and regulations can be especially difficult when a high ratio of units are rented by absentee owners. Tenants usually are not interested in association activities and may be more likely to ignore the rules than residents who own the units they live in. The association may find it worthwhile to establish special procedures for requiring unit renters to transmit their complaints through their landlords and for handling renter violations of the rules. Some associations of condominium projects with large numbers of renters have formed renters' committees. A renters' committee should serve to involve tenants in community functions and make them feel that they are an integral part of the association. Renters should be made to realize that part of their rent pays for the condominium assessment, making them at least indirectly involved in the association. Tenants who are involved in this way are more likely to live within the covenants set forth in the governing documents and other rules and regulations.

No matter how simple or elaborate the procedure for handling violations of the rules, the covenants must be enforced, and they must be enforced from the very beginning of the association's existence. If one unit owner breaks a rule and is not reprimanded, another is sure to follow suit. Soon there will be chaos in the community. A precedent for ignoring rules and violators must never be set. The inevitable result can only be a decrease in the value of the property and an increase in disgruntled association members.

Chapter 10

Establishing Sound
Fiscal Procedures

THE GOVERNING DOCUMENTS of a condominium association charge the board of directors with numerous responsibilities to preserve and maintain the development's common areas and administer the overall operation of the community. Obviously, it needs money to fulfill these obligations, most of which comes from the unit owners through assessments. Because of its fiduciary responsibilities, the board must operate according to sound fiscal policies and procedures.

Virtually all condominium governing documents require the board to elect a treasurer to be responsible for financial records and books of account. In the case of a small association, the treasurer may do the actual bookkeeping. Often, however, these duties are performed under contract by a professional. An accountant or a management agent who has the experience, staff, and systems needed to do the job competently and efficiently may provide these services. The board also may appoint a budget and finance committee to work with the treasurer, management agent, or accountant and to keep abreast of the association's financial operations.

Even if the services of an outside professional are retained, the board of directors must remember that it remains ultimately responsible for all custodial and fiduciary duties. Therefore, even though the board members may not personally prepare the budget, keep the records, or prepare the assessment bills, they must understand the basic principles of record keeping, accounting, and budgeting. The board members are not expected to become accountants. On the other hand, they need not fear the challenge of understanding the fundamentals of financial reporting. The benefits of this knowledge far exceed the burdens of obtaining it. Understanding accounting principles and reasons for internal controls and having the ability to analyze financial statements can permit board members to contribute greatly to the association's management.

Each condominium association is unique in size, resources, staff, and kinds of common areas, and the following discussion of common financial procedures should be read with that fact in mind. Each condominium's unique characteristics must be taken into consideration when the following suggested fiscal policies are adapted to fit the circumstances of a particular association. Each community has its own needs and should mold the suggested policies to fit those needs. The board of directors must recognize the uniqueness of its association while simultaneously imposing adequate and tested safeguards of the resources placed in its care.

The Budgetary Process

A *budget* is an estimated summary of expenditures and income for a given period of time, usually one year. Although a budget typically extends through one fiscal year, it really is an ongoing entity, and even a first unit owner-controlled board of directors will have a budget—the budget prepared by the developer— from which to work. If a management agent is employed by the association, he probably will be responsible for recommending a budget to the board. But, even though the board may not prepare the budget, the directors must be aware of how it was developed. If the board merely approves the agent's budget and sends it to the membership for a vote without analyzing every aspect of it, the board, in effect, is permitting the agent to dictate how the association members will spend their money.

The budget is the mirror that reflects the needs and desires of the unit owners in regard to common areas and common services and the association's ability to adequately finance these needs and desires. Because the primary source of association income is unit owner assessments, the budget determines regular common expense assessments for the year. And because assessments fund virtually all common expenses, understanding the revenue section of a condominium association's budget presents no special problems. It is the expense classifications that present the most problems and require the most time and budgetary experience. The assistance of a management agent who has managed condominiums in the past and has actual experience on which to base budget estimates can be invaluable. Preparing an accurate budget is a difficult job, especially for those unfamiliar with the task. It is not uncommon, therefore, for associations that otherwise are self-managed to employ an agent to recommend an operating budget.

Scheduling Budget Preparation

Because a condominium association's budget can reflect many factors, adequate time should be allocated to its preparation. A budget that is hurriedly drafted and fails to properly estimate and match expenses with income can leave the condominium association financially vulnerable. A timetable for preparing the budget covering approximately four months should be established. During that time, a well-thought-out, well-conceived budget for the coming fiscal year can be adequately planned and accepted.

The calendar for preparing the budget must be planned according to the fiscal year under which the association operates. The governing documents may provide guidelines for determining the beginning and end points of the fiscal year. Some require that the fiscal year run concurrent with the calendar year from January 1 to December 31. Others begin the fiscal year on the date on which transfer of control occurs or on some other specific date. Still other documents give the board of directors discretion to determine when the fiscal year should begin and end.

The money to operate the association comes from all unit owners, and all association members therefore should be given a chance to voice their opinions about the way it is spent. The treasurer, perhaps with the assistance of an accountant or management agent, may be responsible for drafting the budget but should not fail to seek the participation of all association members. His budget timetable should allow time for meetings with the entire membership and with any committees that may wish to request funding for their programs. The best method for obtaining input from all unit owners is to call at least one public hearing on the budget. If a management agent is responsible for drafting a proposed budget, he should not submit his recommendations to the board of directors until such a hearing has been held. Acceptance or rejection of a budget may hinge on whether or not all association members have been given the opportunity to contribute to its development.

The budget calendar should allow the treasurer and/or management agent sufficient time in which to complete all of the steps necessary before the budget can take effect at the beginning of the new fiscal year, including adequate time to coordinate all committee and individual responses, submit the recommended budget to the board of directors, insert revisions made by the board, submit a final working budget to the membership, and print and distribute the approved budget to all unit owners. *(See Appendix A for sample Budget Preparation Calendar.)*

Estimating Expenses

Budgeting is an exercise in economic guesswork. But it must involve educated guesswork based on factual data. The challenge is to secure enough information by which to reasonably calculate costs. The persons responsible for preparing the budget should begin by studying the governing documents and plans of the condominium development. They must know what common areas the association is responsible for repairing and maintaining and what, if any, additional or unusual maintenance or improvements are required.

Another imperative early step is to carefully examine all past invoices, audits, contracts, and financial records, especially those related to the previous year's budgeted and actual expenses. This review should provide some basis for estimating expenses. Of course, there may be changes in expenses from year to year. However, the association, through the board or, in some cases, the developer, may have entered into contracts that will be binding throughout the coming fiscal year, and these contractual expenses can be projected with some degree of accuracy. If a service contract will expire prior to the end of the fiscal year, the cost of that service may be subject to change. This possibility must be considered before assuming that contractual expenses will remain stable. Any possible price increases should be discussed with the contractors.

Although the previous year's records may provide a relatively accurate account of utility costs, utility rates also are subject to change. Therefore, utility companies should be contacted to determine if rate increases are anticipated in the coming year. Any other foreseeable changes from the previous year's actual expenses also should be identified and investigated. In short, preparing a budget requires looking into the future and anticipating all conceivable modifications in expenditures.

Condominium associations throughout the country experience similar problems in estimating expenditures based on incomplete information. For this reason, an exchange of experiences can be valuable. A summary of the operating expenses of one association may be informative to a similar association that is preparing its first budget. Publications of the property management industry are designed to encourage and facilitate this kind of information exchange. One that may be helpful is the *Income/Expense Analysis for Apartments, Condominiums & Cooperatives*, published annually by the Institute of Real Estate Management (IREM).

Itemizing Expenses

A budget may classify items of expense in one of two ways: by *line item* classification or by *program* classification. A line item budget lists expenses by type (for example, salaries, office supplies, insurance, taxes). A program budget lists expenses according to the program or activity for which they will be disbursed (for example, administration, maintenance, operations, reserves). A program budget may be somewhat more difficult than a line item budget to prepare because some costs, such as staff salaries, must be distributed, that is, broken down and allocated to several programs or functions. However, the program budget is preferable because it provides a more accurate method by which to identify actual costs of specific services, and this advantage far outweighs the additional work required to prepare it.

Because the expense requirements of condominium associations differ, the degree of detail required in listing expenses will vary from association to association. The treasurer and/or management agent should tailor an expense format to the association's particular needs, establishing expense categories based on those needs. Once this has been done, the categories should be used consistently in all the association's financial records. (*See Appendix A for sample Budget Worksheet.*)

Although there is no one "right" way to list expenses, IREM has developed a set of program expense categories that are used by professional real estate managers in filing reports with its Experience Exchange Division. These categories are administrative expenses, operating expenses, repair and maintenance expenses, fixed expenses, and reserves. (These are defined and explained more fully in the following pages.)

While neither inclusive nor exclusive, these categories may offer the association treasurer reference points for use in preparing a budget alone or with the assistance of a professional management agent. They may be used on the budget worksheet without change to facilitate the association's budget preparation or adapted to fit the association's unique requirements. Whatever categories are called, of course, is less important than that they be used properly and consistently.

Administrative Expenses. Any expenses that can be attributed to management of the affairs of the condominium association should be classified as administrative expenses. Although smaller associations may depend primarily on volunteer efforts to administer the association, larger associations probably will require staff assistance to handle administrative details. Any *office staff salaries* must be accounted for in the budget. This item of expense should include not only current wages but also payroll taxes, welfare and pension benefits, vacation and sick days, and anticipated wage increases. These supplementary personnel costs could be as much as 18 to 20 percent of the actual salaries.

Every association will have *office expenses*, including those that use volunteers to perform administrative activities in their homes. Office expenses may include such things as postage, supplies, printing, equipment rental, photocopying, and newsletter preparation. Any *telephone* expenses that are directly attributable to the management of the association and paid by it also must be budgeted.

If the condominium is managed by a professional firm or agent, its *management fee* may be considered an administrative expense. If a resident manager is employed, his salary usually is an administrative expense under the management fee category.

The association also may need the service of other professionals. *Legal* expenses, including regular and special fees paid by the association for an attorney's services, typically are categorized as administrative expenses. An attorney may be retained to provide ongoing legal advice to the board of directors in matters ranging from service contract negotiations to the adoption of rules and regulations. In addition, legal counsel may be needed if the association has to file liens to collect delinquent assessments from unit owners. In addition, most governing documents require that an audit of the association's financial records be performed at least annually, and the audit expense of hiring an accountant to perform this service would be considered an administrative expense.

A *miscellaneous* classification can cover other items of administrative expense, such as the cost of renting a room for the annual meeting, hiring a professional administrative consultant, or sending board members to educational seminars on condominium management.

Operating Expenses. The board of directors is responsible for the overall operation of the community, which requires providing certain services, including utilities, to the common areas and, in some projects, to the individual units. Regular services usually are performed on a contractual basis, and these expenses can be budgeted with a fair degree of accuracy. Irregular operating expenses may be more difficult to estimate.

Any costs related directly to the upkeep of an *elevator* are operating expenses. If the payroll is distributed, these costs may include salaries and wages paid to elevator operators.

The cost of *heating fuel* may represent a large portion of the overall operating expenses budget, especially in condominiums located in colder climates. Depending on the type of structure and plan of the building, this figure may represent the cost of heating only the common areas or it may include the cost of heating the entire structure, including the individual units.

The total cost of all *electricity* used in the common areas—including that used to operate elevators, laundry facilities, and lobbies—should be considered an operating expense. The units themselves usually have individual meters, and, if they do, their residents pay the cost of the electricity they use within them.

All *water and sewage* costs for the condominium project must be considered when the budget is planned, and the cost of *gas* used to heat water is another utility expense of many associations. (However, gas used to heat the building should be budgeted under the heating fuel category.)

Exterminating services may be a regular monthly expense or a special expenditure for nonrecurring problems. Exterminating expenses should include an employee's wages and the cost of exterminating supplies, or, if the work is done under contract, the contract price can be used in preparing the budget.

Rubbish removal costs should be anticipated. This item may include not only the cost of actual trash removal but also expenses related to incineration, trash bags used in compactors, trash cans, and dumpsters.

If *window washing* is done under contract, this expense should be listed as an operating expense. If the custodial staff is responsible for cleaning windows, window washing should be considered a repair and maintenance expense.

A *miscellaneous* category can cover any other utilities or operating expenses not otherwise included as specific line items.

Repair and Maintenance Expenses. One of the primary responsibilities of the board of directors is to preserve the physical environment of the condominium project. It is therefore imperative that expenses for repair and maintenance be estimated carefully. The board may further divide each repair and maintenance expense category into payroll, material, and/or contract costs. For example, if money is budgeted for painting the exterior of the building and the association staff is to do the work, the estimated cost of paint and brushes may be budgeted under the materials category and the cost of the labor under salaries. If the work is contracted for and the vendor provides paint as well as labor, the total contractor's cost would be listed under the contract category.

Security costs often are classified as repair and maintenance expenses, whether security is provided for in-house or contracted for. If the condominium employs a doorman, his salary also may be considered a security expense.

Grounds maintenance relates to gardening, landscaping, sidewalk upkeep, street sweeping, snow removal, sprinkler maintenance, and light maintenance. These jobs may be done by employees of the association or through contractual arrangements. The cost of incidental supplies used in performing such maintenance also must be budgeted.

All payroll costs and supplies used to perform routine policing and housekeeping jobs may be listed as *custodial* expense items, while *general maintenance* expenses can include the cost of any repairs that can be anticipated on a continuing basis or which are minor. General maintenance may include such things as the replacement of light bulbs, repair of holes in roofs, and fence mending.

All costs that relate directly to running and maintaining *heating, air conditioning, and ventilation systems* must be estimated and budgeted.

Although the association has no responsibility for decorating individual units, it will have to budget from time to time for *painting* interior and exterior common areas. Costs of plastering, stucco repair, and other related work also should be considered when painting expenses are being estimated.

Expenses for maintaining and repairing all *recreational amenities*, including swimming pools, tennis courts, golf courses, recreational buildings, and so on, must be anticipated. These expenses should include the costs of supplies and equipment, payroll, and contracted services.

Fixed Expenses. Although fixed expenses may not remain as stable as their name implies and may change from year to year, they usually remain relatively constant and can be anticipated with relative accuracy.

Any local and state *real estate taxes* paid through the condominium association must be planned for in the budget. If taxes are segregated and allocated directly to the individual units, they should not be included in the budget.

In addition to real estate taxes, the association may have to pay *other taxes*, such as personal property taxes on furnishings and equipment owned by the association, franchise taxes, licenses and permit fees, or other taxes necessary to the operation of the condominium.

Although it sometimes is considered an administrative expense, *insurance* often is classified as a fixed expense. The amount budgeted for this item should include all costs of fire, liability, compensation, theft, boiler explosion, and any other appropriate insurance coverage for the building structure and the common areas, as well as fidelity bonds and directors' and officers' liability coverage. The association policy may be written on a multiyear basis, in which case the total premium should be prorated so that the cost for one year may be used for budget purposes.

If the condominium lacks certain amenities, the association

may rent them. In that case, annual fees paid for *leased recreational facilities* must be included in the budget.

Few associations pay *ground rent* for the right to occupy the land on which the condominium development rests. If the association does, however, this rent must be budgeted as an expense.

Reserves. Most governing documents require the board of directors to maintain reasonable reserves for working capital, operations, major replacements, and emergencies. Monies set aside for this purpose should be treated in the budget as an expense, since reserves must be included in the unit owner assessments. (The board should note that the reserve category in the budget should include only monies being set aside for future use during the year for which the budget is intended. It should not include monies collected in previous years that are to be disbursed from reserve funds during the budgeted fiscal year.)

· Establishing Reserves

Eventually, every condominium needs major repairs and replacements. As part of its obligation to preserve and protect common areas, the association must be prepared for both expected and emergency repairs and replacements. Establishing reserves can assure unit owners that they will not encounter large special assessments that they may be unable to pay. Instead, more and more boards of directors are establishing appropriate reserves for working capital, operations, contingencies, and replacements.

Capital Reserves. Although most boards recognize the need to establish reserves for capital repairs and replacements, determining how much money should be set aside can present difficulties. Basically, the determination involves a three-step process. *(See Appendix A for sample Capital Replacements Reserve Worksheet.)*

The first step is to list all capital items for which the association is responsible and then to determine how long these capital items, such as the carpeting or furniture in the lobby, the central heating unit, or the fire extinguishers on each floor, can be expected to last. Probable decorating requirements—primarily, the painting of interior and exterior common areas—also should be itemized. (Contractors, engineers, manufacturers, the management agent, and the developer should be able to help estimate how long various items may be expected to last. The Department of Housing and Urban Development is another source of such information.)

After the remaining useful life of each of these items is determined, the second step is to estimate the cost of replacing or repairing them. Replacement costs can be estimated based on the original cost of the item plus an allowance for inflation.

The third step is to divide replacement or repair costs by the remaining years of useful life. The result should tell the board how much should be set aside in reserve each year in order to meet repair or replacement costs when they are incurred.

Suppose, for example, that a condominium has a $142,000 heating and air conditioning unit that has a life expectancy of 12 years. In order to be prepared to replace the unit after that 12-year period, $11,833.33 ($142,000 ÷ 12 years) should be placed in reserve each year. Further, if the annual inflation rate is six percent, an additional $710 ($11,833 × 6%) should be set aside in reserves each year, bringing the total to $12,543.33. As a further example, let us say that the lobby carpeting has an expected life span of seven years and originally cost $18 per square yard. The lobby is seven yards wide and eight yards long, requiring 56 square yards of carpeting at a cost of $1,008 (56 yards × $18 per yard). The yearly reserve requirement for this item therefore would be $144 ($1,008 ÷ 7 years) plus a six percent inflation guard of $8.64 ($144 × 6%), for a total of $152.64.

Capital reserves need not anticipate the cost of every item that eventually may need to be replaced, however, especially certain items whose replacement costs would be extremely high. For example, replacement of an elevator in a high-rise condominium would be a major expense. Even if the elevator had a useful life of 60 years, setting aside reserves to replace a $600,000 elevator would place a great burden on unit owners, many of whom may be hostile to such a reserve assessment, and understandably so, since few could expect to still be living in the development at the time a new elevator is purchased and used. In effect, the current owners would be asked to finance improvements that would benefit only their successors. For this reason, reserves usually are not set aside for items that probably will last as long as the building itself.

Capital improvements and repairs should be listed separately on the capital replacements reserve worksheet to indicate, for example, how much will be needed for painting, roofing, streets and driveways, swimming pools and tennis courts, furnishings and equipment, and other items. Most governing documents require these reserves to be segregated in the financial records and prohibit the association from using them to meet current operating costs.

Operating Contingency Reserves. No board can anticipate every operating expense that an association will have during a fiscal year. To cover major emergencies and avoid the need to impose special assessments, the board should establish a contingency reserve.

The Federal Housing Authority (FHA) recommends that an operating contingency reserve equal three percent of the annual budget being established. For example, if the total operating budget is $120,000 a contingency reserve of $3,600 ($120,000 × 3%) should be established under the FHA guidelines. Older condominium developments, especially those converted from apartment buildings, may be faced with the possibility of experiencing more emergencies than new developments. Therefore, their associations may wish to set aside a greater percentage of the budget for contingency purposes. A contingency reserve of five percent of the total budget should be adequate to protect the older condominium.

Determining and Itemizing Income

The primary source of association income is, of course, *regular unit owner assessments*. The governing documents should specify how assessments may be used. From a practical standpoint, assessments should be used principally to meet the financial needs of the community as a whole. This includes general administration, the repair and maintenance of common areas, and programs and services that are available to all residents. For example, a swimming pool within a condominium development that is maintained as a common expense should be open to all unit owners. If, however, unit owners must pay a fee to use the pool, assessments should not be used for pool maintenance.

Although regular assessments provide the bulk of the association's income, they do not always represent its only source of revenue. Other sources may be amenity rental fees, interest, or special assessments.

Amenity rental fees are special fees that may be paid by unit owners or guests for use of certain of the condominium's amenities and limited common areas, including such things as clubhouse rentals, user fees, tennis court and golf course greens fees, and rental of parking spaces and storage lockers.

Interest on association funds held by lending institutions should be budgeted as revenue. Interest may be generated by any association accounts, including those marked as reserves.

Special assessments may be levied against the unit owners in the event of unexpected expenses. Because special assessments, by definition, are used to cover unexpected expenses, they will not, by nature, be included in the original budget. However, budgets may be reviewed during the fiscal year and modified to take into account any unexpected expenses and consequent offsetting special assessments. Such funds then should be regarded as income and treated separately in the budget from regular assessments.

The association also may have additional sources of income, such as those generated by vending machines and social and recreational activities. These should be grouped in a *miscellaneous* income category.

Financial Statements

Regular comparisons must be made between the budgeted financial picture and the actual financial picture to permit the board of directors to gauge the success and accuracy of its educated guesswork and evaluate whether the objectives of the budget are being met. The economic status of the condominium association is capsulized in a set of financial statements prepared either by the treasurer, management agent, or accountant. The board of directors should study these statements to determine the association's financial strengths and weaknesses and use its evaluations in making decisions about the association's operations. But before any financial statements are prepared, a decision must be made regarding which system of accounting would be more appropriate to the operation of the association.

Systems of Accounting

There are two basic systems of accounting: the *cash method* and the *accrual method*. The cash method records actual cash received or paid out. The accrual method is a more sophisticated method of accounting that keeps track of expenses incurred and income due rather than actual cash inflow and outgo.

The cash method is the easier method to understand and to maintain accurately and consistently. Most people employ a cash method of accounting in balancing a typical checkbook. Assuming that it has no outstanding bills, a cash system will let the association know if it has enough cash to meet its current financial obligations. This accounting method works very well for most condominium associations and is especially useful to those with relatively stable incomes and expenses. No financial system is of value if the board of directors does not understand it. Many management agents, therefore, have found that the cash system of accounting fills most associations' needs.

The accrual method is intended to match revenue that is due but not yet collected with related expenses that may already have been incurred. For example, a retail store may use the accrual method of accounting to match the cost of buying an item, which already has been incurred, with the revenues it will receive from its sale. Most condominium associations probably do not need such a complex system of accounting because their revenues (the owners' assessments) usually already have been collected at the time expenses are incurred. However, large associations that handle large sums of money and have many sources of income and many kinds of expenses may use the more complex accrual method of accounting. Although it is more difficult to understand and requires more effort to set up, the accrual system does provide a more complete picture of the association's financial status.

The Statement of Income and Expense

The *statement of income and expense* will provide most boards of directors with the information they need to properly run their associations and is the only statement that usually is needed by an association utilizing the cash method of accounting. This statement indicates how much income has been earned and what expenses have been incurred within a certain period of time. Known in the corporate world as the profit and loss (P&L) statement, this report provides an overview of the association's financial status. A statement of income and expense must be prepared at least once a year for the purpose of computing income tax returns. However, many boards of directors consider it good business practice to prepare and review a quarterly or even monthly statement. The board should keep in mind, however, that if a management agent or accountant prepares the statement of income and expenses, the more frequently the report is prepared, the higher the cost will be.

The statement of income and expense should show both budgeted and actual figures for the current month or quarter and for the year to date. Comparison of these various data will permit the board to track the association's financial situation and make any adjustments necessary to ensuring the association's financial solvency.

The accounting equation for the statement of income and expense is: *income − expense = net income (or deficit)*. The statement should list revenues and expenses in the same categories used in preparing the budget to facilitate comparison of actual and budgeted income and expense. *(See Appendix A for sample Statement of Income and Expense Worksheet.)*

Other Financial Statements

Some associations, especially those that use the accrual method of accounting, will require additional financial statements, among them a *balance sheet*, a *cash flow statement*, and a *statement of members' equity*. These may be prepared by a management agent or accountant. However, requiring these financial statements to be prepared could result in a major increase in their fees.

While the statement of income and expense presents information about financial operations over a given period of time, the balance sheet tells the association where it stands at a specific point in time by listing its assets, liabilities, and members' equity.

The statement of members' equity tells the unit owners what their vested interest in the association is on a specific date. The members' vested interest does not refer to an actual sum of cash. Rather, it represents the value of the property to the members after all liabilities have been subtracted, based on their percentages of ownership interest.

The cash flow statement records actual inflow and outgo of cash in a given accounting period and is needed when the accrual system of accounting is used. Because the accrual system records income due and expenses incurred rather than actual cash flow, this statement is needed to determine the ability of the association to meet its obligations at a given time.

Financial Record Keeping

A process of financial record keeping must be established to gather all the information needed to prepare a statement of income and expense and any other statements that may be required. The board of directors probably will not need to have a detailed understanding of bookkeeping methods but should understand its fundamental principles and vocabulary to enable it to recognize any errors or omissions in the association's records and to follow the flow of simple transactions through the accounting records.

Five basic records should satisfy the record keeping needs of most condominium associations. These are the *cash receipts ledger*, the *cash disbursements ledger*, the *payroll journal*, the *billing journal*, and the *general journal*, which is used to record all those entries that do not fit into the other four books. These five records of original entry are summarized at the end of each accounting period, and the results are posted in a *general ledger*, which contains account sheets for each item shown on the statement of income and expense. The account sheets in the general ledger then are totaled and balanced and used in preparation of financial statements.

The Chart of Accounts

After selecting a format in which to present the budget and the financial statement, the association should design a *chart of accounts* to facilitate the preparation of useful economic reports. A chart of accounts is a system of coding by number each classification used in the budget and financial statements. Its purpose is to assure uniformity in the accounting system.

The needs of the particular condominium association will dictate the detail and amount of information the board will need to include in its chart of accounts. As a general rule, an account series will be needed for each balance sheet and income and expense statement account. The Department of Housing and Urban Development (HUD) has adopted a chart of accounts for use by its insured multifamily projects, and its expense accounts can be adapted to the needs of most condominium associations. The HUD system is more extensive than the system any association is likely to need, but it does provide a standard and uniform method of accounting that complements the set of categories used by property managers to file reports with the IREM Experience Exchange

Division. *(See Appendix A for HUD Chart of Accounts.)*

The HUD chart uses a four-digit series for coding accounts. Numbers ending in three zeros designate general types of accounts, numbers ending in two designate groups of accounts within each general type, and numbers ending in one zero or another number designate specific ledger accounts. The following illustrates this account number method, with "N" representing a whole number:

N000	General type of accounts
NN00	Group of accounts
NNN0	
or	Ledger accounts
NNNN	

For example:

6000	All Expense Accounts (General account)
6300	Administrative Expenses (Group of accounts)
6310	Office Salaries
6311	Office Expenses (Ledger accounts)
6320	Management Fee

The condominium association should adopt a chart of accounts that is applicable to its own operational needs. This often can be done simply with the help and guidance of a condominium management agent who may, in fact, already have developed a chart of accounts that can be applied to the accounting system of the association. The modular nature of a number-coded chart of accounts permits it to be revised and expanded with relative ease if the needs of the association change.

Fiscal Controls

No association can afford to take an it-can't-happen-here approach to error and fraud. The board of directors and any management agent or resident manager employed by the association will be entrusted with a great deal of money. A system of procedures should be adopted that will provide regular checks on the exactness of accounting data, protect the assets of unit owners, and encourage efficiency. Most condominium management firms will have developed tried-and-tested controls. However, the association that manages itself will have to develop its own. These controls should outline the methods of recording all transactions, directing the flow of cash, and preparing financial documents. How broad and detailed these fiscal controls need be will depend upon the unique characteristics of the given association.

Collecting and Recording Assessments

An association derives most of its income from unit owner assessments. It is therefore essential that procedures for billing, collecting, and recording assessments be adopted and followed.

Individual ledger cards should be prepared for each unit owner and serve as the offical record of each owner's financial status in relation to the association. Each card should list the unit owner's name, the address of the unit, his billing address if he does not live in the unit, a legal description of the unit, and the regular assessment. The card also may be used to record other useful information, such as the owner's telephone number, the number, names and ages of children, and the number and kinds of pets. At each pay period, entries should be made of the assessment due, the period the assessment covers, and any additional charges, such as late payment fees or interest. *(See Appendix A for sample Unit Owner Ledger Card.)*

Several methods are recommended for billing unit owners for regular assessments. Very large associations may have unit bills prepared based on information shown on the ledger cards. As invoices are prepared and mailed, the total amounts billed are posted in a billing journal. When all invoices have been posted, the assessment, late charge, and interest columns of the billing journal should be totaled, and the totals posted in the general ledger.

These massive billings may increase fees for professional management, thereby increasing association costs. Therefore, many associations do not send out individual monthly bills. Instead, some associations send each unit owner an annual notice of the regular assessment, indicating on it when each installment is due. The unit owners are responsible for making these payments on time. Other associations use a coupon book system, supplying coupons to be returned with each assessment payment. Both the annual notice and coupon book methods can save time and postage and billing expenses.

Specific procedures for handling assessment payments as they arrive also should be established. As the envelopes are opened, each check should be reviewed to make sure it shows the correct date, amount, and signature. If it does not, the check should be returned to the sender with a request for a new check. If the check is correct, the return stub or duplicate bill (if used) should be dated and attached to the check.

The back of each check should be stamped "For Deposit Only." Then, each check should be listed in the cash receipts ledger by date, name, and unit number, and the total of the check posted in the cash column and component amounts allocated to the appropriate columns, such as assessment or interest. An adding machine tape should be run to assure that the total of each income account column equals the total of the cash receipts column and that each of these totals equals the total of the checks.

Checks should be deposited daily, and the amount of the deposit entered in the checkbook immediately. When each assessment is paid, the appropriate information should be entered on the individual ledger cards. In addition, it is good practice to file all duplicate bills or stubs in an envelope on which is written the date and amount of the deposit. If any problems arise, deposits then can be checked easily.

At the end of each accounting period (usually the last day of the calendar month) the cash receipts journal should be balanced. The total should be posted to the appropriate account in the general ledger. Individual ledger cards should be balanced as further verification. The total amounts paid shown on the cards should equal the amount shown in the accounts receivable column of the general ledger.

An association may have other sources of revenue. To handle this income, it should adopt procedures similar to those used to collect and record assessments.

Developing Delinquent Assessment Procedures

The board should refer to the association's legal documents for guidance in collecting delinquent assessments. If the documents do not provide sufficient guidelines, the association must adopt formal procedures that should be followed strictly and in all cases of delinquency.

The first step in developing procedures is to establish a time period after which an assessment is considered delinquent. Some associations consider a payment late if it is not received within 10 days of the due date; others may wait until a payment is 30 days past due before considering it delinquent. As soon as a payment is delinquent, a reminder notice should be mailed to the unit owner. If the assessment remains unpaid after a second 10- or 30-day period, the delinquent unit owner should be reminded of his obligation a second time by certified mail and given a certain number of days—five to 10 days often are allowed—within which to pay the assessment. If he does not, the matter may be turned over to the association's attorney for legal action. The appropriate legal action may be prescribed by the governing documents. It usually requires the attorney to write a letter requesting payment and, if this measure fails, to file a lien on the property.

Where professional management is employed, the management agreement should specify the extent of the agent's authority to collect delinquent payments. The agent's authority may be limited to mailing a reminder notice or extend as far as instituting the filing of a lien.

All delinquent payments should be recorded on the individual ledger cards and tied to the ending balance of the general ledger accounts receivable account.

In order to encourage prompt payment of assessments, the association may consider adopting incentives. An association may allow discounts for prompt payment or add penalties and interest after a certain number of days of nonpayment. Some states may prohibit penalties but permit discounts. Of course, any incentive program will be subject to the authority of appropriate state law.

Controlling Expenditures

Internal fiscal controls also are needed for the payment of expenses incurred by the association in carrying out its responsibilities, and it is important that a system for processing invoices be established. Each invoice received by the association should be dated and checked for mathematical accuracy, and the fact that it has not already been paid should be verified. If it has not been paid, the invoice should be stamped with a stamp that provides space in which to record the number and date of the check by which it is paid, the account number or category, and the name of the person who approves payment.

After determining the purpose of the expenditure, the bookkeeper should refer to the chart of accounts and write the appropriate account code number or category in the space provided for that purpose. If the invoice is for goods or merchandise, the person who received the goods or merchandise should initial it to indicate that the goods or merchandise were received in good order. The person authorized by the board to approve the invoice (usually the treasurer of a self-managed association or the management agent of a professionally managed one) should sign it in the appropriate space. The invoice then should be filed in the accounts payable file until funds with which to pay it are available. (It is good public relations policy to hold an invoice no longer than necessary.)

As each invoice is paid, it should be noted in the cash disbursements ledger. This ledger should be balanced at the end of the accounting period, and the total transferred to the general ledger. If any invoices remain unpaid at this time, they should be listed in the general journal.

Checks should be prenumbered to ensure that each is accounted for. Any checks that must be voided should be marked so that they cannot be used again, and blank checks should be kept in a safe place to which only authorized persons have access. When a check is drawn, the check number and the date should be entered on the invoice. After the check has been signed and mailed, the invoice should be filed in a paid invoice file in case it is needed for future reference.

The governing documents may outline certain procedures for cashing checks. In a self-managed association, an officer or some other designated person may be required to sign all checks. Some associations may require two signatures on all checks; others may require two signatures only on those checks that exceed a certain amount (usually $1,000). Where professional management is employed, the board should give the agent authority to endorse most checks. This authority may be limited, however, to require, for example, countersignature on checks in excess of a certain amount. Such procedures should be outlined in the management agreement. However, requiring the board to countersign every check would be a time-consuming practice that would hamper the orderly administration of the financial program. In addition, if the board were to retain the power of signature, its members would have to be bonded. This would result in a double expense for the association, since the management agent already is bonded and the cost of the bond is included in his management fee.

The Audit

Most condominium governing documents require that the association's financial records be audited at least once a year by a certified public accountant (CPA). Even if this requirement is not spelled out, the board of directors should not fail to have this important service performed. The members of the association, through their assessments, provide most, and sometimes all, of the association's income. They have a right to know how their money is being spent and if it is being handled properly. An *audit* is a thorough examination of records and accounts to check their accuracy and determine if the financial statements fairly illustrate the association's financial status. It provides assurance to the association members of the propriety of its money management.

One of the key considerations in choosing an auditor is his degree of experience in auditing condominium association records. The condominium association differs greatly from, for example, a manufacturing company or a grocery store. The auditor should recognize the unique nature of the governing documents, the budget, the method of setting assessments, the simplicity of the bookkeeping process, the association's tax problems, and the way in which the depreciation of common areas is taken into account by reserves. In selecting auditors, the board should contact CPAs and ask them to prepare proposals listing their services and estimated fee schedules. Most accountants will charge either a flat fee or a daily rate.

Even though a condominium management agent may be employed by the association, responsibility for the audit is retained by the board of directors. The use of professional management, however, may result in lower audit costs because the agent's formal and organized bookkeeping system usually saves the accountant time and facilitates the audit.

Because it would be costly and impractical, a complete detailed analysis of every financial transaction is virtually never undertaken by an auditor. The board, therefore, must define carefully the scope of the audit that the association requires. In general, the auditor should review fiscal controls, test procedures used in handling cash receipts and disbursements, make sure that all assessments are billed and collected according to specifications of the legal documents, and verify that all other requirements set forth in the documents are being met. The date and period to be covered by the audit, the date the report is to be delivered, and the number of copies that will be needed also must be determined by the board of directors.

An officer of the association and, if there is one, the management agent should meet with the auditor before he begins his work to give him information on assessments as well as copies of all pertinent contracts and legal documents. The board also may wish to instruct the auditor to prepare his report using the classifications that are used in the budget and statement of income and expense to facilitate comparison of the audit statement with the budget and the financial statement. To avoid any misunderstandings, all of the terms of the audit should be stated in a formal, signed agreement.

Chapter 11

Insuring the
Condominium Community

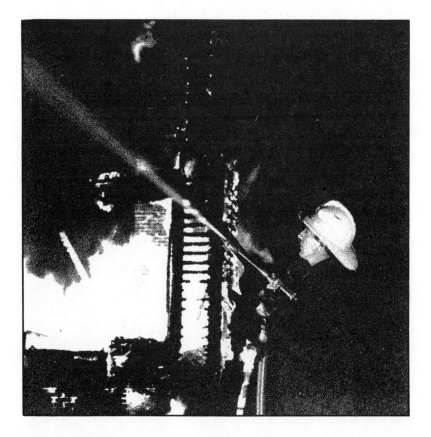

PEOPLE WHO CHOOSE to own and live in condominium units are faced with certain problems that owners of single-family houses do not have. One such problem concerns *insurance*, which relieves the fear of financial loss due to a disastrous event by shifting the risk of such an event to an insurance company. In exchange for assuming this responsibility, the insurance company receives a payment, known as an *insurance premium*. To fully relieve all unit owners of the fear of loss, adequate property and liability insurance must be obtained both for the areas that are owned in common by all unit owners and for the individually owned units.

Securing a complete insurance program is one of the most important tasks assigned a condominium association board of directors by the condominium's governing documents. No matter how large or how small the community, its need for adequate insurance is great. An uninsured loss may be not only emotionally traumatic to all those involved but could undermine the soundness of the association as well. In view of the association's inability to withstand significant unbudgeted expenses, the board must insure it against potential loss. The board is directly responsible for seeing to it that the association is sufficiently protected against all insurable catastrophes. Although a management agent may assist the board by recommending coverages and seeing to it that the insurance policy is maintained in force, assuring that the association has proper insurance coverage ultimately is a responsibility of the board.

The governing documents should indicate what type of insurance the board should obtain. They also may provide some

175

guidelines to determining how much coverage is required. Because state laws tend not to be specific about insurance requirements, the insurance provisions of one set of documents may differ from the insurance provisions of another. Insurance requirements in declarations and bylaws may be extensively detailed or only superficially outlined. Although some provide detailed insurance guidelines, many are sketchy at best. The board that merely complies with loose requirements may fail to provide its association with a sound condominium insurance program. The board must satisfy the requirements specified in the governing documents but also must use its own discretion in determining how much and what kind of insurance coverage is adequate. The first step in tailoring an insurance policy to the needs of a condominium association is to define which potential liabilities belong to the association and which belong to the unit owner. This is not an easy thing to do. Because the condominium concept is so new to the United States, a number of complicated legal questions have yet to be answered.

Some of those who have studied the housing industry believe the modern condominium concept to have been born before its time. Certainly, not all of the complexities of condominium life had been worked out before high-rise and garden condominiums began springing up throughout the country. One wrinkle that needed to be ironed out was the method for writing an insurance policy for condominium property. Major difficulties arose in condominiums where the boundaries of one unit formed the boundaries of other units. If neighboring unit owners both insured the wall separating their units, coverage would be expensively duplicated. If neither insured the wall, there would be a potentially disastrous gap in coverage. The question was: How can interconnecting structures of individually owned units be insured adequately without either leaving major gaps in coverage or duplicating it?

In response to this problem, a system was devised that placed the full burden of insuring the condominium's structure on the association while simultaneously recognizing that every unit owner has the right and obligation to obtain full personal property and liability coverage. Thus, there are two kinds of condominium insurance policies: a master *association insurance policy* and a *unit owner's insurance policy*. The association policy generally combines property and liability coverage for the common areas into one package, serves as the main coverage for the structure of the condominium, and takes precedence over a unit owner's policy in the event of duplicate coverage. The unit owner's policy, which can provide for coverage of real and personal property and liability of the unit owner, was conceived as a complement to the broader association policy and was intended to neither supplement nor replace it.

It is important that the board of directors recognize that various insurance carriers have arrived at various interpretations of how the association can be insured most appropriately and completely. Well-conceived, well-planned association and unit owner insurance policies still may leave gaps or provide overlapping coverage, but experienced condominium carriers do offer integrated programs that can provide a maximum amount of coverage for both the association and the individual unit owner. The board of directors should seek a professional insurance agent who is experienced in drafting condominium insurance policies and who will be able to read the documents and determine the liability exposures of the association based on his experience. He also should keep abreast of all changes in the law that apply to condominium ownership and the responsibilities of association boards of directors.

There is no one standard insurance policy that is right for all condominiums. Operating systems differ greatly among, say, suburban townhouse and downtown high-rise condominiums, while resort condominiums at the seashore have different insurance needs from those high in the mountains. Obtaining specialized, customized service and policies is the key to maximum protection for condominium communities. Board members are not expected to understand the complicated machinery of condominium insurance; only a specialist experienced in writing policies tailored to the service needs of various clients can be depended upon for this kind of expertise. However, to enable them to deal intelligently with such a specialist, board members should have a basic understanding of condominium insurance needs.

The Association Insurance Policy

Drafting an insurance policy of any kind is a difficult, confusing task. Because of the uniqueness and intricacies of joint ownership and operation, drafting an association policy is doubly difficult.

To answer its basic insurance questions, the board should consult with a specialist in condominium insurance who has developed a reservoir of expertise in this area. Although various agents represent different underwriters and therefore offer different coverages, there are a few similarities in the kinds of association coverage that are provided.

Insuring the Condominium Property

In determining the kind of real and personal property coverage the association needs, the board of directors must deal with three primary considerations. It must determine what hazards it needs to protect against, what property requires coverage, and how much coverage is adequate.

What Are the Risks? In determining what perils it should insure the condominium against, the board first must look to its documents. Although fire is the major threat to a condominium, the governing documents may require the board to obtain coverage against a broader range of risk. If there is no such requirement, the board of directors itself may consider it a sound practice to provide additional coverage.

The standard fire insurance policy usually covers direct loss by fire, lightning, and damage by "removal from premises endangered by a peril insured against" (as stated in the New York State Standard Fire Policy, which generally is considered the national standard). Damage by removal can result from breakage, exposure to the elements, or virtually any other cause. Obviously, this basic coverage is incomplete. The board might consider, and possibly be required by the governing documents to consider, *extended coverage*, which expands coverage to include damage caused by seven additional perils: windstorm, hail, explosion, riot and civil commotion, aircraft, vehicles, and some types of smoke.

Coverage can be extended even further with *all-risk coverage*. Many governing documents require this kind of policy, which provides the most comprehensive protection. However, all-risk may be one of the most abused phrases in the insurance industry. Instead of listing the perils that are insured against, the all-risk policy protects the association from losses arising from any cause other than some that specifically are excluded. The term "all-risk" would seem to imply that the association is protected against any direct physical loss to the property, but, because of the exclusions, that is not the case. To further complicate the matter, not every insurance carrier defines all-risk in the same way. Typically, however, all-risk coverage does not protect against damage resulting from wear and tear, earthquake, flood, sewer back-up, war, water seepage, boiler explosion, or nuclear contamination.

The board of directors must know what is excluded from all-risk coverage and understand what the exclusions could mean to the association and how it can fill in the gaps with *endorsements* or riders attached to the policy that extend or otherwise alter its coverage. For example, few all-risk policies cover damage caused by water that is not a result of damage to the exterior of the building. Although this may be a small, recurring liability, it could involve a major expense. For example, a violent thunderstorm could drive rain water under the sliding glass doors of a recreational room and destroy the carpet. *Water damage insurance* policies are available that would cover such a loss, and the board should consider obtaining such coverage (even though it too may list certain exclusions). Similarly, *sprinkler leakage insurance* may be obtained to cover a loss caused by water leaking from an automatic sprinkler system when the discharge of water is caused by something other than fire.

All-risk coverage does not cover earthquake and flood damage. Although this may not present a problem to many condominiums, it will to those built in areas vulnerable to these perils. In those cases, *flood and earthquake insurance* often is available and should be considered if the protection package is to be adequate. Loss due to floods may be especially catastrophic and certainly is worth insuring against if the condominium is situated on a lakefront or in a low-lying area where river flooding may occur.

Another gap in insurance protection can be filled with an endorsement to cover damage caused by vandals or as the result of malicious mischief. Again, the board should consider this endorsement for *vandalism insurance* and any other endorsements that may be appropriate to obtaining the most complete property insurance policy for the association.

What Should Be Covered? Even an all-risk association insurance policy may not adequately cover every piece of property that is the responsibility of the board of directors. However, the appropriate endorsements to the policy can provide a complete blanket of protection.

Many condominiums are built with a great deal of exterior glass. However, all-risk coverage does not always adequately insure against plate glass breakage. There may be glass in common area exterior walls that is the responsibility of the association and should be insured against breakage. Also, in some condominium associations the board of directors is responsible for glass in individual units that forms outside walls. Although many policies include coverage for glass breakage, this coverage usually is limited to $50 per pane and $250 per claim. This limited coverage is scarcely adequate to cover the hundreds of windows in many condominium properties. *Plate glass insurance* policies covering breakage to the full amount of the actual loss, subject to a deductible, are available.

Because all-risk coverage does not protect against boiler explosion, the board should consider obtaining an endorsement to the association policy that would fill this gap. *Boiler and machinery insurance* may provide protection against loss arising out of the operation of pressure, mechanical, and electrical equipment, including damage or destruction of air conditioning and other similar equipment.

Many boards of directors are responsible for swimming pools, fences, signs, piers, light poles, auxiliary buildings, driveways, walkways, and other elements of common property. These items may not be covered under the basic association policy, but coverage can be included in the policy if the appropriate endorsements are added. The same is true of coverage of trees, plants, lawns, and shrubs.

The association also may be responsible for providing coverage for personal as well as for real property. The board must be sure it does not forget to adequately protect lobby furniture, laundry room washers and dryers, office, maintenance, and recreational equipment, and any other association personal property. Damage and destruction of these items are covered by most policies. Many policies depreciate these items for age. However, it is possible for a policy to be written that would cover these items to their replacement value rather than at their depreciated value. Nor do all policies cover theft. Because items that are used in the common areas frequently disappear, it is wise to have theft insurance.

How Much Coverage Is Needed? After deciding what kinds of property coverage are needed, the board must decide how much is needed. The governing documents may provide it with guidelines for determining adequate levels of insurance. The association needs to have enough property coverage to permit it to replace all of the common areas and personal property for which it is responsible. Therefore, in selecting coverage, the board should look for coverage that is related to *replacement cost* rather than *actual value*.

Actual value is defined as replacement cost less depreciation and, at the time of a loss, usually is less than the cost of returning the condominium to its original status. Replacement cost can be determined by an independent appraisal of the property or be projected based on the original cost of construction plus inflation. Depreciation takes into consideration a condominium's age, obsolescence, and degree of deterioration. When a condominium is insured to its replacement cost, the insurance company (assuming that the association has purchased enough insurance) agrees to repair or replace the damaged building without making an allowance for depreciation. To realize the benefit of replacement cost coverage, the association must actually replace the damaged building on the same premises after a loss.

In fact, many condominium documents require the board to insure the condominium at its replacement cost rather than at its actual cost. Although this is the wisest course in most cases, there are exceptions. For example, the actual value of an older apartment building that has been converted to a condominium may be two or even three times less than the replacement cost. Replacement cost refers to the cost of returning a structure to its status prior to damage. It is doubtful that owners of units in an 80-year-old building would—or could—choose to rebuild their condominium complete with solid oak floors and stained glass windows. The board of directors of such an association should consult with an insurance expert, who should be able to advise it regarding how to avoid one of the problems common to insuring conversions.

Most association policies contain a *coinsurance* clause, which restricts the amount the association may recover on a partial loss if the condominium is not insured for at least a certain percentage —usually 80 or 90 percent—of its actual cash value or replacement cost, depending on the kind of coverage. If the policy contains a coinsurance clause with an 80 percent requirement, the board must insure the condominium to 80 percent of its actual value or replacement cost. In return for compliance with the requirement, the association benefits from a reduction in its premium rate. If it does not comply with the coinsurance clause and a loss occurs, the association will not be fully compensated for the loss. The formula used to determine the amount of recovery after such a loss would be:

$$\frac{\text{Amount of Insurance Carried}}{\text{Amount of Insurance Required}} \times \text{Loss} = \text{Recovery Limit}$$

The coinsurance clause therefore places the responsibility for buying the proper amount of insurance on the buyer—in this case, the board of directors.

For example, let us say that a board of directors had purchased $700,000 worth of coverage, which it considered to be in compliance with an 80 percent actual value coinsurance requirement. Thereafter, a fire causes $30,000 worth of damage. If an appraisal then shows that the actual value of the condominium prior to the loss was $1,000,000, the insurance company would not have to pay the full amount of damages since the board did not meet the requirement and the condominium was not insured to 80 percent of its actual value, or $800,000 ($1,000,000 × 80 percent). Instead, the insurance company would pay for only a portion of the damages, based on the previous formula:

$$\frac{\$700,000}{\$800,000} \times \$30,000 = \$26,250$$

The association members therefore would have to pay the difference between the loss ($30,000) and the amount collectible ($26,250), or a $3,750 penalty.

Penalty for possible noncompliance with the coinsurance requirement can be avoided by waiving the coinsurance clause and replacing it with an *agreed amount* clause. This clause represents an agreement by the insurance company to pay the association the face amount of the policy in the event of insured destruction. This face amount is based on the value of the condominium as agreed upon by the board of directors and the insurance company. In effect, the board can partially shift the responsibility for making a correct decision regarding adequate coverage to the insurance company. When a policy includes the agreed amount clause, the insurance company is obligated to pay claims on a replacement cost basis if partial losses should occur. There should be no additional cost for this protection, since, under the agreed amount clause, the property must be insured to at least 90 percent or, most often, 100 percent of its value.

Even if the condominium association's insurance policy includes an agreed amount clause, it is good business practice to require frequent reappraisals of the property. (Some governing documents require such reappraisals to be conducted annually.) Coverage should be updated from time to time to take into account any appreciation of the property indicated by the appraisal.

Most association policies provide for *deductibles* of $100 or more. Deductibles in an association policy will apply either on a per-occurrence basis or on a per-building basis, the former being easier to administer in the case of multiple-building condominium projects. Although the board should be wary of extremely large deductibles, which might negate the purpose of obtaining insurance, inclusion of deductibles in a policy usually results in lower premiums by eliminating numerous small claims that can be relatively expensive for the insurance company to process. Therefore, deductibles may be considered by cost-sensitive associations as a method of lowering premiums.

Repair or Reconstruction? If some calamity results in a complete or near-complete loss of the project and the owners cannot agree whether or not to rebuild, highly emotional debates are sure to erupt. Some association policies require reconstruction to occur on the same site; others do not. Some state laws make reconstruction mandatory unless a certain percentage of a condominium project is destroyed. New York, for example, requires reconstruction unless more than three-fourths of the structure is damaged, in which case the proceeds from the insurance policy are divided among the unit owners according to their percentages of interest. If only a small portion of the condominium is damaged, a unit owner may wish to *partition* the association, that is, to bring legal action to divide the recovery compensation so that he may recover his share individually. Governing documents should prohibit this.

The Insurance Trustee. Most master policies require that an *insurance trustee* be designated by the condominium association.

The trustee (often a bank or trust company) collects funds from the insurance company and disburses them according to the contracts let for repair or replacement of the common areas. State laws outline trustee requirements. In Maryland, a typical example, the trustee clause is invoked only in the event of losses in excess of $25,000. Trustees, of course, never handle compensation for damage to the interior of a unit insured by an individual unit owner's policy.

Protecting Against Liability

To achieve maximum protection for the association, the board must obtain an insurance package that includes liability coverage, as required by most documents. While property insurance should protect the association from losses that are the result of natural casualties, *liability insurance* should protect it from paying damages to a third person for bodily injury or damage to his property. This could result from a civil action charging negligence on the part of the association. The association liability policy should provide coverage for all liability hazards related to the common areas and facilities, as well as offer sound, realistic liability coverage for the administration and operation of the association.

What Are the Liability Hazards? The board of directors should select a *comprehensive general liability insurance* policy, the most complete liability policy available. This policy provides broad coverage for *bodily injury liability*, *property damage liability*, and *medical payments* and, in addition, can be written to include other liability hazards. The board must understand what kind of protection such a policy offers.

First, with bodily injury liability coverage, the insurance company agrees to cover all sums which the association is legally obligated to pay as damages because of bodily injury, illness, or death. In such cases, medical expenses, permanent deformity, pain, suffering, and loss of income may be awarded to the person who is accidentally injured on the condominium's common areas.

Second, with property damage liability coverage, the insurance company agrees to pay the association's liability for legal damages awarded because of damage to or destruction or loss of a person's property as a result of an accident.

Third, it voluntarily pays the medical costs of any guests who have accidents in the common areas for which the association is not legally liable. Such payment does not affect the right of the injured party to bring tort action, that is, to file civil suit, against the association. However, this medical payments coverage is essential to maintaining the good will of the unit owners, since an injured party may be content to have his medical expenses paid and not take legal action to claim damages. (It should be noted that medical payments coverage applies only to guests and does not cover unit owners who have accidents in the common areas.)

Even with these three basic liability coverages, the association still will be vulnerable in some areas. The board of directors should be aware that its comprehensive general liability policy can be tailored to cover other liability exposures. For example, if automobiles of unit owners or their guests are parked on common area parking lots or in a garage, the association may become liable for damage to these vehicles. *Garagekeepers' legal liability* coverage is available to protect the association in such a situation. This coverage can be written to cover (sometimes subject to deductibles) loss resulting from fire, explosion, theft, vandalism, and collision.

The board also may consider it wise to carry *completed operations and products liability* coverage, which protects against liability related to manufactured products or workmanship. An association may need this kind of protection even though it does not manufacture products. For example, it may sponsor a bazaar at which homemade items may be sold, and claims could arise out of alleged injury caused by any such products that are improperly made or improperly labeled.

It is not unlikely that the association at some time will sponsor a social event at which liquor will be distributed on the condominium premises at no charge. Claims could arise from such an occurrence. There is even a chance that the association may be held liable for accidents arising out of the use of liquor dispensed at private parties held by unit owners in common areas, such as in a party room. To avoid such problems, the board of directors should add a *host liquor liability* endorsement to the association policy. This endorsement will cover the association in these situations.

If an employee or a board member has an accident in his own automobile while on company business and the accident involves a third party, a claim could be brought against the association by the third party. This could occur if, for example, there is no or insufficient liability coverage on the employee's or the board member's car. *Automobile nonownership liability* coverage could protect the association in such a situation.

Many condominiums, especially those in warmer climates, either own, hire, or otherwise are involved with boats. The board of directors of such a condominium should see to it that its policy contains an endorsement for *watercraft liability*.

Contractural liability coverage should be included if the association has entered or plans to enter into any contracts that contain indemnification or hold harmless clauses. Under the hold harmless clause, the association assumes the liability of the person with whom it has such a contract. Contractual liability coverage will protect the association against the liability it assumes in this way.

If the association plans to undertake any new construction or extensive repairs, it will need additional protection to cover bodily injury or property damage liability that may result. *Contractor's protective liability* provides the protection that is needed when construction goes beyond routine maintenance or minor alterations.

Insurance companies usually assess a flat charge for *personal injury liability* coverage, and the association should consider obtaining such coverage because its cost is reasonable, while any personal injury liability claims against the association could be quite large. This endorsement covers the association against claims for false arrest, libel, slander, invasion of privacy, or wrongful eviction, claims for which could result from the actions of an employee or board member.

A condominium might have additional liability hazards that can be covered in the association policy. An insurance agent familiar with problems unique to associations should be able to recognize the areas of risk and suggest appropriate endorsements to protect against losses resulting from them.

Special Problems. Because there are certain condominium insurance problems that rarely are associated with the insurance of other kinds of properties, the association policy should contain provisions that address the condominium's unique circumstances. One is a provision that all unit owners be named individually as insureds. Such a provision protects all those named as insureds against personal claims arising out of the ownership, maintenance, or repair of the common areas.

Almost all insurance policies contain a *subrogation* clause, which gives the insurance company the legal right to take action against a third party responsible for damage for which it has made payment. This could create problems in a condominium association, where the company could pay a claim of the condominium management or third party and then, in turn, file suit (subrogation) against an individual unit owner. To prevent this from happening, the association policy should contain a *waiver of subrogation*. This waiver, which recognizes that each unit owner is insured by the policy, protects a unit owner from being held personally liable for something that happens within his unit that causes damage to the entire development.

Another unique situation may occur in the event a unit owner is injured in a common area. The law usually prohibits a person from successfully making a claim against liability coverage that he provided for himself, and this, in fact, would be the situation should a unit owner file suit against the association of which he is a member. Such a case was tested in California in 1971, and the appeals court ruled that a condominium unit owner could indeed sue the condominium management for injuries sustained when he fell over a water sprinkler in a common area. The court held that "unincorporated associations are entitled to general recognition as separate legal entities and that as a consequence a member of an unincorporated association may maintain a tort against his association." Many states have failed to address this issue, and it still is uncertain to what extent the California ruling will apply elsewhere. Some condominium declarations require the association's policy to include a *cross liability* endorsement and, in view of the California precedent, even if such an endorsement is not required, a board should include it in the policy.

Protecting the Board of Directors. Should the board be protected and, if so, how? The personal liability of board members is one of the most frequently overlooked areas of association risk exposure. The board is a unique group. Its members may have had little experience in the administration of a small business. Nevertheless, they are obligated to deal with unfamiliar administrative duties in addition to their involvement in the social and political community. Therefore, there is a great need for *directors' and officers' liability* insurance, a kind of errors and omissions insurance.

The board members and officers of a condominium association are as liable for their acts, or failure to act, as the members and officers of boards of directors of corporations. They are responsible to fellow unit owners, as well as to the public and, as a result, are subject to suit by individual unit owners, prospective buyers, accountants, and others who have business relationships with the association. Among areas of dispute that could result in lawsuits are conflicts of interest; mismanagement of funds; failure to exercise good judgment, diligence, or good faith in the execution of their official capacities; exceeding the authority granted by the declaration or the bylaws; misstatement of the association's financial condition; and failure to obtain competitive bids. Any decision made by the board may be challenged in court, subjecting its members to defense costs as well as to the cost of any financial settlements that may result.

The temptation to sue is particularly strong in condominium communities. Unlike the boards of many nonprofit organizations, the condominium board actually is in business and thus is responsible for major decisions, as well as for substantial dollar amounts. Unfortunately, many board members assume that the association's nonprofit status and the fact that the board serves without pay eliminates financial liability for its decisions. This misunderstanding can lead and has led to disastrous financial predicaments.

To add to the confusion, some condominium documents contain a hold harmless clause that attempts to shelter the board from legal liability for its actions. That such a provision will be upheld in court is questionable. If a board that is "held harmless" by the association is judged liable, responsibility is merely shifted to all members of the association. Therefore, the hold harmless clause found in many declarations is not to be considered sufficient protection for either the individual board member or the total board.

Although the term "directors' and officers' liability" is commonly used, different insurance companies define the term differently. Each carrier uses his own exclusionary language. Typically, however, a directors' and officers' liability policy does not cover dishonesty, undue enrichment, or losses resulting from the denial of the civil rights of an individual.

The Fidelity Bond. Board members also should be covered by a blanket *fidelity bond*, a requirement that may or may not be spelled out in the declaration. Because the treasurer of the board and certain employees are responsible for overseeing the disbursements of funds, the association needs to be protected against loss resulting from fraudulent or dishonest acts. The bond should be in an amount slightly in excess of the total funds that the employees or treasurer can be expected to have access to at any point in time. The bond would reimburse the association for any loss it sustains, up to the amount of the bond, by reason of a dishonest act of a person covered by the bond.

Workers' Compensation. Providing *Workers' Compensation* is a statutory requirement. Therefore, any condominium association that employs building or grounds maintenance or other personnel must be covered by Workers' Compensation to relieve it of any claims for work-related injuries. Workers' Compensation insurance provides for the cost of medical care and weekly income payments to persons injured while working for the association, regardless of who is at fault. In some states, it may even be necessary and prudent to include in the Workers' Compensation policy officers, board members, and other unit owners who could be injured while carrying out association business.

How Much Coverage Is Enough? Governing documents seldom stipulate the minimum amount of liability coverage required. Since property damage and bodily injury liability could involve substantial figures, the board should be careful not to underinsure the association. There are no statutory limitations on the amounts that potentially could be recovered for bodily injury and property damage. The board therefore should act prudently and buy adequate insurance to cover any probable circumstances.

While it is important for the board to select a comprehensive general liability policy, coverage can be extended under an *umbrella liability policy*. This provides coverage for claims that are too large to be covered under comprehensive general liability and also might cover losses not listed in the basic association policy. Umbrella liability coverage usually is available in increments of $1 million. The board of directors should consider appropriate coverage, depending on its own needs. While such needs cannot be accurately anticipated, the board should consider all possibilities and work with an expert in determining a realistic amount of liability coverage.

Contracting for the Association Policy

After the board has learned what kinds of coverage are available, it should draw up a bid specification, taking into account any insurance requirements specified in the governing documents and the association's peculiar insurance needs. If an annual evaluation of the property is performed, it should be included in the bid package. All other pertinent data, including floor plans and governing documents, should be added to the package. Three or more insurance agencies (preferably those with experience in insuring condominiums), should be invited to bid. Most companies will bid on one-year contracts, subject to renewal. The board also should specify which carriers it wishes to be covered by.

Before making a final selection based on the bids it receives, the board should investigate the potential agents' and companies' ability to serve the association. Their claims service and staff capabilities and, if applicable, their unit owners' billing services should be checked thoroughly. Many associations require that an insurance company representative attend either annual meetings or insurance committee meetings. For this reason, it is essential that the agent be willing to come into personal contact with the unit owners.

Once the insurance company has been selected, a method for handling large claims should be established. Such an agreement will expedite claims and protect the interests of all persons involved.

It also is a good idea for the board of directors to contract with the insurance carrier to provide engineering assistance in reducing hazards within the development. Most insurance companies will provide this service without charge because it reduces their risk. Special attention should be paid to structural problems and those that could result from use of the swimming pool.

After an insurance company has been selected by the board of directors, it is the agent's responsibility to prepare, in layman's language, a statement of coverage. This statement should outline the association insurance policy and recommend what each unit owner should cover by his individual unit owner's policy. The board of directors should distribute this statement to all owners and may wish to make itself available to them to answer questions. However, it is the obligation of the agent to respond to any inquiries that the unit owners may have concerning the master policy and its relation to the individual unit owners' policies.

The Unit Owner's Insurance Policy

Because coverage provided by the master condominium association policy is limited to those losses involving only common areas, the individual owner is responsible for losses affecting his own unit. Until recently, most condominium unit owners purchased the kind of insurance sold to rental apartment dwellers. However, because of the many differences between the two types of tenancy, this kind of insurance was inadequate to cover the unit owner's unique needs. A condominium unit owner's policy in various forms now is available throughout the country, and unit owners should be sure that they are covered by a policy designed especially for them.

The condominium unit owner's policy may cover five areas: the personal property of the unit owner (with some exceptions, as noted in the policy); unit realty that may not be covered by the association policy; additional living expenses incurred by the unit owner in the event he is forced to live elsewhere temporarily while repairs to damage are made or new permanent quarters are found; personal liability, including legal defense against suits arising from bodily injury or property losses sustained by another; and medical payments to others for injuries resulting from accidents on his premises.

However, the unit owner may not be adequately protected by these coverages and may need to endorse his policy to provide the missing protection. If the condominium association policy covers the entire physical structure, the unit owner's policy should cover the remainder of his needs. However, although most association policies cover all real property, not all do. In some cases it may be the unit owner's responsibility to insure some real property within his unit, such as permanent fixtures or additions or alterations made at his expense. The unit owner's policy may be endorsed to provide insurance coverage beyond the limits of the basic policy.

The basic owner's policy, like the association package, can be endorsed to cover all risks, with certain exclusions. Here again, the comprehensiveness of the all-risk coverage depends upon the carrier. This all-risk approach is particularly desirable because, in the condominium structure, a unit owner has relatively little control over events that may originate in a neighbor's unit.

Some condominium owners rent their units to others. If a rented unit is furnished, an endorsement is available to cover theft of personal property belonging to the individual unit owner. Also, such appurtenant structures as poolside cabanas, hobby shops, or storage sheds often are installed at the owner's expense, and that unit owner may endorse his policy so that these structures are properly and adequately covered.

Unit owners also may want to consider obtaining *loss assessments coverage* to cover the requirement that losses incurred by the association and not otherwise insured must be met through a special assessment of the unit owners. Let us say, for example, that a condominium association carries only $450,000 liability protection for occurrences within the common areas. Then, a guest is fatally injured when she falls down a stairway, her widower sues the association for $1 million, and the courts eventually award him $650,000. In this instance—and such large judgments are not unlikely—the insurance company would pay the $450,000 covered by the association policy, but the association still would owe $200,000. If there were 60 unit owners in the association, each would be assessed his share of the amount owed based on the percentages of ownership, or about $3,300 each. The loss assessment endorsement, however, should cover the unit owner's portion of this amount, as well as protect him against certain other kinds of special assessments. To keep premiums low, payment under this coverage may be subject to a deductible.

A tenant who rents an apartment and is displaced by fire or other damage resulting from some other occurrence usually will relocate in a relatively short period of time, but a condominium unit owner probably will need to wait until repairs are made and his original unit can be reoccupied. Considerable time may elapse before the unit is once again livable, and a family that must spend many weeks or months in a hotel or other temporary living quarters may find bills running up quickly. Although the basic unit owner's policy may provide some protection against such an occurrence, an appropriate endorsement can provide increased protection to cover excessive expenses.

A condominium unit owner may have additional needs that may be met by special endorsements to his policy, and an insurance agent should be able to provide advice as to coverage of these other unit owner liabilities.

Chapter 12

Tax Considerations

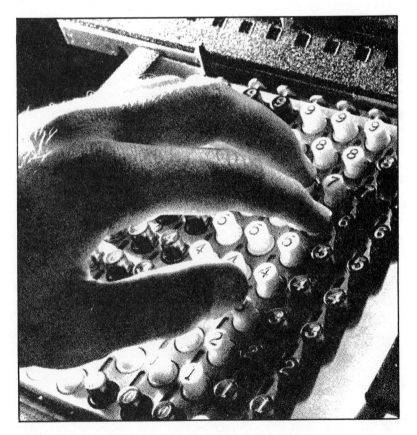

FILLING OUT TAX returns, receiving tax bills, and paying all kinds of taxes are inescapable facts of American life. The new condominium unit owner will need to know both how the property he has purchased will be taxed and how he will be treated by the Internal Revenue Service. Understanding the federal income tax status of the total condominium community requires the unit owner to think on two separate and distinct levels. On the one hand, he should know how he will be regarded as the owner of an individual condominium unit; on the other, he should understand the tax treatment of the condominium association, of which he and all other unit owners are members.

The Federal Tax Status of the Condominium Association

Finding a way to tax the income of condominium associations was a very complicated and lengthy process. The very purpose of the association clouded the issue. The difficulty of trying to apply federal income tax laws to a nonprofit organization formed to operate and manage property owned by all of its members raised some interesting and unique questions. The federal tax treatment of the condominium association was blanketed in confusion until the passage of the Tax Reform Act of 1976.

The Tax Reform Act changed the way condominium associations and other homeowners' associations are taxed by making it possible for them to be treated as tax-exempt organizations. Prior to the adoption of the act, one of a condominium association's main concerns usually was its federal income tax status. Of course, there was no problem if money collected from assessments was spent on the condominium's operation during the tax year. The issue of how to treat reserves held for capital improvements and operating expenses, however, raised serious questions. If income tax had to be paid on reserve funds, condominium unit owners, in effect, were being taxed on money they were setting aside for maintenance of their homes. The Tax Reform Act resolves many of these questions, allowing the condominium association to elect tax-exempt status if it meets certain qualifications and regulations.

Electing Tax-Exemption

Under Section 528 of the Internal Revenue Code, a condominium association that is organized and operated to provide for the acquisition, construction, management, maintenance, and care of a condominium's common areas can qualify for tax exemption if (1) at least 60 percent of the association's gross income comes from unit owner assessments, (2) at least 90 percent of its expenses go for managing, maintaining, and caring for common areas, (3) substantially all of the units are used as residences, and (4) no part of the net income benefits any individual member of the association. In addition, Section 528 requires that substantially all of the units must be used as residences.

If it meets these requirements, an association can elect tax-exempt status by filing federal income tax return form 1120-H, the U.S. Income Tax Return for Homeowners Associations. This must be done annually. If form 1120-H is not completed and the tax-exempt option is not taken, the association will be taxed as a corporation.

Section 528 of the Internal Revenue Code requires the condominium association to distinguish between income that is exempt from taxation and income that is taxable. In general, any regular membership dues, fees, and assessments received from residential unit owners for operations reserves are considered exempt income and can be applied toward meeting the 60 percent qualification. Sources of income that are not exempt and are subject to federal income tax are (1) interest earned on reserve funds, (2) fees received from nonmembers for the use of association facilities, such as a swimming pool, tennis court, or party room, (3) assessments for work done on a privately-owned portion of a condominium unit, (4) income received from members as customers for services, such as maid service or house cleaning, rather than in their roles as unit owners, and (5) fees received from unit owners for special use of facilities that is not normally available to association members, including such things as hourly tennis court fees, laundry room and vending machine income, and rental fees for use of a party room. To further define the latter category, the Internal Revenue Code makes this distinction: If regular membership assessments do not entitle a member to use a particular facility, then income generated by that use is subject to tax. For example, if a unit owner pays a $110-a-month assessment but, in addition, must pay $1.50 each time he uses the swimming pool, the money collected in the form of swimming pool user fees is taxable income.

The condominium association should be aware that obtaining tax-exempt status does not necessarily mean that it will not have to pay any income taxes at all. Income that does not come from unit owner assessments still will be subject to tax. However, Section 528 does permit it to take two deductions. First, it can deduct any expenses that are directly related to producing any of the association's income. For example, if a condominium realizes $1,500 in fees for the use of the swimming pool, the $1,500 would be subject to tax. But if the association spends $300 to print identification cards for the pool's users, the $300 could be deducted and only $1,200 of this income would be taxable. Second, every tax-exempt condominium association is allowed a specific deduction of $100 from its taxable income. This $100 deduction is allowed so that associations with only a small amount of otherwise taxable income will not be subject to tax.

When an association elects tax-exempt status, the first $25,000 of its taxable income is taxed at the rate without the surtax amendment of 48 percent. As an example of how this works, consider the hypothetical condominium association that had the following income and operating expenses one year:

Income
    Assessments $ 98,000
    Interest   1,100
    User Fees   900
        Total Income $100,000
        Operating Expenses $ 92,000
        Income Over Expenses (Reserves) $ 8,000

If expenses of $120 could be allotted to the user fee income, the income tax would be determined as follows:

Nonexempt Income (Interest + User Fees) $ 2,000
Deduction of Expenses to
   Generate User Fees $120
Specific Deduction   100
   Total Deductions $ 220
Taxable Income $ 1,780
Tax Rate   48%
Tax Due $ 854.40

Tax-Exempt Status or Corporate Status?

If a condominium association does not elect the tax-exempt status, or if it does not qualify under Section 528 to do so, the association must file a tax return in the same manner as a corporation and be taxed at the corporate rate of 22 percent (in the case of a tax year ending after December 31, 1978) of income over expenses, including reserves. This is how the corporate tax rate would affect the same condominium association:

Income $100,000
Operating Expenses $ 92,000
Taxable Income $ 8,000
Tax Rate   22%
Tax Due $ 1,760

Obviously, this association would benefit from electing the tax-exempt status.

    If the association elects tax-exempt treatment, it is not permitted to benefit from special deductions provided for corporations or the net operating loss deduction. Thus, the association that elects tax-exempt status under Section 528 will not be able to deduct from its taxable income any losses that it may have had in the previous year. Accordingly, in some situations, an association might lower its income tax by not electing tax-exempt status and by being taxed as a corporation.

To understand how this factor can affect an association, let us consider its impact on the same hypothetical condominium association. Let us say that in the previous year the association had operated at a $9,000 loss (such losses are not unusual for fledgling associations). In effect, its operating expenses exceeded its income by $9,000. If this condominium association filed its tax return as a corporation, its $8,000 net income in the same year could be entirely offset by the previous year's net operating loss and the association would not have to pay any taxes. In addition, because net operating losses incurred in tax years ending after 1975 may be carried forward seven years following the taxable year of the loss, the remaining $1,000 would be available as a deduction in the next six years, provided the association filed its return as a corporation.

Although it does not often occur, it is possible for an inexperienced condominium association to operate at a loss but still have to pay income tax. If the association elects the tax-exempt status for the year it operated at a loss, any revenue that is not tax-exempt—such as user fees and interest—would be subject to the 48 percent tax-exempt organization tax rate. This could be avoided if the association filed its return as a corporation.

In addition, there is a way that an association can file as a corporation and avoid income tax even if its assessments exceed its expenses. If the excess assessments are refunded to the unit owners or are applied to the next year's regular assessments, they will not be subject to corporate tax. Either action requires a special vote of the membership. Of course, this alternative does fail to recognize the importance of establishing reserve funds.

There is yet another method for avoiding income tax on certain reserves. If an association chooses the corporate tax treatment, special assessments designated for specific capital expenditures are not included in the gross taxable income, provided that they meet certain requirements. These special assessments can be excluded from taxation if the assessment has been appropriately approved, if the funds are set aside in a special bank account and not commingled with regular assessments, and if the funds are

used for the purpose for which they were assessed. In effect, this
alternative excludes capital reserves from being treated as income
for tax purposes. To understand how this works, again consider
the hypothetical condominium:

Income	
Assessments (Operations)	$ 91,000
Assessments (Capital Reserves)	7,000
Interest	1,100
User Fees	900
Total Income	$100,000
Income Subject to Tax	
Assessments (Operations)	$ 91,000
Interest	1,100
User Fees	900
Total Income Subject to Tax	$ 93,000
Operating Expenses	$ 92,000
Taxable Income	$ 1,000
Tax Rate	22%
Tax Due	$220

Since the election for tax-exempt treatment must be made
each year, a condominium association should review its financial
status annually. An election under Section 528 might be advanta-
geous one year, while the association might be in a better tax
position by accepting the corporate tax treatment the following
year. The condominium association should weigh all of the vari-
ables before it reaches a decision. There are ways to avoid or
lower the tax bill, if all of the alternatives are known and understood. Certainly, no condominium association should pay federal
income taxes on assessments collected to operate and maintain
the condominium community.

Although the Tax Reform Act of 1976 resolved certain
issues, it also created some new questions that will be answered
only as Section 528 is interpreted by the courts. Because modern
condominium ownership is still a relatively new concept, obtaining
the assistance of a qualified tax attorney or a certified public accountant—preferably one who has had experience in condomin-

ium legal practices—is essential to making the right decision about the association's tax status.

The Federal Tax Status of the Unit Owner

The person who owns his home has certain advantages that the apartment renter clearly does not have. Specifically, the home owner can benefit from a set of federal income tax shelters. In the eyes of the Internal Revenue Service, there is no essential difference between a condominium unit owner and a single-family home owner. As a result, families and individuals can turn to condominiums as a way to take advantage of income tax incentives.

Taking Advantage of Deductions

The person who owns and uses his condominium unit as his principal residence throughout the year can enjoy the same tax shelters as his friend who owns a conventional house. Assuming that both itemize their deductions, the three principal tax deductions available to both the condominium owner and the single-family home owner are deductions for interest, property taxes, and casualty and theft losses.

Because a condominium unit owner obtains his own individual mortgage on his unit, he can deduct any mortgage interest paid during the tax year. Similarly, if he has a mortgage on his share in the common areas of the condominium, he also can deduct the interest paid on that mortgage. Although it is very rare for individual unit owners to obtain a blanket mortgage, if they did, each unit owner could deduct his portion of the interest on that common mortgage. And any time that a unit owner borrows money to make repairs, improvements, or additions to his individual unit, he can deduct the interest that he pays on that debt.

Like the home owner, the condominium unit owner also can deduct property taxes for the year in which they are paid. He can deduct real estate taxes assessed against his individually owned unit, he can deduct his share (based on his percentage of ownership interest) of any real estate taxes assessed against the condominium's common areas, and he can deduct real estate taxes on any other separate interest that he owns in the condominium project. Under some state laws, for example, a condominium unit owner may hold title to a parking space or a storage locker. If he does, he can deduct real estate taxes levied on such a piece of property.

The unit owner should keep in mind that deductions for property taxes are available only if the unit owner has a fee simple absolute interest in the land. *(See Chapter I for a discussion of this term.)* If he has a leasehold interest, he is not entitled to deduct the real estate taxes that are assessed against the land, even though he is obligated to pay these taxes. However, real estate taxes assessed against any buildings or additions and improvements can be deducted by the unit owner.

Again like the conventional home owner, a unit owner whose property is damaged or destroyed by fire or other casualty, in excess of $100, may have incurred a deductible loss, and the same is true of losses due to theft. A deductible casualty loss is determined by comparing the value of the property in question immediately before the casualty with its value immediately after the casualty. If there is no better way to determine this difference in value, it may be based on the cost of repairing or replacing the property to the condition it was in just before the casualty occurred. If the decrease in the value of the property as a result of the casualty is less than its *adjusted basis*, in other words, its original cost, the decrease in value is used to determine the deductible loss. If the decrease in value is greater than the original cost, then the latter is used. If an item is stolen, either its fair market value at the time of the theft or its original cost, whichever is less, is used to determine the deductible loss. In all cases, any insurance compensation and a $100 loss limitation is subtracted from the total loss to arrive at the deductible loss.

A single example should illustrate how the deductible loss is determined. Let us say that a fire has damaged an interior wall that is part of the unit owner's property, a sofa that he originally purchased for $900, and a painting purchased for $25. It is established that the value of the sofa just before the fire was $300, but after the fire it was worth only $10. The painting, which was totally destroyed by the blaze, had greatly appreciated since it was purchased and, just prior to the fire, was valued at $750. The decrease in the value of the sofa (the value before the fire minus its value after the fire) was $290 ($300 - $10), and of the painting, $750 ($750 - $0). The wall was repaired for $565. Since the loss is based on either the adjusted basis or the decrease in value, whichever is less, the loss on the sofa would be $290 and the loss on the painting would be $25. The loss on the wall, set by the repair cost, would be $565. Thus, the total loss would be $880. If the unit owner received $330 from his insurance company, his casualty loss deduction for income tax purposes would be $450. Here is how that figure is determined:

	Sofa	Painting	Wall
(1) Adjusted basis (original cost)	$900	$ 25	—
(2) Value before casualty or theft (if available)	300	750	—
(3) Value after casualty or theft (if available)	10	0	—
(4) Decrease in value (Line 2 minus Line 3) or Repair or replacement cost (if Line 2 and Line 3 are unavailable)	290	750	$565
(5) Loss	$290	$ 25	$565
(6) Total loss (if more than one item of property is damaged, destroyed, or stolen)	$880		
(7) Insurance or other recovery compensation	$330		
(8) $100 limitation	100		
(9) Total Line 7 plus Line 8	430		
(10) Casualty loss deduction (Line 6 minus Line 9)	$450		

The person who uses his condominium unit as his primary place of residence cannot deduct personal expenses, such as maintenance assessments, assessments for the use of recreational amenities, costs for repairing and maintaining his unit, insurance, depreciation, utility fees, or wages of domestic help. Nor, like the home owner, can he deduct depreciation on his unit. However, if a condominium unit owner uses his unit as income-producing property and rents his unit to a tenant, then the property can be depreciated for income tax purposes. The unit owner also can claim the normal landlord deductions for expenses related to its maintenance. These deductible expenses could include regular assessments and fees, insurance, repairs, maintenance, and utilities. Of course, all rents that are collected on a rental unit must be reported by the owner as income.

Selling a Condominium Unit

Just like the home owner who sells his house and makes a profit on the sale, the owner of a condominium unit used for residential purposes who sells it at a gain will have to pay a *capital gains tax*. A loss on the sale of the condominium unit has no effect on individual income tax and no deduction for it is allowed.

However, again like the home owner, the condominium unit owner who realizes a gain can defer payment of the capital gains tax if he meets certain qualifications. Specifically, (1) he must buy or build a new residence, no matter whether it is a house, mobile home, houseboat, cooperative, or another condominium; (2) he must purchase and move into his new residence within 18 months of the sale of his unit (additional time is allowed for occupancy of a home that is being built); and (3) the adjusted sales price of the new residence must be equal to or greater than the adjusted sales price of the unit he sold. This postponement also is available to a home owner purchasing a condominium unit as a residence.

The unit owner should be mindful that, while this capital gains tax may be postponed, it may not be forgotten or ignored. The long-term advantage of postponing this tax is that a home owner can indefinitely defer the capital gains tax by continually reinvesting in more valuable homes. If it is postponed until the owner reaches the age of 65, all or part of the gain may be excluded from his gross income in accordance with certain requirements set forth in the Internal Revenue Code.

When the capital gains tax is postponed, the gain is subtracted from the cost of the new residence to determine the income tax basis of the new residence. For example, if a unit owner realizes a gain of $17,000 on the sale of his condominium unit and six months later purchases a new unit for $52,000, the nonrecognized gain of $17,000 is subtracted from the purchase price of his new unit, making its *basis* or value for tax purposes $35,000.

The Condominium's Real Estate Tax Status

In addition to paying federal income taxes, the unit owner also will be faced with paying real estate taxes. One of the characteristics of condominium ownership is that the individual units are taxed separately; the project is not taxed as a single piece of property.

Because real estate taxation practices have their roots in state condominium laws, there are likely to be some differences from state to state in the method used to assess condominium properties. Most state laws consider each condominium unit and its undivided interest in the common areas as one parcel of real property. In such cases, the unit owner's property is subject to an individual assessment and individual taxation as if it were any other kind of real property. Although this is the usual practice, it is not uncommon for assessors to value the entire project as though it were a single property and then determine the individual real estate tax assessments based on the percentages of interest. Even when this is done, however, separate tax bills are sent to each unit owner.

The condominium association usually does not receive a tax bill. However, the general guideline is that if a parcel can be sold, it can be assessed, and the association may hold title to a property that can be sold, such as an office for use of the condominium manager, an apartment used by a janitor, or a garage. In these cases, the association may, at least in some states, receive a tax bill.

Because each unit owner can deduct all property taxes he pays—including his share of the property taxes on the condominium's common areas—the association should document each owner's portion of an assessment whenever taxes are assessed against common areas and paid by the association as a common expense, to support each owner's deduction claim.

Appendix A

Governing Document Content Checklist

SUBJECTS TREATED IN GOVERNING DOCUMENTS	DECLARATION	ARTICLES OF INCORPORATION	BYLAWS	UNIT DEED	HOUSE RULES AND REGULATIONS
Definitions of Units and Common Areas					
Assignment of Percentages of Ownership Interest					
Establishment of Administrative Procedures					
Outline of Maintenance Responsibilities					
Establishment of Fiscal Procedures					
Delegation of Management Authority					
Outline of Insurance Requirements					
Establishment of Rules, Regulations, and Restrictions					
Method for Transferring Controls					

Condominium Association
Record of Administrative Requirements

Condominium Association _____

RECORDATION OF DOCUMENTS

Declaration

Date _____ Municipality _____ Book _____ Page _____

Bylaws

Date _____ Municipality _____ Book _____ Page _____

Articles of Incorporation

Date _____ Municipality _____ Book _____ Page _____

ANNUAL MEMBERSHIP MEETING REQUIREMENTS

Date _____

Notice Required _____ Proxy Due Date_____

VOTE REQUIREMENTS

Amend Declaration _____ Amend Bylaws _____

Decide Operational Issues _____ Approve Special Assessments _____

SPECIAL MEETING REQUIREMENTS

Notice Required _____ Limitation of Issues _____

Board Vote Needed to Call_____ Owner Vote Needed to Call_____

BOARD OF DIRECTORS REQUIREMENTS

Number_____ Initial Terms _____

Offices _____

Requirement to Remove Officer _____

Requirement to Remove Director _____

Method for Replacement of Director _____

BOARD MEETING REQUIREMENTS

Minimum Number of Meetings _____

Notice Required _____ Votes to Pass Motion _____

Nomination Application

I, _____
(Print Name)

hereby submit my name for consideration for nomination for the Board of Directors

of _____ Condo-

minium Association, the election of which is to be held at _____ on
(Time)

_____ at _____ .
(Date)   (Location)

Occupation _____

_____

Education _____

_____

Experience _____

_____

Outside Activities _____

_____

I think I would be an asset to the Board of Directors because _____

_____

_____

Endorsements

Name	Address	Signature
_____	_____	_____
_____	_____	_____
_____	_____	_____
_____	_____	_____
_____	_____	_____

Signed _____

Address _____

Date _____

Ballot

To elect _____ Directors of the Board of Directors of

_____ Condominium Association

Date _____   Vote _____ times

Candidates   Indicate
(list alphabetically)   Vote Here

_____   _____

_____   _____

_____   _____

_____   _____

_____   _____

_____   _____

_____   _____

_____   _____

_____   _____

Policy Resolution

Policy of _____ Condominium Association

Adopted by the Board of Directors _____
                                              (Date)
Topic _____

Resolved: _____

_____

_____

_____

_____

_____

_____

Filed in Minute Book Page _____

Attested by _____
                        (Secretary)

Notice of Annual Membership Meeting

The annual membership meeting of _____

Condominium Association will be held at _____ on _____
                                          (Time)   (Date)
at_____ for the purpose of electing_____
              (Location)
Director(s) and the transaction of such other business as may properly come before

the meeting.

                                        Signed_____
                                                  (Secretary or Management Agent)

Proxy

I/We, _____ being the owner(s)

of the condominium unit located at _____

in the _____ condominium do hereby

authorize and appoint _____
                                (Name of Proxy)

of _____ to be my/our proxy,
              (Address of Proxy)

to represent me/us on the issues to be discussed at the membership meeting of

_____ Condominium Association

to be held on _____at _____
                    (Date)   (Location)
and to vote on my/our behalf on the issues submitted to vote at this meeting or, in the

event a quorum shall fail to attend, at such time and place as the adjourned meeting

shall be resumed. This proxy shall remain in full force and effect until such time as it

shall be revoked by me/us in writing.

_____	_____
(Date)	(Signature of Owner)
_____	_____
(Date)	(Signature of Owner)

                                Notary Seal

Committee Interest Questionnaire

Please complete this questionnaire if you are interested in playing an important role in

the activities of _____Condominium Association.

Name _____

Address _____

Telephone _____ Date _____

I would like to work on the following committee (in order of preference):

_____ Architectural Control Committee

_____ Landscape and Grounds Committee

_____ Budget and Finance Committee

_____ Insurance Committee

_____ Maintenance Committee

_____ Rules and Regulations Committee

_____ Social Committee

_____ Newsletter Committee

_____ Welcoming Committee

_____ Recreation Committee

I would accept chairmanship of the committee I am volunteering for:

_____ At this time

_____ In the future

I have a (considerable) (moderate) (small) amount of time to devote. The most con-

venient time for me is (weekends) (days) (evenings) (whenever needed).

I have the following skills which may be of value to the operations and activities of the

community (typing, shorthand, specific vocational experience, etc.): _____

_____

_____

Service Contract Record

COMPANY	TYPE OF SERVICE	FREQUENCY OF SERVICE	TERMINATION DATE	AMOUNT (MONTHLY)	CANCELLATION PROVISION
	Pool				
	Gardening				
	Janitorial				
	Elevator Maintenance				
	Security Services				
	Trash Removal				

Parliamentary Rules Governing Motions

Name of Motion	Can Speaker Be Interrupted?	Is a Second Needed?	Can It Be Debated?	Can It Be Amended?	What Vote Is Needed to Pass?	Can It Be Reconsidered?
Ranking Motions						
Privileged Motions						
Fix the Time to Adjourn	No	Yes	No*	Yes	Majority	No
Adjourn	No	Yes	No	No	Majority	No
Recess	No	Yes	No*	Yes	Majority	No
Question of Privilege	Yes	No	No	No	Chair Rules	No
Orders of the Day	Yes	No	No	No	Enforceable on Demand	No
Subsidiary Motions						
Lay on the Table	No	Yes	No	No	Majority	No
Previous Question	No	Yes	No	No	Two-thirds	No; unless vote on question has not been taken
Limit Debate	No	Yes	No	Yes	Two-thirds	Yes
Postpone Definitely	No	Yes	Yes	Yes	Majority	Yes
Refer to Committee	No	Yes	Yes	Yes	Majority	Yes
Amend	No	Yes	Yes	Yes	Majority	Yes
Postpone Indefinitely	No	Yes	Yes	No	Majority	Yes
Main Motions						
General Main Motion	No	Yes	Yes	Yes	Majority	Yes

Parliamentary Rules Governing Motions,*cont.*

NAME OF MOTION	CAN SPEAKER BE INTERRUPTED?	IS A SECOND NEEDED?	CAN IT BE DEBATED?	CAN IT BE AMENDED?	WHAT VOTE IS NEEDED TO PASS?	CAN IT BE RECONSIDERED?
Nonranking Motions						
Main Motions to Renew Questions						
Take from the Table	No	Yes	No	No	Majority	No
Rescind	No	Yes	Yes	Yes	Two-thirds	Yes; If Negative Vote
Amend Something Previously Adopted	No	Yes	Yes	Yes	Two-thirds	Yes; If Negative Vote
Discharge a Committee	No	Yes	Yes	Yes	Majority	Yes; If Negative Vote
Reconsider	Yes	Yes	Yes	No	Majority	No
Incidental Motions						
Point of Order	Yes	No	No	No	Chair Rules	No
Suspend the Rules	No	Yes	No	No	Two-thirds	No
Object to Consideration	Yes	No	No	No	Two-thirds in Negative	No
Division of Question	No	Yes	No	Yes	Majority	No
Division of Assembly	Yes	No	No	No	Enforceable on Demand	No

*Not debatable when another question is before the assembly.

Preventive Maintenance Schedule

Item _____ Date _____

DESCRIPTION OF MAINTENANCE JOB	FREQUENCY			
	INSPECT	CLEAN	LUBRICATE	REPLACE

Frequency Code: D–Daily; W–Weekly; M–Monthly; Q–Quarterly;
S–Semiannually; A–Annually.

Custodial Maintenance Schedule

AREA	DESCRIPTION OF MAINTENANCE JOB	FREQUENCY
Lobby		
Laundry		
Halls and Corridors		
Elevators		
Stairways		

Frequency Code: D–Daily; W–Weekly; M–Monthly.

Emergency Telephone Number Checklist

Condominium Association _____

Address _____

		TELEPHONE	
		OFFICE	HOME/NIGHT
Board of Directors	_____	_____	_____
	_____	_____	_____
	_____	_____	_____
	_____	_____	_____
	_____	_____	_____
	_____	_____	_____
Association Employees	_____	_____	_____
	_____	_____	_____
	_____	_____	_____
	_____	_____	_____
	_____	_____	_____
Accountant	_____	_____	_____
Attorney	_____	_____	_____
Architect	_____	_____	_____
Developer	_____	_____	_____
Insurance Agent	_____	_____	_____
Management Agent	_____	_____	_____
Service Contractors	_____	_____	_____
Air Conditioning	_____	_____	_____
Heating	_____	_____	_____
Fuel	_____	_____	_____
Equipment	_____	_____	_____

Emergency Telephone Number Checklist, *cont.*

| | | TELEPHONE | |
		OFFICE	HOME/NIGHT
Elevators	_____	_____	_____
Antennae	_____	_____	_____
Electrician	_____	_____	_____
Glass	_____	_____	_____
Landscaping	_____	_____	_____
Lawn Service	_____	_____	_____
Laundry	_____	_____	_____
Locksmith	_____	_____	_____
Painter	_____	_____	_____
Pest Control	_____	_____	_____
Plumber	_____	_____	_____
Roofer	_____	_____	_____
Security Service	_____	_____	_____
Security System	_____	_____	_____
Snow Removal	_____	_____	_____
Street Lighting	_____	_____	_____
Trash Removal	_____	_____	_____
_____	_____	_____	_____
_____	_____	_____	_____
_____	_____	_____	_____
Miscellaneous			
Fire Station	_____	_____	_____
Police Station	_____	_____	_____
_____	_____	_____	_____
_____	_____	_____	_____

Grounds Care Program
Specifications for Bid

LAWN CUTTING

(1)   Initial cut in first week of April; final cut in middle of November.
(2)   Total cuts: Thirty (30); additional per cut cost should be indicated.
(3)   Cut height: Two and one-half (2½) inches.
(4)   Grass clippings: Swept and removed from all streets, curbs, sidewalks, and entrance ways and from surfaces of any walls, windows, or doors to which adhered with such cutting; grass clippings are to be raked and removed from all lawn areas if their length shall exceed three (3) inches.
(5)   Inability to cut due to weather: Credit for incomplete cuttings or cuttings not performed shall be prorated on the basis of the percentage of the area incompleted with adjustment made at the close of the season.
(6)   Lawn cutting shall be confined to between the hours of 8:30 a.m. and 5:00 p.m. and shall be performed on weekdays only unless otherwise agreed to by the Board of Directors.
(7)   Grass around all buildings, flower beds, trees, and other obstacles within the lawn area shall be hand trimmed with each cutting, and the cuttings raked and removed.

EDGING

(1)   Inclusive of all sidewalks, entrance ways, and curbs.
(2)   Complete edging is to be accomplished in single operation during the first week of June, August, and October and in the last week of November.
(3)   Depth of edging: Minimum of two (2) inches.
(4)   Width of edging: Minimum of one-half (½) inch.
(5)   Edged dirt and grass is to be swept up and removed as generated.

PRUNING

(1)   All shrubs and trees are to be pruned upon completion of their growth season to maintain proper shape and uniformity of appearance.
(2)   Clippings are to be removed as generated.

Grounds Care Program
Specifications for Bid, *cont.*

LAWN CARE PROGRAM

  Early Spring: Soil test for nitrogen, phosphorous, and potassium needs; soil test for pH requirements; lime and fertilize as required: aerate and roll; apply chemicals for weed and fungus control; milky spot treatment for Japanese beetles.

  Early Summer: Fertilize; aerate and roll; apply chemicals to control weeds, fungus, cinch bugs, sod webworms, and pre-emergence crabgrass control; spray trees for beetles and webworms.

  Late Summer: Fertilize; roll; apply chemicals for weeds, cinch bugs, sod webworms, and pre-emergence crabgrass control.

  Fall: Fertilize; lime; seed; aerate and roll; apply chemicals for weed and fungus control.

MULCHING OF TREES AND FLOWER BEDS

(1) Turn monthly.

(2) Apply and spread additional mulch as needed.

GENERAL SPECIFICATIONS

(1) Contractor agrees to maintain Workers' Compensation and Public Liability insurance in the amounts of $50,000; $100,000; $300,000 in full force throughout the term of the contract and to furnish vendee with certificates of said insurance in evidence thereof.

(2) Contractor shall furnish vendee with one estimate for application of the above program to the condominium development grounds for one season.

(3) Contractor shall furnish all tools, equipment, materials, and labor at his expense.

          Bid Amount _____

Pie Diagram
Assessment Presentation

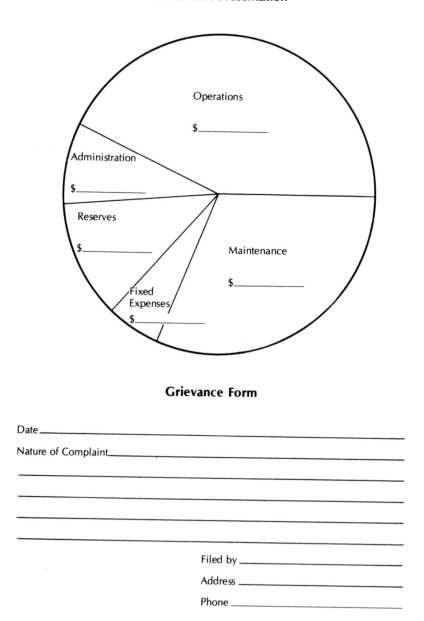

Operations

$_____

Administration

$_____

Reserves

$_____

Fixed
Expenses

$_____

Maintenance

$_____

Grievance Form

Date _____

Nature of Complaint _____

_____

_____

_____

_____

Filed by _____

Address _____

Phone _____

Condominium Association Complaint Log

DATE	TIME	OWNER	ADDRESS	TELEPHONE	FORM OF COMPLAINT	DESCRIPTION OF COMPLAINT	DISPOSITION	COMPLETED

House Rules and Regulations

(1) Any common sidewalks, driveways, entrances, or passageways shall not be obstructed or used by any unit owner for any other purpose than ingress to and egress from the units.

(2) Except as to the areas termed limited common areas, no article shall be placed on or in any of the general common areas except for those articles of personal property which are the common property of all the unit owners.

(3) Unit owners, members of their families, their guests, residents, tenants, or lessees shall not use sidewalks, driveways, entrances, or passageways as play areas.

(4) No vehicle belonging to or under the control of a unit owner or a member of the family or a guest, tenant, lessee, or employee of a unit owner shall be parked in such manner as to impede or prevent ready access to any entrance to or exit from a building.

(5) No owner, resident, or lessee shall install wiring for electrical or telephone installation or for any other purpose, nor shall any television or radio antennae, machines, or air conditioning units be installed on the exterior of the project, nor shall any similar improvements that protrude through the walls or the roof of the condominium be constructed, except as may be expressly authorized by the Association.

(6) No work of any kind shall be done upon the exterior building walls or upon the general or limited common areas by any unit owner. All such work is the responsibility of the Association.

(7) Owners and occupants shall exercise reasonable care to avoid making or permitting to be made loud, disturbing, or objectionable noises and in using or playing or permitting to be used or played musical instruments, radios, phonographs, television sets, amplifiers, and any other instruments or devices in such manner as may disturb or tend to disturb owners, tenants, or occupants of other units.

(8) Disposition of garbage and trash shall be only by the use of garbage disposal units or by use of common trash and garbage facilities.

House Rules and Regulations, *cont.*

(9) No rugs or other materials shall be dusted from windows, balconies, decks, or patios by beating or shaking.

(10) No cats, dogs, or other animal, bird, or reptile (hereinafter for brevity termed "animal") shall be kept, maintained, or harbored in the development unless the same in each instance is expressly permitted in writing by the management agent or, if there is no management agent, then by the Board of Directors. Where such written permission is granted, such permission is revocable if the animal becomes obnoxious to other owners, in which event the owner or person having control of the animal shall be given a written notice to correct the problem, or if not corrected, the owner, upon written notice, will be required to dispose of the animal. The written notice provided for herein shall be issued by the management agent or, if there is no management agent, then by one or more of the members of the Board of Directors.

(11) The Association assumes no liability for nor shall it be liable for any loss or damage to articles stored in any common or other storage area.

(12) Any damage to the general common areas or common personal property caused by a unit owner or a child or children of a unit owner or their guests or the guests of a unit owner shall be repaired at the expense of that unit owner.

(13) No unit shall be occupied by more than four persons, which number shall not include more than two children, without the consent of 100 percent of the percentage ownership of the units as that term is defined in the Declaration of this Condominium. For these purposes the term "children" refers to persons who have not attained the age of 13 years.

(14) No owner shall display any sign visible from the exterior of any unit, nor place on or remove from the project grounds plants of any description without the prior consent of the Board of Directors.

The foregoing House Rules and Regulations are subject to amendment and to the promulgation of further regulations.

Guidelines for the
Architectural Control Committee

The Architectural Control Committee (hereafter referred to as the Committee) shall be made up of volunteers appointed by the President of the Board of Directors. The Committee will help to administer the rules and regulations as set forth in the Declaration and Bylaws. The Committee shall vote on requests for all external changes and shall present its recommendations to the Board of Directors (hereafter referred to as the Board) for its approval or disapproval.

APPLICATION PROCEDURES

(1) A written request describing any improvements to be made to the property must be sent to _____

(2) The descriptions must include all vital information pertaining to the changes to be made.

(3) When a color change is requested, a color swatch is required.

SPECIFIC PROJECT REQUIREMENTS

(1) Awnings and above-ground decks of any kind are not felt to enhance aesthetic qualities of the community and therefore shall be prohibited.

(2) Any additions to the parent structure shall be prohibited.

(3) Any exterior paint change must be approved by the Committee.

(4) Any extensions of the rear patio must be approved by the Committee.

(5) All front and side iron railings must remain the original black color. The back railings and porches may be painted a different color if approved by the Committee. All iron railings and porches must be well kept and be attached properly to the unit.

(6) All fences must be wood and be of a natural wood color or stain. Fences that enclose a yard must be no higher than five (5) feet and be of a natural wood color or stain.

(7) Hedges are considered fences and therefore are not generally allowed forward of the rear line of the house. Chicken wire may be used to reinforce a hedge only for the first growing season of the original hedge, then it must be removed.

(8) A privacy fence that is perpendicular to the unit may be erected to a height of six (6) feet and a depth of twelve (12) feet. This fence may not enclose an area but must be along the side of property lines.

Guidelines for the
Architectural Control Committee, *cont.*

(9) Any type of plastic, metal, or wood flower bed fencing that does not exceed a height of twelve (12) inches may be used to enclose a flower bed that does not extend to the sidewalk. If a front yard has been turned into a flower bed, it must be enclosed by brick-in-the-ground edging or be left unedged.

(10) Exterior lighting shall not be directed in such manner as to create annoyance to neighbors.

(11) Trash containers shall not be permitted to remain conspicuous except on days of trash collection. No trash containers may be kept on general common areas.

(12) No pools other than small wading pools that can be put in storage nightly shall be used on any lot at any time.

(13) No structures such as dog houses, storage sheds, etc., shall be constructed on any lot at any time.

(14) Children's play equipment such as small plastic slides is permitted so long as it can be stored at night.

(15) Small portable sandboxes are permitted so long as they are well kept, covered at night, and removed at the end of the summer season. If not kept in good condition, the Committee will request repair or removal.

(16) Swing and gym sets on individual lots shall not be permitted.

(17) No outside televisions or radio antenna shall be permitted.

(18) Realty signs shall not be permitted on general common areas. No realty sign shall be attached to a unit. Realty signs must not remain on individual lots after sale of units.

(19) No clothes lines of any kind shall be permitted.

(20) All latticework must be against the surface of the rear or sides of the building. It may be left the natural wood color or painted a harmonious color with Committee approval.

(21) No garden shall be bordered with chicken wire. Vegetable gardens are restricted to the rear portion or yard of the limited common area of any unit and shall be limited in size to one-third (⅓) of that area.

(22) Small wooden bird feeders shall be permitted so long as they are placed on poles between five (5) and eight (8) feet high and are kept presentable. Multibird houses shall not be permitted.

(23) Minibikes shall not be permitted on any common area per local law.

(24) No motor vehicle shall be kept on any common area except the parking area.

(25) No boat or trailer shall be parked on any parking area or street.

Approval of any project does not waive the necessity of obtaining a county building permit.

Architectural Improvement
Application and Review Form

Unit Owner_____Date _____

Address of Unit _____Phone _____

Nature of Improvement _____

_____

_____

_____

Color (if applicable) _____

Location (if applicable) _____

Dimensions (if applicable) _____

Construction Material (if applicable)_____

Supplier_____Approximate Cost _____

(A sketch of all improvements must be attached to the application to show location

and dimensions.)

Send to _____

Address _____

Date Submitted_____Signed _____

For Internal Use Only

Date Received _____

Inspected on _____Inspected by _____

Approved on _____Disapproved on _____

Reason for Disapproval _____

_____

_____

Architectural Control and Use Violation Log

UNIT ADDRESS	UNIT OWNER	DESCRIPTION OF VIOLATION	DATE NOTED	FIRST NOTICE	INSPEC- TION	SECOND NOTICE	SECOND INSPECTION	ATTOR- NEY	COM- MENTS

Budget Preparation Calendar

DATE	ACTION TO BE COMPLETED
	President assigns members of Budget and Finance Committee to work with standing committees in preparing appropriate budget requests.
	Committees submit budget requests to treasurer.
	If association employs staff, treasurer submits salary recommendations to board of directors.
	Public hearings conducted, at which time committee chairmen formally make their requests, explain them, and answer questions regarding them. All unit owners invited.
	Budget conferences between board and committee chairmen conducted.
	Final budget decisions, including official estimates of revenue from assessments and other sources, are made by treasurer with assistance from management agent.
	Treasurer submits proposed budget to board.
	Modifications made by board are incorporated into budget.
	Printing of budget with amendments completed under treasurer's supervision.
	Board reviews final budget and passes resolution to adopt it.
	Fiscal year begins, and budget takes effect.

Capital Replacements Reserve Worksheet

ITEM	REPLACEMENT ÷ COST	REMAINING USEFUL LIFE	= ANNUAL RESERVE REQUIREMENT
Painting, Interior	_____	_____	_____
Painting, Exterior	_____	_____	_____
Water Heater	_____	_____	_____
Carpet and Flooring	_____	_____	_____
Street and Driveway	_____	_____	_____
Heating-Air Conditioning System	_____	_____	_____
Swimming Pool	_____	_____	_____
Tennis Court	_____	_____	_____
Furnishings and Equipment	_____	_____	_____
Light Fixtures	_____	_____	_____
Fire Extinguishers	_____	_____	_____
_____	_____	_____	_____
_____	_____	_____	_____
_____	_____	_____	_____
_____	_____	_____	_____

Total Annual Capital Replacements Reserve Requirement _____

Budget Worksheet

EXPENSES				TOTAL ANNUAL	TOTAL MONTHLY
Administrative Expenses					
Office Salaries				_____	_____
Office Expenses				_____	_____
Management Fee				_____	_____
Legal				_____	_____
Audit				_____	_____
Telephone				_____	_____
Miscellaneous				_____	_____
Operating Expenses					
Elevator				_____	_____
Heating Fuel				_____	_____
Electricity				_____	_____
Water/Sewer				_____	_____
Gas				_____	_____
Exterminating				_____	_____
Rubbish Removal				_____	_____
Window Washing				_____	_____
Miscellaneous				_____	_____
Repair and Maintenance	*Pay-roll*	*Mate-rials*	*Con-tract*		
Security	_____	_____	_____	_____	_____
Ground Maintenance	_____	_____	_____	_____	_____
Custodial	_____	_____	_____	_____	_____
General Maintenance	_____	_____	_____	_____	_____
Heat/AC/Vent	_____	_____	_____	_____	_____

Budget Worksheet, *cont.*

	Pay-roll	Mate-rials	Con-tract	TOTAL ANNUAL	TOTAL MONTHLY
Painting, Interior	___	___	___	___	___
Painting, Exterior	___	___	___	___	___
Recreational Amenities	___	___	___	___	___
Miscellaneous	___	___	___	___	___
Fixed Expenses					
Real Estate Tax				___	___
Other Tax				___	___
Insurance				___	___
Recreational					
Facilities, Leased				___	___
Ground Rent				___	___
Reserves					
Capital Replacements				___	___
Operating Contingencies				___	___
Total Expense Budget				___	___
INCOME					
Regular Unit Assessments				___	___
Rental Fees				___	___
Interest				___	___
Special Assessments				___	___
Miscellaneous				___	___
Total Income				___	___

Statement of Income and Expense Worksheet

	MONTH ACTUAL	MONTH BUDGETED	YEAR-TO-DATE ACTUAL	YEAR-TO-DATE BUDGETED
INCOME				
Regular Assessments				
Rental Fees				
Interest				
Special Assessments				
Miscellaneous				
Total Income				
EXPENSES				
Administrative Expenses				
Office Salaries				
Office Expenses				
Management Fee				
Legal				
Audit				
Telephone				
Miscellaneous				
Operating Expenses				
Elevator				
Heating Fuel				
Electricity				
Water/Sewer				
Gas				
Exterminating				
Rubbish Removal				
Window Washing				
Miscellaneous				

Statement of Income and Expense Worksheet, *cont.*

	MONTH ACTUAL	MONTH BUDGETED	YEAR-TO-DATE ACTUAL	YEAR-TO-DATE BUDGETED
Repair and Maintenance				
Security				
Ground Maintenance				
Custodial				
General Maintenance				
Heat/AC/Vent				
Painting, Interior				
Painting, Exterior				
Recreational Amenities				
Miscellaneous				
Fixed Expenses				
Real Estate Tax				
Other Tax				
Insurance				
Recreational Facilities, Leased				
Ground Rent				
Reserves				
Capital Replacements				
Operating Contingencies				
Total Expenses				
Net Gain (Loss)				

Unit Owner Ledger Card

Unit Owner_____

Address of Unit_____

Billing Address _____

Monthly Assessment _____

DATE	DESCRIPTION OF PAYMENT	BILLED	RECEIVED	BALANCE

Miscellaneous Information

Telephone Number _____

Children_____ Pets _____

Other _____

_____

_____

Chart of Accounts

from the U.S. Department of Housing and Urban Development

6300 ADMINISTRATIVE EXPENSES

6310	Office Salaries
6311	Office Expenses
6312	Office Rent
6320	Management Fee
6330	Manager or Superintendent Salaries
6340	Legal Expenses
6350	Auditing Expenses
6360	Telephone and Telegraph
6370	Bad Debts
6390	Miscellaneous Administrative Expenses

6400 OPERATING EXPENSES

6410	Elevator Payroll
6411	Elevator Power
6420	Fuel
6421	Engineer Payroll
6430	Janitor Payroll
6431	Janitor Supplies
6440	Bus Operator Payroll
6441	Gasoline, Oil, and Grease
6450	Electricity
6451	Water
6452	Gas
6460	Exterminating Payroll
6461	Exterminating Supplies
6462	Exterminating Contract
6470	Garbage and Trash Removal
6490	Miscellaneous Operating Expenses

6500 MAINTENANCE EXPENSES

6510	Protection (Security) Payroll
6511	Protection Fee, Costs, or Contracts
6520	Grounds Payroll
6521	Grounds Supplies and Replacements
6522	Grounds Contract
6530	Cleaning Payroll
6540	Repairs Payroll
6541	Repairs Material
6542	Repairs Contract
6543	Repairs—Extraordinary and Nonrecurring
6550	Elevator Maintenance
6551	Air Conditioning Repair and Maintenance
6560	Decorating Payroll
6561	Decorating Supplies
6562	Decorating Contract
6570	Motor Vehicle
6580	Maintenance Equipment Repairs
6590	Miscellaneous Maintenance Expenses

6700 INSURANCE AND TAXES

6710	Taxes
6720	Insurance

Appendix B

NATIONAL ASSOCIATION OF REALTORS®
Special Committee on Condominiums
Condominium Legislation—Recommended Criteria

PREAMBLE

Condominiums are and should remain an important form of ownership. As applied to homes, the form affords an apartment dweller both the opportunity for the efficiency and convenience of that type of dwelling and the security and benefits of being an owner. To a detached or townhouse owner, the form provides an organized method of control by all owners over the conduct of the affairs of an entire project. The industry has just begun to explore the use of this type of ownership in commercial and industrial situations. However, the popularity of condominiums has revealed abuses, inequities, and problems affecting the consumer. Further, an analysis of the present statutes reveal inadequacies not only in "consumer protection" but in other areas affecting the formation, operation, and use of this form of ownership.

The person who forms a condominium to sell units as part of his ordinary business or in contemplation of a profit is often referred to as a "developer." A person forming a condominium of a pre-existing building is often described as a "converter." As used herein, the term "sponsor" connotes both these entrepreneurs.

Based upon this analysis, the Special Committee on Condominiums of the NATIONAL ASSOCIATION OF REALTORS® recommends the following:

DIVISION I—BASIC CONSUMER PROTECTION—RESIDENTIAL CONDOMINIUMS

1.   Disclosure—Filing

(a) Statement—The consumer needs education about and information on the scope and nature of the residence he is about to purchase and the costs involved. Certain "abuses" have come to light and must be eliminated; they are dealt with in other paragraphs in this Division. In many areas, disclosure will be sufficient to protect the consumer and acquaint him with the facts he requires to make an informed decision.

Disclosure of material information is to be made by the sponsor.

(b) Filing with an Agency—Not all jurisdictions will find filing with a governmental agency necessary. It must be emphasized that there are great costs involved and that ultimately those costs will be borne by the consumer.

Before the sponsor may sell any unit, the disclosure statement must be filed with a state governmental agency.

(c) Scope of Applicability—The condominium form of ownership has applicability to many situations which makes it a useful device. It is most commonly employed as the method of establishing the apartment dweller/home owner type of unit. It is in these projects that consumers have suffered abuses and the thrust of remedial efforts must be focused in this area.

"Residential condominiums" are to be governed by disclosure/filing requirements and other provisions outlined under these criteria. A residential condominium is a project or portion of a project devoted to and used primarily for residential purposes, each apartment or unit being intended for use by a single family.

(d) Small Condominiums Exempt—Not all residential projects should be covered; however, it is not intended that "loopholes" be permitted. A series of small buildings grouped together by a sponsor which are in reality one large development under an umbrella association should not escape the more stringent requirements. The most salient criteria might be that of the contiguity of the land on which the projects or units are built.

Disclosure/filing should not be applicable to condominium projects containing twelve units or less.

2.   Budgeting and Reserves

(a) Pro Forma Operating Statement

A statement shall be prepared and certified to by an independent professional experienced in such matters projecting the operating costs for the first year of operations.

(b) Creation of Reserves

Initial reserves are to be established and funded by contributions to be made by the individual unit owners either at the closing of each purchase by a lump sum payment or after closing by monthly payments as part of the regular assessment.

(c) Sponsor's Assessment

The sponsor shall pay regular monthly assessments for all units substantially completed.

3.   Management Agreements and Service Contracts

(a) Length of Term—Under paragraph 7 below, it is contemplated that the association will be in the control of the individual unit owners no later than three years after the sale of the first unit (except for the "expandable condominium"). Accordingly, under the rule suggested in this paragraph 3, the individual unit owners will have an opportunity to choose their own management. The same rule would apply to contracts for landscape maintenance, fuel supply, and similar routinely needed services. It is the experience of the Institute of Real Estate Management, an institute of the NATIONAL ASSOCIATION OF REALTORS®, that a three-year term is a reasonable period for these types of contracts in the initial stages of a condominium's formation. Longer terms may not necessarily be of benefit to the project and are not always justifiable. However, a shorter term may be too restrictive on the sponsor or the management company or service contractor he might employ. In any event, there should be termination for just cause.

Management agreements and service contracts entered into by the sponsor or the condominium association while the sponsor controls its decisions shall have a termination date or be cancellable three years after the closing of the sale of the first unit, except for "expandable condominiums" which are referred to below.

4.   Recreational Leases

A residential condominium project constructed around and focused on an amenities package (which might even include a golf course) designed to meet the needs of that project should not be burdened with a device where a sponsor can enjoy a future benefit in a disguised fashion. On the other hand, where a given project is adjacent or close to a recreational facility and an individual unit owner can decide not to participate and thereby incur no charge, there is no hidden cost.

(a) Prohibited—Exception

Leases of recreational or other facilities to the residential condominium association by the sponsor or related parties should be prohibited unless all of the cost of operations are payable on a "membership" basis and "membership" is not compulsory or part of the regular monthly assessment to the unit owner.

(b) Disclosure of Certain Leases

Any "tie-in" between the sponsor and a related party in a permitted recreational lease must be disclosed in the statement required in paragraph 1.

5. Leases to the Sponsor or Others of Portions of the Common Elements or Association-Owned Units (such as Food Shop or Restaurant)

A merchant or restaurateur may be reluctant to invest in the trade fixtures needed to make his establishment of high quality, knowing that it may be years before the given project would reach a sustaining level, which may be well after all the units are sold out. It is not unusual to see leases providing for up to five years' free rent for such tenants. Disclosure will reveal those leases designed to hide a benefit to the sponsor as contrasted to those that are legitimate business transactions.

(a) Disclosure of Lease Terms

The terms and identity of the lessee and any relationship to the sponsor must be disclosed in the statement required in paragraph 1 above.

6. Warranties of Quality for Newly Constructed Condominiums

(a) Required—It is contemplated that all assignable manufacturers' and contractors' warranties will be assigned in addition to the warranty.

Warranties by the sponsor should be required as follows:
(i) For the individual unit and limited common elements, one year from the date of closing.
(ii) For the common elements, six months from the date the association is "turned over" to the individual unit owners or two years from the substantial completion of the common elements, whichever is earlier; but in no event less than one year from the closing of the first sale.
(iii) For the common elements, until the association is "turned over" to the individual unit owners, the individual unit-owner members of the association board may enforce the warranty in the name of the association, and if there be no individual unit owners on the board, then the individual unit owners may enforce the warranty in the name of the association.

(b) Warranty or Insurance Program—The NATIONAL ASSOCIATION OF REALTORS® Home Protection Committee has established criteria for a warranty-type program. It is intended that a program meeting such criteria base will be offered by private industry.

The sponsor can discharge his obligation under this paragraph by furnishing a warranty insurance policy of a financial responsible institution affording coverage for the matters to be warranted.

7. Control by Individual Unit Owners

During the period before the control passes to the individual unit owner, it is recommended that sponsors as a matter of good practice encourage the formation of an "Advisory Council" to meet with the official board in a consultative capacity. In this way several of the individual unit owners become knowledgeable in the operation of the condominium and are prepared for the eventual "transfer." "The inexperience of unit owners in self-government" is at the heart of many consumer complaints regarding condominiums. If this approach is followed, the individual unit owners will develop the expertise necessary to the proper administration of the board's affairs.

(a) Time and Units Sold

Control of the condominium association must be transferred to the individual unit owners no later than three years after the closing of the first unit or when 75 percent of the units are sold and closed, whichever is the first to occur, except for the "expandable condominiums," which are governed at paragraph 9 below.

(b) Rights of Individual Unit Owners

Prior to the transfer of control referred to above, the individual unit owners shall have the right to elect at least one board member after 25 percent of the units are sold and closed, and after 50 percent of the units are sold and closed the individual unit owners shall have the right to elect a "full" minority of the board, a majority less one.

8.   Permanent Mortgage by the Sponsor of Portions of the Residential Condominium's Common Elements or Association-Owned Units

The use of this type of mortgage (a mortgage on an apartment for on-site staff, recreation room, or other property of the association) is another form of the below market lease referred to at paragraph 5 above. This can be a beneficial device if used to finance "front end costs" such as the cost of the recreation room. Raising funds in this manner should reduce the per unit price as it spreads the payment for this capital item over a period of time. Such mortgages must be disclosed so that a purchaser can understand the "total cost of his unit and future monthly assessment."

(a) Required Disclosure

Prior to the first sale of any unit, such mortgage is permissible if (i) it is disclosed in the statement required at paragraph 1 above, (ii) it is fully amortized over the term of the loan, and (iii) it contains a "prepayment without penalty" clause.

(b) Consent Required after Sale of Units

After the sale of the first unit, such a mortgage is permissible only with the consent of 75 percent of the individual unit owners and purchasers.

9.   Expandable Condominiums

(a) Time Limit

Additional units may be added to a condominium project in accordance with a "plan" contained in the initial declaration, but all additions must be made within seven years of recording the declaration. The right to continue to "expand" may terminate earlier if the sponsor fails to meet the terms of the plan.

(b) Certain Exceptions to Other Time Limits

For an "expandable" condominium, the time limits of paragraphs 3 and 7 above are extended by an additional four years, provided, however, that if the right to expand is terminated for failure to comply with the plan, then such limits are cut off as of such termination.

(c) Special Rule for Control

For "expandable" condominiums the provisions of paragraph 7(b) concerning the individual unit owners' right to elect one condominium board member shall be effective after 25 percent of the units built in the first phase are sold and closed.

(d) Special Rule for Warranties of Quality

The time limit applicable to 6(a)(ii) above shall be applicable to the common elements as they are built in phases, the warranty on each phase being treated as if each phase was a separate condominium. However, the right of actions shall be in the individual unit owner members of the condominium association board who may enforce the warranty in the name of the association.

10.   Conversions

(a) Notification of Tenants

A notice of the formation of a residential condominium must be given to each tenant.

(b) Termination of Occupancy by Landlord—Clearly, a landlord cannot terminate a tenant's right of possession if there is a lease. The rule under this paragraph assures the tenant a minimum of 120 days to move, with or without a lease. If there is a lease affording longer possession rights, its provisions will be honored. The financing of this type of project prohibits prolonged periods of delay in "completing the conversion." The interest rates usually charged between the time of purchase of the building and closing of the unit sales is on the basis of a construction loan rate and not at the rate of a loan secured by an income-producing property, often a difference of up to five percent. The longer the period of these "interim" loans, the higher the ultimate cost to the purchasers.

During the 120 days subsequent to notice above, the tenant's possession may not be "disturbed" notwithstanding that there is no lease for all or any part of that period.

(c) Furnishing of Services and Payment of Rent

For the 120-day period above, the landlord must continue to furnish services to the tenant on the same basis as was done prior to the notice, and the tenant shall continue to pay the same rent as prior to the notice.

(d) Option to Purchase

Each tenant will have the option to purchase his apartment for a period of 90 days from the notice required above on the same terms or better than the apartment will be offered to the general public.

11.   Use of Earnest Money Deposits

(a) Trust Accounts

All earnest money shall be held in separate trust accounts to be designated and shall not be pledged, assigned, or used otherwise by the sponsor.

12.   Suit by Condominium Association on Behalf of Unit Owners

At this time, in several jurisdictions, it is unclear whether the condominium association may sue for damages or an injunction in matters affecting the individual units of a residential condominium. Hence, in a zoning case concerning a parcel adjoining a residential condominium project or a situation where the sponsor has breached his warranties of quality in all or some of the units but not the common elements, all of the several unit owners affected would need to sue in their own names, each hiring a lawyer, etc. The law general recognizes the concept of a "class action" and an analagous rule should be to encourage for condominium use, where appropriate, to simplify and make available the benefits of joint effort which is the foundation of the condominium concept.

(a) A residential condominium association may sue on behalf of the individual unit owners in those cases where more than one individual unit owner is or shall be affected or has or will be damaged by the same party and arising from the same or similar wrong, breach, or act.

(b) Upon filing such an action, notice thereof by certified mail shall be given to all the unit owners on whose behalf such action was filed and any individual unit owner may withdraw from the action provided, however, the defendant may request that the rights of any such individual unit owner shall be determined in that action.

(c) Any award resulting from such an action shall be held for the benefit of those individual unit owners on whose behalf the action was brought after deduction of the costs and expenses of the case. In the event some unit owners seek or request that the condominium association file an action on behalf of those owners and others similarly situated and the costs and expenses of such action exceed the award made, those owners making such request shall bear those costs and expenses. However, in those cases where none of the affected individual unit owners request that such action be brought on their behalf and the costs and expenses of any such action brought by the condominium association exceed the award made, unless expressly agreed otherwise, such amount shall be treated as an expense of the entire condominium association.

13.   Mechanic's Lien

In the event a mechanic's lien affects two or more units of a residential condominium, whether such lien attached prior to or after the formation of the condominium or recording the declaration, the owner of any unit so affected may remove the unit and the applicable percentage of the common elements from such lien by payment or posting a bond for that portion of such lien affecting such unit and common elements based upon the percentage of common elements involved.

14.   Actions among the Unit Owners and/or Condominium Association

In actions brought by unit owners against other unit owners or the condominium association or by the condominium association against some or all of the unit owners, wherein the party defendant prevails, upon a finding that such action was brought without substantial cause or that it was brought in bad faith, the court may award the cost of reasonable attorneys' fees to the defendant.

DIVISION II—SPONSOR'S RIGHTS

1.   The efficient completion of the project and "sell out" are, in many respects, more important to the individual unit owners than to the sponsor. Hence, the condominium association or individual unit owners should not hinder or interfere with the program of the sponsor.

The sponsor may reserve the right to maintain sales offices, signs, and model units until all units are sold and in addition thereto an easement to complete construction of the condominium and to fulfill warranty obligations.

DIVISION III—CONDOMINIUM FORMATION

1.   Common Elements

(a) Percentage Assigned to Each Unit

Any reasonable formula determined by the sponsor based upon square footage or values or a combination thereof should be permitted.

2.   Leaseholds

(a) Permissible

The formation of a condominium of a leasehold estate should be permitted.

(b) Special Rules for Residential Condominiums

(i) The essential information of the lease provisions such as length of term and rent must be disclosed.

(ii) The leasehold must provide that any individual unit owner may pay his separate rent so that his rights are not dependent on the payment of *rent by other units or the association.*

3.   Statutory Short Form Document

For basic provisions, a statutory form of declaration and bylaws should be available to aid in simplifying the examination of these basic documents.

4.   Time Sharing

"Time sharing" condominiums where different periods of time are owned by different persons should be established by statute.

Division IV—Condominium Association

1.   Board Organization

(a) Number of Members

The number of members sitting on the board shall be five but no more than seven.

(b) Meetings

All board of directors meetings should be open and notice should be posted at least ten days prior to the meetings.

(c) Personal Liability of Individual Unit Owner Board Members—Individual residential condominium unit owners are basically home owners living cooperatively. Any owner contributing his time to the affairs of all should be held to a reasonable standard of care. Clearly, good faith and honesty should be demanded but otherwise a board member should not be expected to exercise his duties with any greater expertise or diligence than he would apply to managing his home. This standard is in contrast to the high standard of care imposed on trustees under the "prudent man" rule.

A member of the board of directors in performing his duties shall act in good faith exercising the same care as he would in the conduct of his own affairs.

(d) Officers and Directors Liability Insurance

Such insurance should be a required expenditure of the association.

2.   Budget Responsibility

(a) Board to Oversee

The board shall vote the annual budget which shall remain effective until such a budget is reduced by action of the association at a membership meeting, special or regular. The action of any such meeting shall expressly set forth the budget under which the condominium shall operate and must be passed by at least a 66 2/3 percent vote of the unit owners. Notwithstanding any other provision of the bylaws on calling meetings, by a written petition, holders of five percent of the votes shall have the right to have such a meeting called within 30 days after such petition is delivered to the chief executive office of the association.

3.   Meeting of Members

(a) Annual Only

The unit owners, except for special cause, should not have a regular meeting more frequently than annually.

(b) Voting

For a "residential condominium," each unit should have one vote to cast on issues to be presented to the unit owners. For units having more than one owner, the owners should designate one of their number as the "voter" for their unit.

(c) Cumulative Voting—To give voice to the few, the concept of cumulative voting has been employed not only in business corporations in some jurisdictions, but also in the election of some public officials.

In elections for the association board, the bylaws may provide that the unit owner may cumulate votes and cast as many votes for one candidate as the number of offices to be filled multiplied by the number of votes of the unit owner or to distribute such votes on the same principle to as many candidates as the unit owner may decide.

DIVISION V—INSURANCE

1.   Individual Condominium Unit Policies

The "Homeowners No. 6" or broader form of protection should be made available in all jurisdictions.

2.   Other Insurance

Associations should purchase, if available, the following forms of coverage: (a) Workmen's Compensation, and (b) liability for motor vehicles used by the association that are owned, rented, or non-owned.

DIVISION VI—UNIT MORTGAGES

1.   Priority

The regular assessments of the condominium association should have priority over all liens (including rent for leasehold condominiums) except real estate taxes.

DIVISION VII—BANKRUPTCY AND RECEIVERSHIPS

1.   Priority of Assessment

In the event the sponsor or any individual unit owner, voluntarily or involuntarily, is within the jurisdiction of the bankruptcy court, the assessments, regular and special, must be paid even if other creditors, except the U.S. government, are prejudiced.

2.   Receiver

In the event a receiver or trustee is appointed by a court to act under court supervision for the units owned by the sponsor, the condominium association may request that such receiver or trustee act in behalf of the condominium association for the administration of the common elements.

3.   Association Not Acting

In those cases where the condominium association fails in a material respect to administer the common elements in accordance with the condominium documents, 25 percent of the individual unit owners may request a court to appoint a receiver to perform the functions of the association under court supervision.

(Editor's Note: Condominium Legislation—Recommended Criteria was developed by the Special Committee on Condominiums of the NATIONAL ASSOCIATION OF REALTORS® to provide guidelines for drafting state condominium legislation. The criteria originally were approved by the Board of Directors of NATIONAL ASSOCIATION OF REALTORS® on May 6, 1975. Additions subsequently were approved on November 11, 1975, February 10, 1976, and May 2, 1977. The criteria will continue to be subjected to regular scrutiny, and modifications and/or additions made to reflect changes in and a greater awareness of the condominium industry.)

Glossary

Accounting System of gathering financial information and keeping a record of business transactions in order to prepare statements concerning assets, liabilities, and operating results.

ACCREDITED MANAGEMENT ORGANIZATION® (AMO) Designation awarded by the Institute of Real Estate Management to firms that prove themselves in compliance with certain standards, including organizational stability, management portfolio, and fiscal and operational reliability and education.

Accrual Accounting Method of recording expenses incurred and income due in the periods to which they relate rather than actual flow of cash.

Actual Cash Value Amount of money that would be required to repair or replace existing building or improvement with another of like kind in the same condition, thereby taking into account depreciation; replacement cost less depreciation.

Additional Living Expense Insurance Coverage that would reimburse the insured for living costs in excess of normal living expenses if loss of or damage to property forced him to maintain temporary residence elsewhere.

Address the Chair Speak to the presiding officer of a business meeting.

Ad Hoc Committee Special committee appointed to carry out a specific nonrecurring task and disbanded when that task is completed.

Adjourn Officially dismiss or end a meeting.

Adjusted Basis Original cost or book value of an asset for income tax purposes.

Adjusted Sales Price   Amount paid or payable for an item less actual selling expenses and other expenses incurred to assist in the sale.

Administrative Expenses   Cost of goods or services that can be attributed to the management of affairs of a condominium.

Agent   One who has the authority to act for or represent another; see **insurance agent, management agent**.

Agreed Amount Insurance   Policy under which coinsurance clause is waived if insured carries insurance of an agreed amount and under which insurer agrees to pay face amount on the policy in the event of total loss of property covered or upon occurrence of a stated contingency.

All-Risk Insurance   Policy under which a loss resulting from any cause other than those causes specifically excluded by name is considered to be covered.

Amend   Modify or change; under parliamentary procedure, modify a motion by adding, deleting, or substituting words.

Amendment   Revision of a governing document or, under parliamentary procedure, a motion.

Amenity   Facility that is part of common areas and increases physical comfort, such as a swimming pool or tennis court.

Amenity Rental Fee   Fixed charge paid by unit owner or guest for use of common facility and/or limited common area.

Annual Membership Meeting   Once-a-year assemblage of unit owners required by governing documents to conduct association business, such as electing a board of directors.

Appraisal   Survey of a property and estimate of its value by an expert in property analysis.

Architectural Controls   Standards and restrictions that limit what a unit owner can do to change the outward appearance of his unit and outline procedures a unit owner must follow if he wishes to make changes to the exterior of his unit.

Articles of Incorporation   Formal document that, when filed, sets up an association as a corporation under the laws of the applicable state.

Assembly   Group of persons gathered for some common purpose.

Assessment   Amount charged against each unit owner, based on percentages of budgeted common expenses, to fund the opertion, administration, maintenance, and management of a condominium.

Asset Item that has purchasing power, often because it can be converted into cash; *pl.*, entries in a balance sheet listing these items or properties.

Association See **condominium association**.

Association Insurance Policy Written contract combining liability and property protection into one package and designed to cover common areas of a condominium, usually including the structure, and take precedence over unit owners' policies; also called master insurance policy.

Audit Examination of financial records and accounts to verify their accuracy and determine if financial statements adequately reflect an association's financial status.

Automobile Nonownership Liability Insurance Protection against loss arising out of an association's legal responsibility and as a result of an association employee or officer having an accident while on association business in an automobile neither owned or hired by the association.

Balance Sheet Financial statement that indicates the financial status of an association at a specific point in time by listing its assets, liabilities, and members' equity.

Ballot Paper used to cast secret vote.

Basis See **adjusted basis**.

Billing Journal Form used to chronologically record preparation of invoices.

Blanket Fidelity Bond Contract covering loss of association money or real or personal property when such a loss is due to dishonesty of an employee.

Board of Directors Official governing body of a condominium association elected by members of the association; also called board of managers or board of trustees.

Bodily Injury Liability Insurance Protection against loss arising out of insured's legal responsibility and as a result of injury, illness or disease, or death of another person.

Boiler Pressure tank in which water is heated and from which it is circulated either in the form of steam or as water.

Boiler and Machinery Insurance Property and liability coverage for loss arising out of the operation of pressure, mechanical, and electrical equipment.

Budget Estimated summary of expenditures and income for a given period.

Bylaws   Secondary laws of an association that govern its internal affairs and deal with routine operational and administrative matters; also called code of regulations.

Call for Orders of the Day   Require an assembly to conform to prescribed order of business.

Capital Expenditures   Funds spent for additions or improvements to physical plant or for equipment.

Capital Gains Tax   Fee levied on profit realized on the sale of a capital asset, including an owner-occupied dwelling, such as a house or condominium unit, or land.

Capital Reserves   Funds set aside for probable repair and replacement of common areas and facilities.

Cash Accounting   Method of recording revenue when actual cash is received and expenses when actual cash disbursements are made.

Cash Disbursements Journal   Book of original entry for chronologically recording all checks issued.

Cash Flow Statement   Report that indicates actual inflow and outgo of cash and its related sources and uses in a given accounting period.

Cash Receipts Journal   Book of original entry for chronologically recording all cash taken in from all sources.

CERTIFIED PROPERTY MANAGER® (CPM)   Designation awarded by the Institute of Real Estate Management to professional property managers who have met standards of performance, experience, education, and ethical conduct.

Certified Public Accountant (CPA)   Accountant who has met certain state legal requirements.

Chairman   Person who presides over an assembly, meeting, committee, or board.

Chart of Accounts   System of coding by number each classification used in a budget and financial statements.

Coinsurance   Insurance policy under which insured shares losses if property is insured for less than a certain percentage of its value.

Commingling of Funds   Combining or mixing monies.

Commit   Send an issue to committee for study or action and resubmission to an assembly at a future time.

Committee   Group of people officially delegated to perform a function, such as investigate or report or act on a matter.

Common Areas Property owned jointly by all unit owners that ordinarily includes land and structure or portions of structure not otherwise described as units; also called common elements.

Common Expenses Costs of managing, maintaining, administering, repairing, replacing, and operating a condominium.

Communications Program Organized method of transmitting information.

Community Associations Institute (CAI) Independent nonprofit research and educational organization formed in 1973 to develop and distribute guidance on condominium and homeowners' assocations.

Completed Operations and Products Liability Insurance Protection against loss arising out of insured's legal responsibility and as a result of alleged injury from manufactured products or workmanship.

Condominium Form of ownership in a multifamily housing development that combines exclusive ownership of a dwelling unit and joint ownership of common areas.

Condominium Association Private, automatic, usually nonprofit organization responsible for the total operation of a condominium community; also called council of owners or council or association of co-owners.

Condominium Management Agreement Formal contract between a professional property management firm and a second party, either an association board or a developer, to manage a condominium in exchange for a stated rate of compensation.

Condominium Unit That part of a condominium development, probably a space of air or three-dimensional area located within the walls, floor, and ceiling of a condominium structure, privately owned and independently and exclusively used by a unit owner; also called condominium apartment.

Contingency Event that may occur but is not necessarily expected.

Contract Voluntary and legally binding agreement between parties calling for them to do or not do some specific thing for some consideration, usually monetary.

Contractors' Protective Liability Insurance Protection against loss arising out of insured's responsibility and as a result of new construction or extensive repairs undertaken by the association.

Conversion   Transfer of multifamily rental development to condominium form of ownership through sale of individual living units; multifamily dwelling whose ownership has been so transferred.

Cooperative   Corporation that holds real estate, specifically a multifamily dwelling, shareholders in which have the right to live in one of its units.

Corporate Surtax Exemption   Release from obligation to pay additional tax levied on the amount by which a corporation's net income exceeds a certain sum.

Corporate Tax Rate   Proportionate fee levied against the net income of corporations.

Countersignature   Second or confirming signature.

Cross Liability Endorsement   Attachment to an insurance policy that provides protection for an association should a unit owner be awarded damages as a result of an accident in common areas.

Cumulative Voting   System by which votes are amassed to allow unit owner to cast as many votes as there are offices to fill.

Custodial Maintenance   Upkeep of an area through performance of cleaning, policing, and related routine housekeeping chores.

Damages   Money paid or ordered to be paid as compensation for injury or loss.

Debate   Discussion of a question pending before a deliberative body.

Declaration   Legal document that, when filed, commits land to condominium use, creates a condominium association and serves as its constitutional law, physically describes a condominium, defines the method of determining each unit owner's share of the common areas, and outlines responsibilities and restrictions; also called declaration of codes, covenants, and restrictions or master deed.

Deductible   Specific amount to be subtracted from a loss and written into an insurance policy as a means of effecting a decrease in premium.

Deferred Maintenance   Upkeep that may be scheduled at a future date without allowing a minor problem to become a major one.

Delinquency   Overdue assessment payment.

Depreciation   Decrease in value of property because of physical deterioration resulting from wear and tear, functional inability to serve its use as well as a new property designed for the same purpose, or locational obsolescence resulting from external and environmental factors.

Default   Failure to fulfill or live up to terms of an agreement.

Developer   One who converts a tract of land or other property to a specific use.

Direct Loss   Physical loss of or damage to property concerned.

Directors' and Officers' Liability Insurance   Protection against loss arising out of alleged errors in judgment, breaches of duty, and wrongful acts of a board of directors and/or officers in carrying out their prescribed duties.

Discharge a Committee   Remove a matter from a committee's consideration and put it before an assembly.

Division of Assembly   Requirement that, in the event there is some doubt as to the accuracy of an announced voice vote or vote based on a show-of-hands count, a recount be taken by having members stand.

Division of a Question   Separate consideration of parts of a motion or an amendment to it.

Easement   Right to use land owned by someone else for certain limited purposes, such as for party driveways, drainage, etc.

Emergency Maintenance   Necessary repairs that cannot be predicted and require immediate attention.

Endorsement   Attachment to an insurance policy that in some way modifies its coverage.

Equity   Owner's interest in a property, usually determined by the value of the property less mortgage, liens, or other encumbrances against it.

Equity Accrual   Buildup of an owner's interest in a property because of mortgage loan amortization or appreciation in its total value.

Errors and Omissions Insurance   Protection against loss arising out of an alleged error or oversight on the part of an insured professional while performing his prescribed duties.

Escape Provision   Clause in a contract that, under certain circumstances, allows either party to cancel the agreement prior to its expiration date.

Escrow   Agreement that something, usually money, given to a third party be held until certain conditions are met.

Estate   Nature of an owner's right or interest in his property and its use.

Expandable Condominium   Development under condominium form of ownership designed to permit additional multifamily living structures to be built within it if the demand for them exists.

Extended Coverage Insurance   Policy that extends basic fire policy to cover property loss caused by additional perils, usually including windstorm, hail, explosion, riot and civil commotion, aircraft, vehicles, and smoke.

Fair Market Value   Most probable selling price of property or item.

Fee Simple Absolute Interest   Most complete type of private ownership of real estate which gives title holder the right to possess, control, use, and dispose of it as he chooses.

Federal Housing Authority (FHA)   Federal agency that functions as an insurer of mortgage loans.

Fidelity Bond   Formal agreement under which an employer would be reimbursed for loss, up to an amount specified, that may result from a dishonest act of covered employee occupying a position of trust.

Fiduciary Relationship   Agreement based on trust in which one person or group of persons handles financial transactions for another or others.

Financial Statement   Report that indicates certain information concerning financial position of an association.

Fiscal Controls   Procedures for regulating and verifying financial activities.

Fiscal Year   Twelve-month period for which an association plans use of funds.

Fixed Expenses   Costs that remain relatively stable.

Fixture   Item of personal property that is annexed, attached, or affixed to or installed in real property, such as plumbing fixtures or wall-to-wall carpeting.

Fraud   Deliberate deception practiced in order to secure unlawful gain.

Garagekeepers' Legal Liability Insurance   Protection against loss arising out of insured's legal responsibility and as a result of damage to vehicles left in care, custody, and control of association.

Garden Condominium Multifamily dwelling under condominium ownership that usually is no more than three stories tall, has units arranged horizontally and vertically, and is built around a courtyard; also called low-rise condominium.

General Journal Book of original entry to record miscellaneous entries that do not apply to other journals.

General Ledger Record to which all accounts in the form of debits and credits are transferred as final entries from the journals, thus indicating accumulated affects of transactions.

General Maintenance Upkeep that can be anticipated and performed on a regular basis or is minor in nature.

Governing Documents Set of legal papers, filed by a developer with the appropriate local government office, that commit land to condominium use and create and govern a condominium association.

Graduate, Realtor Institute (GRI) Designation awarded by state organizations of the National Association of Realtors to persons who have demonstrated competency in prescribed educational course material.

Ground Rent Payment for the use and occupancy of real property, according to the terms of a lease.

Hazard Source or cause of a disaster, such as fire, flood, or worker's injury; also, perilous conditions that may create or increase the probability of loss.

Hearing Examination, usually informal, of an accused person.

High-Rise Condominium Multifamily dwelling under condominium ownership that utilizes an arrangement of units placed one on top of the other.

Hold Harmless Clause Contractual provision that shifts liability inherent in a situation to another party; see **indemnification**.

Horizontal Property Another name for a condominium.

Host Liquor Liability Insurance Protection against loss arising out of insured's legal responsibility as a result of an accident attributed to the use of liquor dispensed but not sold by an association and/or used in common areas.

House Rules and Regulations Guidelines related to day-to-day conduct in common areas and relationships between unit owners.

Incidental Motion   Motion that involves question of procedure arising out of another motion and over which it takes precedence.

Income Tax   Charge levied by federal government against taxable income of an individual or corporation.

Indemnification   Condition, usually contractual, of being protected against possible damage, loss, or suit; see **hold harmless clause**.

Inflation   Sharp and continuing rise in price levels due to an abnormal increase in available currency and credit greater than the proportionate increase of available goods.

Insurance   Protective measure that shifts risk of financial loss due to certain perils to an insurance company in return for payment of premiums.

Institute of Real Estate Management (IREM)   Organization founded in 1934 to develop professionalism in the field of property management by setting standards of performance, experience, and ethics and making available to the industry educational courses and publications.

Insurance Agent   Representative of an insurance company, licensed by the state, who negotiates and effects insurance contracts and services policyholders.

Insurance Claim   Sum of money demanded for a loss in accordance with the terms of an insurance policy.

Insurance Trustee   Person or institution who administers recovery funds collected from insurance company.

Insured   One covered by insurance; a policyholder.

Insurer   One who provides insurance; an insurance company.

Interest   Charge for a financial loan, usually based on a percentage of that loan.

Interim Period   Time during which unit owners are living in a condominium but developer controls the association.

Internal Revenue Code   Laws that govern the filing of tax returns with the United States Treasury.

Investment   Outlay of money in order to realize income or profit in the future.

Invoice   List of goods shipped or services rendered with an account of applicable costs; a bill.

Journal   Financial record book in which certain business transactions are recorded chronologically and for the first time.

Judgment Court decree of indebtedness to another and amount of that indebtedness.

Leasehold Interest Position of a tenant in a leased property, including the right of use and possession for a definite and specific period of time in return for compensation.

Ledger Card Official record of a unit owner's assessment payments.

Liability Legal responsibility and obligation; *pl.*, financial obligations entered in a balance sheet.

Liability Insurance Coverage for damages arising out of insured's legal responsibility and resulting from injuries to other persons or damage to their property.

Lien Claim or attachment, enforceable at law, to have a debt or other charge satisfied out of a person's property.

Limit Debate Place restrictions on the amount of time to be allowed for debate of an issue or the amount of time each speaker may debate an issue.

Limited Common Areas Property that physically is part of a condominium's common areas but is reserved for the exclusive use of a particular unit owner or group of unit owners.

Line Item Budget Format listing of expenses by type.

Loss Amount of an insured's claim; amount of decrease in value of his property.

Loss Assessment Insurance Unit owner protection that would cover special assessments he may be obligated to pay because a loss incurred by the association was not otherwise adequately insured.

Main Motion Proposal that brings business before an assembly for discussion or action.

Maintenance Upkeep of property or an item in its proper and functional condition.

Maintenance Program Schedule of all repair, inspection, cleaning, lubrication, and other tasks necessary to keep something in proper working order.

Management Agent Representative of a professional management firm.

Management Agreement See **condominium management agreement**.

Management Plan Program for operating a condominium.

Master Association   Organization of unit owners of more than one condominium created to maintain, operate, manage, and finance recreational facilities of which they share the use; also called common association.

Mechanical Maintenance   Repair, inspection, lubrication, and cleaning of machines and tools to keep them in proper working condition.

Medical Payments Insurance   Coverage that voluntarily provides for payment of medical and similar expenses of persons injured in common areas regardless of the question of fault or legal liability.

Meeting   Assemblage of association members gathered to discuss issues and make decisions on them through motions.

Metes and Bounds   Legal description of real property in which boundaries are defined by directions and distances.

Mid-Rise Condominium   Multifamily housing structure under condominium ownership that usually is six to nine stories high and has a single front entrance and lobby and common corridors.

Minutes   Official record of proceedings of a meeting.

Mortgage   Temporary and conditional pledge of real property as security for a financial obligation.

Mortgagee   Lender in a mortgage loan contract, such as a bank or other lending institution.

Mortgage Insurance   Protection designed to pay off mortgage loan upon death or disability of insured.

Motion   Formal proposal put before an assembly on which action must be taken.

Mulch   Protective covering, usually organic, placed around plants to protect against weed growth and help soil retain moisture.

National Housing Act, Section 234   Passed in 1961, permitted Federal Housing Authority of the Department of Housing and Urban Development to insure loans made by private lenders for construction, rehabilitation, and/or purchase of single-family or multifamily housing for rent or ownership, thereby extending mortgage insurance to condominiums.

Newsletter   Printed periodical report devoted to news of and for a special interest group, such as a condominium association.

Noncumulative Voting   Assignment of one vote per person.

Objection to Consideration of a Question   Expression of opposition to discussing and taking action on a main motion.

Obtain the Floor   Be formally recognized by the chairman of a meeting and given the exclusive right to speak.

Occupancy Restrictions   Limitations on who may and may not buy and/or live in condominium units.

Operating Contingency Reserves   Funds set aside to cover unusual and emergency expenditures that cannot be anticipated when an annual budget is drafted.

Operating Expenses   Costs incurred to maintain a property and keep it productive of services.

Order of Business   Sequence in which issues are to be taken up at a meeting.

Organization Meeting   First meeting of an association at which directors are elected.

Ownership Interest   Legal share, expressed in percentages, each unit owner has in common areas.

Parliamentarian   Adviser to presiding officer who acts as the authority on rules of conducting a business meeting.

Parliamentary Procedure   Established rules of parliamentary law and unwritten rules of courtesy used to facilitate the transaction of business in deliberative assemblies.

Partition   Legal action brought by a unit owner to separate his share, based on ownership interest, of a condominium's common areas or common monies.

Payroll Journal   Book of original entry for chronologically recording all salary and related transactions.

Pending Question   Motion before an assembly that has not yet been put to a vote.

Peril   Cause of a possible loss against which insurance may be obtained.

Personal Injury Liability Insurance   Protection against loss arising out of personal insults, such as slander, liable, or false arrest, allegedly delivered by the insured.

Personal Property   Possessions that are temporary or movable, as opposed to real property which is fixed; personalty.

Physical Maintenance   Repair, inspection, and cleaning of a physical plant in order to keep it in proper condition.

Plat   Survey plan or map and descriptions of a tract of land showing property lines, easements, etc.

Point of Order   Demand that chairman enforce parliamentary rules which are being violated.

Police   Regular patrol of an area, keeping it neat in appearance.

Policy Resolution   Formal statement submitted to an assembly for a decision; subsequent to passage, outline of plan of action.

Postpone Definitely   Delay action on a pending question until some future time.

Postpone Indefinitely   Kill a main motion for the duration of a meeting by forestalling vote on it.

Preamble   Introduction to a contract that identifies its purpose and establishes its legality.

Premium   Compensation to insurer for accepting risk of loss; cost of insurance.

Preventive Maintenance   Program of inspection and regular care that allows potential problems to be detected and solved early or prevented altogether.

Previous Question   Demand to close debate and vote immediately on an issue.

Privileged Motion   Motion with highest authority that interrupts consideration of other matters and relates to urgent or special subjects.

Professional Management   Handling by an experienced and trained individual or firm of a full range of administrative, maintenance, and operational tasks for a condominium association.

Program Budget   Format of listing expenses according to program or activity for which they will be disbursed.

Property Damage Liability Insurance   Protection against loss arising out of insured's legal responsibility as a result of damage to or destruction of another's property.

Property Insurance   Protection of insured's real or personal property against loss or damage caused by specified perils.

Property Tax   Fee levied by local governments against real estate, business equipment, and inventories.

Prorate   Divide, distribute, or assess in proportionate shares.

Proxy   Authorization given to one person to vote in place of another.

Question   Matter being considered by an assembly.

Quorum   Minimum number of members that must be present or votes that must be represented at a meeting in order for business to be transacted legally.

Question of Privilege   Interruption of pending business to state an urgent request or make a motion on an immediate problem.

Real Estate   Land and all permanent improvements on it; realty.

Record of Original Entry   Financial record of initial transaction of business; a journal.

Recreational Lease   Long-term agreement under which a developer retains ownership of a condominium's recreational facilities and allows unit owners to use them for a specified time in exchange for compensation in the form of rent.

Recess   Short break in a business meeting.

Reconsider   Bring a motion before an assembly as if it had not been considered previously, thereby cancelling the effect of the earlier vote.

Refer   See **commit.**

Rent   Compensation given in exchange for the use of space or real property.

Replacement Cost   Amount of money required to repair and replace an existing property with property of the same material and construction without deducting for depreciation.

Rescind   Cancel or nullify a previous action by an assembly.

Reserves   Funds set aside for special purposes, specifically, to enable an association to meet nonrecurring and/or major expenses.

Resident Management   Plan for running a condominium whereby a person works exclusively for an association, handling all of its affairs.

Risk   Chance of a loss from a hazard.

Robert's Rules of Order   Recognized formal guidelines for conducting a business meeting.

Second   Indication from a second member that he agrees a certain motion warrants consideration of the membership.

Secondary Motion   Motion that relates to a main motion or involves emergency or procedural questions.

Self-Management   Plan of running a condominium whereby unit owners carry out policy decisions of and handle affairs for an association.

Service Contract   Formal agreement that certain work necessary for the continuing operation of a condominium be performed in exchange for specified compensation.

Single-Deed Estate   Real property covered by one title.

Single-Family House   Detached dwelling designed for occupancy by one family.

Special Assessment   Fee levied against unit owners to cover unexpected expenses.

Special Meeting   Unscheduled meeting called by board or membership to discuss urgent business.

Sprinkler Leakage Insurance   Protection against loss caused by accidental discharge of water from an automatic fire prevention sprinkler system.

Standing Committee   Group of people formed to handle on-going business on a certain subject.

Statement of Income and Expense   Financial report that indicates how much income has been earned and what expenses have been incurred over a certain period of time and compares budgeted and actual figures for the period in question and the year-to-date.

Statement of Members' Equity   Financial report that indicates vested interest of unit owners, or value of their property after all liabilities have been deducted, on a specific date.

State the Question   Restatement of a motion by chairman, thus opening it to debate.

Subcommittee   Subordinate committee composed of members appointed from a main committee to handle a specified task within the main committee's responsibilities.

Subrogation   Legal process of substitution by which an insurance company seeks from a third party, who may have caused a loss, recovery of the amount paid to the policyholder.

Subsidiary Motion   Motion that takes precedence over main motions and affects the way a main motion is handled.

Suspend the Rules   Set aside parliamentary procedures in order to take up a matter in such a way as to otherwise be in violation of them.

Sweetheart Contract   Agreement between two parties of excessive length or excessive rates of compensation.

Table   Temporarily set aside a pending question when a more urgent matter arises; lay on the table.

Tabloid   Small format newspaper.

Taxable Income   That portion of revenue that is subject to taxation.

Tax Exemption   Freedom from liability on taxes that apply to others.

Title   Ownership of property and instrument that is evidence of that ownership.

Tort Action   Legal filing of civil suit arising out of a wrongful act, damages, or injury involving liability.

Townhouse Condominium   Multifamily dwelling under condominium ownership that utilizes an arrangement of units attached side by side, often rowhouses with individual entrances.

Transition Period   Time immediately after developer transfers control of an association to unit owners and during which they must learn to accept responsibilities of running a condominium.

Tribunal   Court for hearing disputes.

Trustee   See **insurance trustee**.

Umbrella Liability Insurance   Protection against losses in excess of amounts covered by other liability insurance policies.

Underwriter   Employee of insurance company who reviews applications for coverage, decides if it should be given, and determines appropriate rates.

Undivided Interest   Ownership that is inseparable and cannot be divided or severed, such as a condominium unit and its share of common areas.

Unit   See **condominium unit**.

Unit Deed   Legal instrument that, when filed, transfers title of a condominium unit and its undivided portion of common areas from one owner to another.

Unit Owner   Person or persons, corporation, partnership, or other legal entity that holds title to a condominium unit and its undivided interest in common areas; also called apartment owner or co-owner.

Unit Owner Insurance Policy   Policy specifically designed to provide property and liability coverage to meet needs of owners of condominium units.

Urban Land Institute (ULI)   Independent nonprofit research and educational organization incorporated in 1936 to improve the quality and standards of land use and development.

Use Restrictions   Rules and regulations, often prohibitive in na-

ture, that regulate human behavior in common areas and between neighbors.

Utilities   Community services rendered by public utility companies, such as gas, electricity, and telephone.

Waiver   Surrender of a right or privilege.

Watercraft Liability Insurance   Protection against loss arising
out of legal responsibility as a result of accident involving boats.

Water Damage Insurance   Protection against property loss
caused by water, with certain exceptions.

Workers' Compensation   Provision, required by state law, to
cover cost of medical care and weekly income payments to injured workers or their dependents for industrial injuries or
diseases, regardless of blame.

Index